HISTORY
AND MEMORY

MANCHESTER
1824

Manchester University Press

❦ HISTORICAL APPROACHES ❦
Series editor
Geoffrey Cubitt

The Historical Approaches series aims to make a distinctive contribution to current debate about the nature of the historical discipline, its theory and practice, and its evolving relationships to other cultural and intellectual fields. The intention of the series is to bridge the gap that sometimes exists between learned monographs on the one hand and beginners' manuals on the other, by offering works that have the clarity of argument and liveliness of style to appeal to a general and student readership, while also prompting thought and debate among practising historians and thinkers about the discipline. Titles in the series will cover a wide variety of fields, and explore them from a range of different angles, but will have in common the aspiration of raising awareness of the issues that are posed by historical studies in today's world, and of the significance of debates about history for a broader understanding of contemporary culture.

HISTORY
AND MEMORY

Geoffrey Cubitt

Manchester University Press

Manchester and New York

distributed exclusively in the USA by Palgrave

Published by Manchester University Press
Oxford Road, Manchester M13 9NR, UK
and Room 400, 175 Fifth Avenue, New York, NY 10010, USA
www.manchesteruniversitypress.co.uk

Distributed exclusively in the USA by
Palgrave, 175 Fifth Avenue, New York,
NY 10010, USA

Distributed exclusively in Canada by
UBC Press, University of British Columbia, 2029 West Mall,
Vancouver, BC, Canada V6T 1Z2

British Library Cataloguing-in-Publication Data
A catalogue record for this book is available from
the British Library

Library of Congress Cataloging-in-Publication Data applied for

ISBN 978 0 7190 6077 9 *hardback*
ISBN 978 0 7190 6078 6 *paperback*

First published 2007

16 15 14 13 12 11 10 09   10 9 8 7 6 5 4 3 2

Typeset
by Florence Production Ltd, Stoodleigh, Devon
Printed in Great Britain
by the MPG Books Group

CONTENTS

ACKNOWLEDGEMENTS

While its defects are mine, this book bears the mark of numerous conversations and intellectual exchanges with colleagues and friends over a lengthy period. I hope that those involved will recognize that it is only despair at the possibility of listing all who should be listed, and not lack of appreciation, that leads me not to name names. One group, however, can be acknowledged collectively: as designer and tutor of an undergraduate course on 'History and Memory' in the History Department at the University of York, I have had the privilege of discussing the kinds of issues that this book addresses with successive cohorts of students whose intelligent enthusiasm and openness to fresh ideas and approaches have been a constant stimulus to thought. Without this experience, it is unlikely that this book would have been embarked on. Nor, perhaps, would it have been finished without the sympathetic patience and benevolence under fire of those who have been respnsible for monitoring research in my department over the last few years, and of successive editors at Manchester University Press. To all of these, I am most grateful.

But the biggest debts come last. Living with the crises and frustrations of other people's efforts at book production is a strain at the best of times. My wife Katy and son Richard have had to live with this project for longer than the second can remember and than the first had a right reasonably to expect. I am indebted to them both – to Katy for the burdens of responsibility she has borne and the tolerance and practical support she has given to a husband and colleague in need (as well as for the inspiration of her own work on relevant topics); to Richard for offering regular emphatic reminders that life should consist of more than history and memory, and publication deadlines. This book is not an adequate recompense for what they have had to put up with, but it is dedicated nonetheless to the two of them together, in the hope of doing better in future.

INTRODUCTION

Great claims have been made for memory, both as a capacity and as a concept. Without the ability to remember, it has been suggested, 'we should be locked in an infinitesimal present, speechless and without thought'[1] – unrecognizable, in short, as the conscious, purposeful, communicating creatures we like to think of ourselves as being. Memory is 'the enabling capacity of human existence', 'the scaffolding upon which all mental life is constructed', an 'apparently seamless and omnipresent function' at the heart of our existence.[2] Claims of this kind are impressive, but double-edged. On the one hand, they give the concept of memory a right of entry into almost any field of human enquiry. On the other, they give it a significance that is potentially so general as to leave us feeling none the wiser: if memory is the common element in everything, we may feel, knowing about it may not give us a special purchase on anything in particular. In practice, until quite recently, this was probably the view that most historians would have been inclined to take: while few would have denied that memory was an ingredient in the things that historians studied, few would have felt that it was an ingredient on which they had to focus.

Things have changed. In the last quarter century, memory has become, to all appearances, one of the central preoccupations of historical scholarship. A variety of things have contributed to this explosion of interest: the interest of social historians in gaining access to the experiential aspect of social processes and situations, the increasingly subtle methodological engagement with the mental and social dynamics of remembering by practitioners of the emerging discipline of oral history, the drive among cultural and social historians to explore the workings and the interactions of orality and literacy, the interest of cultural and intellectual

historians in the representation of the past as a vital feature of
political and religious ideologies, the (loosely-speaking) post-
modernist emphasis on the mental construction both of reality
and of subjectivity, the efforts of modern and contemporary
historians analytically to grasp the traumatizing effects of total war
and of genocidal atrocities on individuals and on societies, the
involvement of such historians with efforts in the post-Soviet era
to recover and to re-evaluate the pasts that Communist regimes
had systematically suppressed, are only some of the more obvious
impulses. But the 'turn to memory' (as I shall call it, following a
now established usage) has come to seem more than the sum of
these contributions: memory has become, in some quarters at least,
a key term in the lexicon of historical study – an almost obligatory
concept for the validation of new modes of historical enquiry and
for the revamping of old ones. 'Where we once spoke of folk history
or popular history or oral history or public history or even myth',
Kerwin Lee Klein has written, 'we now employ memory as a metahis-
torical category that subsumes all these various terms'.[3] Gabrielle
Spiegel likewise detects a 'rush to valorize memory as an alternative
historiographical discourse'.[4] The movement that both of these
authors are describing is a complex one. In turning to memory,
historians have been turning not just towards an interest in new
kinds of subject matter, but towards new ways of organizing and
labelling and describing their objects of study, and new ways
of conceptualizing the nature of their own discipline and the
knowledge it is geared to producing..

  History's turn to memory has not been an isolated disciplinary
occurrence. Parallel upsurges of interest in phenomena of memory
and in the use of memory as an organizing intellectual category
have been felt, roughly contemporaneously, not just in disciplines
such as psychology, for which the study of remembering has been
a long-established area of interest, but in a host of others whose
engagement with it is roughly as new as history's own – literary
studies, sociology, anthropology, cultural studies, folklore studies,
art history, archaeology, museology, musicology, to name only a
few.[5] In turning their attention to memory, historians have entered
a peculiarly busy interdisciplinary arena. This arena remains,
however, largely unregulated. Memory studies are not, and are not
obviously in the process of becoming, a coherent and unified field
of enquiry, of the kind that possesses agreed definitions and a

measure of methodological co-ordination: rather, 'memory' is a term that is played out – and played with – across a proliferating range of disciplinary and discursive areas, producing insights and connections that are often stimulating or suggestive, but frequently in need of further elaboration. Any attempt at a general survey of such a field is bound to be partial and impressionistic, and to be almost instantly outdated – and such a survey is not what this book will be attempting.[6] What is attempted is simply an introduction to some of the issues that the recent wave of interest in history and other disciplines has brought to the fore, and an exploration of some of the intellectual connections that thinking about memory's significance for history can prompt us to develop. Although the book is intended primarily for historians, and seeks to address the kinds of issues that I believe historians should be interested in, there is no intention here of formulating an approach to memory that will be distinctively and peculiarly a historian's approach; rather the aim is to show how a range of approaches, some rooted in historians' current practice, others developed in other disciplines, may be helpful to historians in conceptualizing the issues that memory poses in and for their discipline. I am aware that the book reflects my own experience as a historian whose knowledge and experience is principally of the modern period, and that specialists in other periods may find it deficient in the attention it pays to scholarship in their own fields, but the book is nevertheless offered in the belief that the issues it raises are relevant to many of the concerns of historians generally, and not just to those working on recent centuries.

To say that this book is concerned with history's relationship to memory is, of course, a deceptively simple statement, since 'memory' and 'history' are both words that have multiple senses. In practice – holding the term 'memory' steady for a moment and allowing 'history' to move around – I am concerned in this book with three different kinds of history–memory relationship. I am concerned, firstly, at a general level, with memory's role in what *change* we call the historical process – the process by which things in the *across* past have happened, and by which one historical state of affairs has turned into another, up to and including the historical moment *time* that we call the present. I am concerned, secondly, with the practicalities of making memory an object of historical study – with the conceptual and methodological approaches that may help historians to define and to approach memory as an element in historical situations. And I am concerned, thirdly, with how people have envisaged and debated the perceived relationships between memory and history as forms of knowledge, each purporting in some way to connect present consciousness with past reality. Thinking about each of these three different kinds of history–memory relationship has implications for thinking about the two others.

But this is only half of the complexity we have to unravel, for in any of these three connections, 'memory' itself can be understood in different ways. According to some of these understandings, memory is something essentially personal and individual; according to others it is basically connected to social institutions and cultural forms; to some it is a survival of past experiences; to others, it is essentially a reconstruction of those experiences from a present standpoint. In investigating the different kinds of history–memory relationship, I shall also, of necessity, be investigating the connections and differences between these different ways of conceptualizing memory itself.

It will be clear that exploring the complexities that have just been outlined requires us to operate on two levels. On the one hand, we will be concerned with history and memory as practicalities – with the processes, activities, experiences or forms of knowledge that these two terms have been used to describe. On the other, we will be concerned with the terms themselves, in their functioning as concepts and discursive instruments – with the ways in which the two words 'history' and 'memory' have been put to use in thinking and arguing about human relationships to the past and about the status of our past-related knowledge. For, if part of the significance of history's recent turn to memory lies in the new approaches that have been adopted in historical study, another part of it lies in the way thinking about memory impinges on thinking about history itself, as a form of knowledge. History and memory are proximate concepts: they inhabit a similar mental territory. Sam Wineburg speaks of them as 'colliding worlds'. What this seems to mean for him is that, when we understand the terms as he understands them – as referring, in the case of memory, to 'knowing the past using the ordinary sense-making capacities we use to know most things', and in the case of history, to 'knowing it as the result of disciplined habits of mind' – they stand for ways of knowing about the past which may be in conflict or in tension with each other, but which are so partly because they also connect and overlap with each other.[7] What I mean here is slightly different – that when we consider the conceptual fluidity and variability of definition with which both 'history' and 'memory' have been invested, we can see them as conceptual terms that have constantly interacted with each other, moving in and out of each other, circling each other warily or amorously, sometimes embracing, sometimes separating, sometimes jostling for position on the discursive terrain that is their common habitat. More will be said about this history of interaction, and about the issues that run through it, in Chapter 1. Here the meanings assigned to the term 'memory' will be fluid and multiple, because their fluidity and multiplicity has been a feature of the debates and polemics I am describing. In the remaining chapters of the book, by contrast, I shall be using the word 'memory' in more concrete ways, to describe and connect a disparate range of practices and processes and phenomena, some occurring within individuals and some within the structures of society and culture, which are involved in producing consciousness of the past at various social levels. In these chapters, my attention will shift gradually from a focus on memory's manifestations in human individuals to one on social interactions, collective structures and public representations, though my overall intention is to show how approaches to memory on these different levels can be interwoven. In these chapters, the word 'memory' is deployed as an analytical instrument or descriptive category, and the meanings I assign to it therefore have to be more tightly defined.

One here enters thorny territory. Memory owes its current prominence in the scholarly lexicon at least partly to its flexible range of meanings, and the value that has been placed on this multivalency has sometimes attracted adverse comment. One does not have to go as far as Norman Finkelstein, who recently denounced 'memory' as 'surely the most impoverished concept to come down the academic pike in a long time', to be wary of the facile conflations and elisions of meaning that have sometimes been smuggled into scholarly thinking through an over-complacent use of this conceptual vocabulary.[8] Andrew Lass has warned that the heuristic value of the term 'memory' is diminished by the habit of using it as 'a catchall term for a wide variety of phenomena' which, while they may be 'intertwined in complex and significant

ways', are strikingly distinct in others.[9] Noa Gedi and Yigal Elam
have carried the criticism further, protesting at the way in which
the term 'collective memory' has been allowed to displace such
useful concepts as 'myth' and 'tradition' and 'stereotype': the
substitution of one vague and general term for a range of more
specific ones is usually indicative, they pointedly remark, 'of
conceptual degeneration, and not, as some would like to think, of
sophistication'.[10] Even a scholar less sceptical about the potential
richness of 'memory' as a conceptual category, Alon Confino, warns
that this category is 'depreciated by surplus use' and sees it as
currently 'more practised than theorized'.[11] Like these authors, I
am anxious in the present book not to be beguiled by memory's
endlessly obliging availability as a term of reference. A word may
be allowed to mean many things, but it is usually unwise to allow
it to mean all of them simultaneously. We need differentiating
markers: we cannot – or should not – pursue an interest in 'memory'
across a range of fields that has individual psychology at one
end and the cultural dynamics of societies at the other, without
expecting to break our conceptual stride occasionally. Nor should
we assume that the emergence of 'memory' as an analytical category
is the kind of conceptual revelation that can only usher other
conceptual vocabularies (such as that of tradition) towards
redundancy; its value may lie rather in the ways it intersects with
such vocabularies and allows us to re-examine them.

But if it is important to be discriminating in the way we use the
terminology of memory and remembering, it is important also to
recognize that memory is not something it is easy to delimit. In
the last analysis, memory is not an object, but a concept – a mental
category that we make use of in making sense of complex and
elusive aspects of human behaviour and experience. Like any
concept worth its salt, it is only serviceable at the risk of getting
frayed at the edges. If we must regard it as a thing, we should think
of it as a thing like a chemical element, never appearing in a pure
state, but always mixed up in other things – in our processes of
learning and perception, in our sense of identity or selfhood, in
our awareness of time or place, in our habits of narration and our
capacity for social interaction, in our sense of tradition or our
potential for development. But memory's multifaceted involvement
in human life means that any intellectual approach to it is bound
to be a partial one: we gain an analytical point of entry by restricting

the focus of our inquiry. Methodological starting-points vary accordingly: for some, what matters in the study of memory is a phenomenological analysis of the actual sensation of remembering; for others, a measurement of the speed and accuracy with which certain kinds of data can be recalled under specified conditions; for others, an analysis of the narrative forms that are used to convey recollections of past experience; for others, an investigation of the social contexts within which people develop or practice the skills and habits of recollection; for others, the correlation of the effects of remembering with patterns of neural activity. Often cultivated within the structures of different academic disciplines, such approaches come to embody not just different perspectives on a common object of study, but separate and not always easily compatible understandings of what that object of study consists of, and of how the study of it is connected to broader structures of human knowledge. Some of these understandings have traditionally viewed memory as something 'individual' or 'personal', others as something 'social'; some have focused on inner subjectivity, others on external manifestation. If we need precision in distinguishing between these different understandings, we need also to avoid the kind of peremptory rigorism that too swiftly converts the working understandings of memory that have been developed in one corner of the interdisciplinary forest into inflexible definitions that can prevent us from exploring the multiple connections between different aspects of human life and experience that an interest in memory can alert us to. Memory is not, in the end, a thing to be pinned down, like a moth in a cabinet; it is a term whose usefulness lies in being tested and debated. Nor, of course, should we assume that the definitions of memory which work for us would automatically be transferable to other cultures or have made sense in earlier historical periods. What we need are not immutable definitions, but ways of bringing different understandings of memory into contact with each other, of exploring their frictions and intersections, of comparing their different purposes and assumptions.

Doing this requires us also to remember that memory's existence is always somewhat mysterious, and that thinking about it is therefore always, in some measure, an imaginative business. We approach an understanding of it through the use of models, through analogy, through metaphor – in short, through figurative and associative thinking.[12] Are we to think of memory as a structural framework, or as a productive process, or as a stream of images? Are we to describe it as the debris of a past that has receded, or as the thread that connects past and present existences? Are we to compare it to a wax tablet which bears the imprint of the mind's past experiences, or to a storehouse of images, or to a labyrinth, or to a holographic image? The choices we make of such imagery set tramlines for our further thinking, and bind our understanding of memory into our broader culture. Imaginative connections, thus established, can outlive the conditions that give rise to them. Analogies can get reversed over time. The long-established habit of imagining memory as a storehouse has been transmuted into the reverse suggestion that storage systems might be understood as forms of memory: talk of society's 'archival memory' or of 'computer memory' persists, even though the storehouse analogy is no longer widely used in scholarly thinking about individual memory. Indeed, the sense of the analogy now moves in the opposite direction: models drawn from computer science, which have little to do with traditional images of the storehouse, are now used to describe the operations of memory in the individual. It is by such means that 'memory' as a concept gets stretched into new areas, and applied in new ways, shifting its focus as efforts at comprehension – both of memory and of other things – generate new imaginative connections. In keeping a critical eye on such extensions and displacements of meaning, we should not ignore the extent to which we ourselves, as thinkers about memory, are caught up in the mental experimentation that we are describing. 'Memory' has no fixed, stable, unitary meaning to which we can invariably recur: it is always, and legitimately, a concept in flux and under review.

In practice, of course, any discussion of memory must have limits, and must prioritize some of the term's possible meanings over others. In its broadest contemporary uses, the term 'memory' has an extremely general application: it designates what André Leroi-Gourhan has called 'the support on which sequences of acts are inscribed'[13] – in other words, whatever enduring instincts or dispositions are assumed to give rise to observable regularities or patterns in the way things are or the way things happen. Thus understood, 'memory' may be mental or physical, natural or artificial, conscious or unconscious, individual or social: it may be embodied in animal instinct, or in cultural programming, or in electronic systems ('computer memory'), or at the limit, even in the molecular structures that produce effects of 'shape memory' in certain physical materials. While such a capacious conception of memory has its uses, most recent studies of memory in the humanities and social sciences have been premised on a narrower understanding: without necessarily agreeing on the further elaboration of the concept, they have taken 'memory' to refer to relationships to the past that are grounded in human consciousness. Defining memory in terms of consciousness does not, of course, prevent us from recognizing that consciousness may be supported by – and may seem sometimes inextricably entangled with – some of the other things that the broader conception of memory also encompasses, such as bodily habits, cultural and educational structures, or artificial intelligence systems. But it gives us a preciser point of focus: for present purposes, the study of memory is the study of the means by which a conscious sense of the past, as something meaningfully connected to the present, is sustained and developed within human individuals and human cultures.

This is still, by some standards, a broad definition. Much of the controversy that the recent turn to memory has generated has had to do with whether the use of 'memory' as an analytical category should be further restricted, by confining it to cases of strictly personal recollection. The historian Sarah Foot speaks for those – not all of them hostile to all aspects of the turn to memory – who have insisted on such a restriction:

> The act of memory I take to be a personal one, particular (exclusive) to the mind recalling past events [. . .]. That memory is itself constructed by many of the same mechanisms of selection and omission that will shape collective accounts and formal histories is taken to be self-evident. Yet the notion of a common past, a pool of shared remembrance to which the members of a specific social, political or, for example, religious community have access by virtue of their individual and collective ownership of the elements of which it is constructed, I wish to differentiate from 'memory'. For such commemoration – whether oral or written – is memorial (in the sense of celebrating recollection, co-mingling remembrance), but not reminiscent, in that the mental process involved in its recovery is that of a learned pattern, not the process of drawing out an experienced one. This distinction cannot be absolute – relived experiences are often, when retold, gilded with learned glosses supplied by other witnesses or auditors of earlier, unrefined versions – yet the cognitive acts are discrete.[14]

The argument is a clear one, yet shadows of the possibility of arguing differently are present in the stream of words somehow evocative of memory ('commemoration', 'memorial', 'remembrance') that Foot makes use of in describing the more collective relationships to the past that she wishes memory to be cognitively distinguished from. It must be recognized also that, while the 'personal' or 'individualistic' understanding of memory is supported by many of our everyday experiences and assumptions, long-established tendencies in common parlance can also support a broader or different understanding. When we speak of the need to preserve something for memory, or of a past event as having faded from memory, or when we inscribe a monument 'in memory' of something or someone, we do not necessarily feel that this way of talking requires us to specify the individuals whose mnemonic capacities are being referred to: memory, in such expressions, seems to be disembodied, less an activity of individual minds than an afterlife of things and events, a diffuse medium in which they can persist as objects of consciousness after losing the fuller qualities of concrete actuality.

Certainly, less 'individualized' understandings of what the term 'memory' can refer to have been characteristic of much of the work that the turn to memory has produced.[15] In some cases, there has been an adjectival revisioning, producing 'social memory', 'collective memory', 'cultural memory' or 'public memory' as the ostensible object of analysis; in others, 'memory' (without qualification) has simply been allowed to cover a range of phenomena, many of which are not obviously 'personal' in character. Memory, we are told, is 'the part of the past which, in its intimate connection to people and things, seems to lend dignity to the idea of the group'.[16] Collective memory is 'what remains of the past in the lived experience of groups, or what these groups make of the past';[17] or is 'the collective construction of the past by a present community';[18] or is 'defined as the representation of the past, both that shared by a group and that which is collectively commemorated, that enacts and gives substance to the group's identity, its present conditions and its vision of the future';[19] while the study of social or collective memory 'is really the study of the common cultural pool which informed a vision of the collective past, explaining how and why present society came into being'.[20] Definitions such as these simply by-pass the question of what individuals remember. Other advocates of a broader conception of memory have, however, been more explicit about where individual remembering stands in relation to this conception. 'Memory is more than the act of recollection by recollecting persons', writes Edward Shils. 'Memory leaves an objective deposit in tradition.'[21] Such a formulation perhaps leaves room for terminological negotiation: is the deposit that memory leaves in tradition itself a continuation of memory (as Shils's wording implies) or is it (as Foot might argue) a form of knowledge of which memory was once the vehicle but whose articulation now depends on a different form of mental action? In Michael Schudson's conception of memory, by contrast, there is no such room for ambiguity: the point is not merely that memory exceeds the limits of individual recollection, but that 'in an important sense, there is no such thing as individual memory at all', since most of the information about the past that individuals rely on in orientating themselves in the present is not stored in their own individual minds, but is 'distributed across social institutions and cultural artifacts'. The individual, for Schudson, merely 'piggybacks on the social and cultural practices of memory' that his or her society has developed.[22]

In seeking to understand the differences that have arisen between scholars over the appropriate conceptual definitions of memory as a field of study, we should not ignore the obvious point that different conceptual emphases may sometimes be a legitimate reflection of the different issues that arise in the study of different periods or different types of society. The contrasting attitudes of Foot and Schudson, for example, may have as much to do with differences between the cultures they are studying – those of Anglo-Saxon England and late twentieth-century America respectively – as with broader differences of intellectual ideology. As Foot herself makes clear, Anglo-Saxon society was a society largely dependent on oral communication: even the written texts that helped to give the sense of the past a durable shape (and that constitute the historian's obvious sources for studying that sense of the past) were generally encapsulations of material drawn from personal recollection or from reminiscences communicated within limited social circles.[23] It is not surprising if the student of such a society feels the need of a working definition of memory that allows her to analyse the specific contributions of individual memories to larger structures of knowledge. The need to do this may well be less apparent to the student of a modern society dominated by the media of mass communication and the mechanisms of a consumer culture: when Schudson reasons that the real substance of the American people's memory of the Watergate affair is to be located not in the 'individual and idiosyncratic recollection' of which individual Americans may sometimes be capable, but in newspapers, books, television programmes and other such publicly disseminated cultural productions, he is – just like Foot, though to opposite effect – fashioning a concept of memory that reflects his perception of the cultural dynamics of the society he is considering.[24]

This is not to say that medievalists always insist on memory's 'personal' aspect, or that students of modern societies always prefer to define it culturally or institutionally. Larger intellectual issues, of a kind that cut across such questions of specialism, may also be at stake. The conception of memory as something essentially personal and intrinsic to individual selfhood seems, at a general level, inextricably connected to the broader currents of individualizing thought that we associate with the Enlightenment and its later liberal legacy. Moves to 'socialize' or to 'culturalize' or to 'collectivize' conceptions of memory may be viewed, by the same token, as part of the calling in question of the hegemony of these individualizing modes of thought that has arisen on assorted intellectual fronts over roughly the last half century – leading in some cases to the attempted revival or re-examination of older 'collectivist' styles of sensibility (a tendency that can be detected in some versions of the idea of collective memory), and in others to the elaboration of modes of thought which seek to reflect on the implications for consciousness and identity of a post-modern, hyper-mobile, media-dominated cultural environment (a tendency evident, for example, in recent writings on 'prosthetic memory' or on 'digital memory').[25] In exploring memory's shifting and sometimes conflicting conceptual definitions, we are engaging with some of the ways in which contemporary culture wrestles with notions of society, of identity and of cultural change.

The premise for this book's own consideration of issues of memory is that neither the 'personal' or 'individualistic' view of memory nor the view that locates it in social, cultural or institutional formations and practices can claim a natural priority over the other. To say this is not to say that we can blur the distinctions between them, but that investigating the tension between them, and reflecting on possible ways of mediating between

Individual + collective

them, can be a way of posing and exploring important questions about the ways in which human relationships to the past are constructed, and the implications of such constructions both for individuals and for societies. The challenge for broader thinking about memory lies in the quest for connections – in the exploration of the complex relationships that may exist between the ways in which individuals remember the pasts that fall within their personal experience, the ways in which they define or experience their social involvement, and the ways in which representations and understandings of a social or collective past are generated within the larger society.

Meeting this challenge has not always been made easier by the conceptual confusion in which terms such as 'collective memory', 'social memory' and 'cultural memory' have sometimes been shrouded. The first of these terms to enter common usage, 'collective memory', has meant, for some, simply the representations of a collective past that have been produced within a given community; for others, a kind of power of recollection that is somehow vested in a group's institutional structures; for others, a sort of area of common ground that manifests itself in the personal memories of a group's individual members; for others, the collaborative strategies that people sometimes adopt when they try to remember things in a group setting.[26] 'Social memory', which entered common usage slightly later, has been used sometimes virtually interchangeably with 'collective memory' (in one or more of the latter's multitude of senses),[27] but at other times as a way of administering a corrective to the other term's supposedly misleading tendency to over-reify the collective aspects of existence. Fentress and Wickham, for example, while maintaining that what makes certain memories social is the fact of their being 'attached to membership of social groups of one kind or another', are resistant to a language of 'collective memory' that they see as unduly neglectful of the individual: 'social memory', in their view, allows for a more nuanced exploration of 'the question of how individual consciousnesses might relate to those of the collectivities those individuals actually made up'.[28] But others, again, have worked the distinction differently, taking 'social memory' to be a term that 'reflects the influence of social factors on individual memory', and 'collective memory' to be one that indicates 'distributed processes of memory or transactive memory with social functions'.[29] 'Cultural memory', finally, has been used sometimes as a virtual synonym for 'material heritage' (in the sense of physical remains that are perceived to have symbolic significance for a particular group or society), sometimes to denote a society's 'memory' for particular cultural codes or devices, sometimes to designate memory that is deemed to be somehow encapsulated in cultural devices, and sometimes simply as a kind of gloss, which explains 'that memory can be understood as a cultural phenomenon as well as an individual or social one'.[30]

It is important, amidst this sometimes bewildering variability of usage, to spell out the meanings that I myself will be assigning to some of these terms. I think of this book as having to do both with *individual memory* (which in particular contexts I may call personal or autobiographical memory) and with *social memory*. In defining what I mean by the latter, and in analysing its workings, I shall have also to engage with and refer to, but will try to maintain a critical distance from, a conception of *collective memory*. How are these terms to be understood?

By *individual memory*, I mean what most people mean by it – memory that is located in the minds of individuals, and through which those individuals have knowledge of things that fall within their personal experience. Memory of this kind is an integral part of the mental functioning of individuals, and is closely linked to concepts of personality and selfhood, and it is these aspects of it that I shall principally focus on in Chapter 2. But individual or personal memory is also part of the mental equipment that allows human beings to function in social settings: its forms are influenced by its social uses, and it makes a contribution to social knowledge and social understanding that can be explored from a social as well as an individual angle. Understanding how individual memory is a resource both for individuals within society and for societies themselves, and how it is connected to larger social processes, will be the primary purpose of Chapter 3.

By *social memory*, I do not mean some kind of functional analogue of individual memory – a unitary mnemonic capacity that does for a group or society what individual memory does for the individual. For me, the term is a general one, which covers the process (or processes) through which a knowledge or awareness of past events or conditions is developed and sustained within human societies, and through which, therefore, individuals within those societies are given the sense of a past that extends beyond what they themselves personally remember. My exploration of social memory therefore begins as a facet of the discussion of the social dimensions of individual remembering in the early parts of Chapter 3, is carried further through the discussion of the workings of memory in social groups in later parts of that chapter, and is then completed by the discussion of the ways in which representations and understandings and senses of the past are produced within the larger society that forms the substance of Chapters 4 and 5.

Social memory, as I understand it here, needs to be defined in relation to individual memory on the one hand, and to conceptions of collective memory on the other. There is no intention, in my usage, of defining a 'kind of remembering' that is social in ways which exclude the workings of the memory that is individual. The ways in which individuals, as participant members of societies, formulate and articulate memories of their own experience are a vital ingredient in the processes that produce knowledge and awareness of the past within those societies. They are not, however, the only things that contribute to those processes, and social memory is therefore not, in my understanding of it, reducible to a kind of sum total or cumulative effect of individual remembering. Rather, processes of social memory are ones which characteristically also involve the operation of a wide variety of cultural devices, and of elements of institutional or social structure, whose effect is often to loosen the connections that given bodies of data may have to specific contexts of individual recollection. The past that people acquire a sense of through their participation in and exposure to these processes is not an accumulation of individual pasts that in principle might be disaggregated, but a past (or a set of pasts) that is (or are) envisaged as being somehow general and collective. The ways in which the possible ingredients for such a sense (or senses) of the past are developed and assembled within society may, of course, simultaneously have an impact on the ways in which individuals remember their own experience: one of the ways in which they find meaning in that experience may be by focusing on its perceived connections to the wider and longer experiences of the groups and societies of whose pasts they are made socially and culturally aware. The processes of social memory are ones which are always cross-weaving the social and the individual, producing pools of retrospective knowledge and understanding that are available both for social use and for personal appropriation.

It is important to envisage social memory as a process (or set of processes), rather than a mental product (or set of products) or a collective mental capacity. Social memory, as understood here, is not particularized: its definition does not include the idea of its being, in essence, attributable as a kind of definable property to specific groups or communities. Thus, if we have occasion – as often happens – to think about how these processes work within a particular social formation, we can speak of the workings of social memory *within* that formation, but should avoid talking of the social memory *of* that formation, as if the formation itself had a kind of mnemonic intellect that linked it unproblematically to a past that was distinctively and definitively its own. Similarly, when referring to the specific representations of the past that may be current within a given society at a given moment, I shall try to speak of these as representations which the processes of social memory may have put into circulation at a particular time, and which themselves have a role in the further development of those processes, rather than speaking as if the representations themselves had a status as 'memories' of a kind that such a supposedly collective mnemonic intellect might be capable of possessing.

The point of making these distinctions is, of course, to avoid the excessive reification of collective identities, and the naïve (or perhaps sometimes disingenuous) presumption of their continuity, that certain uses of the term 'collective memory' (and indeed of 'social memory') have tended to encourage. When we speak of individual memory, we use the word 'memory' fairly fluidly, allowing it to refer sometimes to the general capacity which allows the individual to recollect past experience, sometimes to the more specific mental processes through which this capacity is actualized, and sometimes to the images or impressions that are the specific products of this recollective effort. But we can do this only because our talk of individual memory is premised on an assumption of essential continuity in the remembering subject: we assume, in other words, that there is a mind which registered the initial experience, that it is the same mind that is now recalling that experience, and that the processes that somehow bridge the gap between past experience and present consciousness are ones of which that same mind is the essential location. In the processes of social memory, such a presumable continuity of mind is decisively lacking – and it is lacking not only because groups or societies are not mental entities in the sense that individuals are (that they do not, in other words, naturally possess a unitary central co-ordinating intelligence that allows them to synthesize the various impressions that arise within them into a coherent and pragmatically useful operational system of knowledge), but also, and equally fundamentally, because the continuity of the social entity over time is always inherently problematic. We are always separated from those we have been brought to regard as our social ancestors, not merely by the obvious rupturings of personal awareness that the deaths of successive waves of individuals must produce (but that the overlapping of generations might do something to mitigate), but by shifting conceptions of social identity and shifting patterns of collective organization. To evoke a collective past is always to annexe earlier experiences to a present social conception, and the language of collective memory tends to obscure the extent to which the perceived relevance of such a past to today's social identities must always be an imaginative or ideological construction. Michel-Rolph Trouillot has put the point forcefully:

> Do Europeans and white Americans remember discovering the New World? Neither Europe as we know it, nor whiteness as we now experience it, existed as such in 1492. Both are constitutive of this retrospective entity we now call the West, without which the 'discovery' is unthinkable in its present form. Can the citizens of Quebec, whose license plates proudly state 'I remember', actually retrieve memories of the French colonial state? Can Macedonians, whoever they may be, recall the early conflicts and promises of panhellenism? Can anybody anywhere actually remember the first mass conversions of Serbians to Christianity?

The point here is not simply that people cannot personally have memory of things that happened centuries before they were born, but also that the notion of a collective memory that passes from generation to generation as a fundamental constituent of social identity masks what are often radical discontinuities in social consciousness. In the cases cited, Trouillot argues, 'the collective subjects who supposedly remember did not exist at the time of the events they claim to remember. Rather, their constitution as subjects goes hand in hand with the creation of the past.'[31]

In my own usage, therefore, *social memory* and *collective memory* are not synonymous terms. *Social memory* is a set of processes that are not necessarily neatly bounded by the dividing lines between different human communities, and that within any community are likely to generate a diversity of understandings both of what pasts ought to be evoked or described or celebrated, and of the particular contents that representations or evocations of each of those pasts should incorporate or articulate. *Collective memory* is the species of ideological fiction, itself often generated by and within these processes of social memory, which presents particular social entities as the possessors of a stable mnemonic capacity that is collectively exercised, and that presents particular views or representations of a supposedly collective past as the natural expressions of such a collective mnemonic capacity.

To identify collective memory (in the sense just outlined) as a fiction is not, however, to say that we can easily do without the term altogether. In the first place, the term itself, understood sometimes in this sense and sometimes in others, is so ingrained in recent scholarly discourse that it is often impossible to summarize or to criticize the thinking of scholars who have contributed to the understanding of social memory processes without at least registering their use of it. Secondly, and perhaps more importantly, the fiction that I am using the term to describe may itself sometimes have played an important part in social memory processes. Even if nations, for example, are not, in reality, the carriers of an organic kind of collective memory which binds their present members together in a homogeneous connection to a primordial and continuous past, the idea that they are may be influential in structuring the way that understandings of the past are developed and formulated within particular societies.

Social memory is a process (or set of processes), and processes are composed of social and cultural practices, which combine over time to produce effects in human consciousness and human social relationships. My understanding of social memory is close, in this respect, to that recently formulated by Jeffrey Olick in his call to scholars to resist 'substantialist temptations' by 'viewing social remembering as the ideological projects and practices of actors in settings'. For Olick:

> People, alone or together, remember, recollect, commemorate, etc. These various mnemonic practices, however, create only the

appearance of substance rather than an actual entity scholars should treat as (the?) collective memory. Actors make claims on behalf of memory, assert what they think it is and what they want to have as parts of it; scholars study remembering and the variety of other practices associated with it (e.g. commemoration, museification, heroization, etc.), but avoid taking claims made on behalf of or in terms of collective memory as indicators of a substantial entity – "the collective memory". The scholar's job [. . .] is to chart the uses of the claim, not to participate in its ontological transubstantiation from concept into reality.[32]

Viewed from such an angle, social memory consists of a host of interlocking practices, many of them continuous or repetitive, some of them subtly transformative of people's sense of identity. Some of these practices are premised on, or geared specifically to promoting, concepts of collective identity or corporate continuity that foster the fiction of collective memory; others are geared to more mundane social purposes.

Although the basic understanding of social memory that is adopted here views it in terms of process and practice, it seems sometimes a legitimate extension to use the term 'social memory' (or just 'memory') to refer also to the regime or distribution of past-related awareness that social memory processes bring into existence. Thus we might speak of a certain event remaining in memory for generations, or of the 'social memory of the American Civil War, for example. But it should by now be clear what is meant by this. To speak of the Battle of Gettysburg having a place in American memory in the present day is not, obviously, to say that there are individuals still alive who personally remember it. Nor is it to say that there is a unitary memory of the battle that is somehow lodged in a kind of American public mind. Nor, finally, is it to say that all Americans somehow share the same view of the battle and of its significance. What is meant is simply that, through the complex and variegated processes which I am calling those of social memory, some kind of awareness of the battle is widespread in contemporary American society. Such an observation is, of course, only a starting-point for further analysis. In going further, we may well need to explore, for example, how far the possession of such an awareness of Gettysburg is regarded by Americans as somehow integral to being an American, how far it is typically couched in terms which present the battle as an episode that was vitally significant in the establishment of a national identity or the strengthening of a national community, how far different political and cultural agencies have tried to impose (and how far they have been successful in imposing) a particular understanding of the battle, or particular ways of thinking and talking about it, as normal – or even normative – within American society. These questions may well be of vital significance for our practical understanding of how social memory processes have operated in particular cases, and of their role in the formation of different conceptions of collective identity, but particular answers to them are not implicit in the way I define social memory generally.

What is presented in this book is an investigation of issues and connections, and a review – though not a comprehensive one – of some current scholarly approaches. There is no pretension here of doing full justice to the richness of current historical scholarship on memory, and there are many areas – among them oral history, the gendering of memory, memory and material culture, and memory and museums – where I have been reduced to merely touching on fields of interest that deserve far ampler elaboration. My excuse, such as it is, is that the basic task I have set myself is not that of evaluatively summarizing the development of this now massive and varied historiographical field, or of presenting its edited highlights. Rather, I have sought to find a way of presenting or suggesting the kind of connections between different areas of interest that might help historians (and others) to move towards a more integrated approach to the larger question of how understandings of and relationships to the past are produced and formulated, both at an individual and at a more collective or institutional level, within human societies.

Moving in this direction does not, I want to suggest, depend on our finding a definitive way of resolving the kinds of arguments about 'history' and 'memory' as general intellectual categories or presumed modes of knowledge that are discussed in Chapter 1. Indeed I shall suggest that while analysing such arguments can give us important insights into the issues that are underlyingly at stake in efforts to define history's character and social function as a discipline, the multiplicity of emotionally and politically inflected meanings that the terms 'memory' and 'history' have taken on make it unreasonable to expect a neat conceptual resolution of the history–memory problem. For all the problematic and sometimes irritating multiplicity of its ideological uses, however, the term 'memory' has had an important pragmatic value in recent scholarly endeavour: it has helped scholars to research new areas, to approach familiar fields from unfamiliar angles, to make new connections, to establish new interdisciplinary interactions, in ways that both deepen and extend our historical understanding.

The suggestion is sometimes heard that the focusing of historians' attention on issues of memory is really a kind of retreat from history's traditional concerns with the analysis of past societies and of historical processes towards a 'presentist' study of the way the past is represented or imaginatively constructed. Katharine Hodgkin and Susannah Radstone have suggested, for example, that historians who have engaged in memory studies have done so 'primarily because the concept of memory seems to offer a more cautious and qualified relation to the past than the absolute assertion that for some is associated with history'. From this standpoint, the essence of a turn to memory is seen to lie in its embracing of an awareness that is taken to be 'provisional, subjective, concerned with representation and the present rather than fact and the past'.[33] As an observation on some historians' current motivations (which is what it is offered as), this may have value, but what it holds out is, in my view, a rather one-dimensional vision of where the study of memory might eventually carry us. Refraining from 'absolute assertion' about the past need not mean abandoning the effort to deepen our understanding of historical processes. If a reified 'past' can no longer be considered a stable object of scrutiny, the 'present' has scarcely more stability. The present is not a moment of fixity to which 'representations' of the past may have their significance neatly confined; it is always a moment of emergence, in which things that have been going on for some time go on going on, acquiring changing layers of significance as they do so. And this, for all the problems of the undertaking, is an important part of what historical studies should seek to shed light on. This does not mean ceasing to be interested in 'representations' (rather the opposite), but it means seeking to develop an understanding of representations that is processual – that explores the contexts and productive processes of their emergence, their relationship to earlier representations and to gradually evolving frameworks of understanding, and the ways in which they themselves feed back into the ongoing process by which a sense of the past and of its present significance is always being generated, negotiated, modified, communicated, and put to service as a basis for action, within society. Recent work on memory has, I believe, begun to make some purposeful advances in this direction, and it is to the continuation of these advances that this book seeks to make a contribution.

All of this is important because the sense of the past, and the complex processes of memory that sustain and develop it, make a contribution to the historical process that is not peripheral, but integral and often crucial. How people behave in particular situations is often determined less by some very immediate set of circumstances, or by some cumulative totality of previous history that weighs upon them, than by the specific – and often emotionally laden – understandings that they and others have of what has happened in the past and of what the past implies for the present. Historical processes are not reducible to orderly sequences of self-contained moments, each politely receding as its successor comes in view. As Macbeth ruefully perceived, deeds – some deeds at least – are apt not to be done when they are done. Events and experiences linger in consciousness unevenly and sometimes almost imperceptibly, periodically resurfacing, sometimes exerting an influence long after the conditions that ostensibly produced them have been seemingly surpassed. Episodes such as the Battle of Kosovo or the American Civil War, experiences such as those of slavery or of ethnic cleansing, leave their mark in patterns of expectation, in hostilities and insecurities, sensations of humiliation or delusions of grandeur, that are transgenerational and often unpredictable in their effects. The impressions such episodes and experiences create overlap and intersect with ones generated by things that come earlier or later, giving to the historical process a texture not of orderly sequence but of tangled simultaneity. Understanding how the flow of the past has produced each successive present moment and understanding how each such moment has construed the past that it deems to be significant cannot be separate undertakings: the task is always to connect them.

Notes

1 R. F. Atkinson, *Knowledge and Explanation in History: an Introduction to the Philosophy of History* (Ithaca, 1978), p. 47.

2 Quotations from G. Goethals and P. Solomon, 'Interdisciplinary perspectives in the study of memory', in P. Solomon et al (eds), *Memory: Interdisciplinary Approaches* (New York, 1988), p. 1; G. Fischbach and J. Coyle, 'Preface', in D. Schacter (ed.), *Memory Distortion: How Minds, Brains, and Societies Reconstruct the Past* (Cambridge, Mass., 1995), p. ix; R. Terdiman, *Present Past: Modernity and the Memory Crisis* (Ithaca and London, 1993), p. 9.

3 K. L. Klein, 'On the emergence of *memory* in historical discourse', *Representations* 69 (2000), p. 128.

4 G. Spiegel, 'Memory and history: liturgical time and historical time', *History and Theory* 41 (2002), p. 151.

5 For samplings of recent work on memory issues in some of these fields, see edited collections such as the following: R. Van Dyke and S. Alcock (eds), *Archaeologies of Memory* (Oxford, 2003); J. Climo and M. Cattell (eds), *Social Memory and History: Anthropological Perspectives* (Walnut Creek, CA, 2002); S. Crane (ed.), *Museums and Memory* (Stanford, 2000); S. Radstone (ed.), *Memory and Methodology* (Oxford, 2000); S. Radstone and K. Hodgkin (eds), *Regimes of Memory* (London, 2003); P. Antze and M. Lambek (eds), *Tense Past: Cultural Essays in Trauma and Memory* (New York, 1996).

6 There have, however, been admirable synoptic overviews of parts of the field: see for example J. Olick and J. Robbins, 'Social memory studies: from "collective memory" to the historical sociology of mnemonic practices', *Annual Review of Sociology* 24 (1998), pp. 105–40; D. Schacter, 'Memory distortion: history and current status', in D. Schacter (ed.), *Memory Distortion: How Minds, Brains, and Societies Reconstruct the Past*, pp. 1–43.

7 S. Wineburg, *Historical Thinking and Other Unnatural Acts: Charting the Future of Teaching the Past* (Philadelphia, 2001), p. 248.

8 N. Finkelstein, *The Holocaust Industry: Reflections on the Exploitation of Jewish Suffering* (London, 2000), p. 5.

9 A. Lass, 'From memory to history: the events of November 17 dis/membered', in R. Watson (ed.), *Memory, History and Opposition Under State Socialism* (Santa Fe, 1994), p. 102 (n.1). Lass's remark is framed in the context of his critique of Paul Connerton's conception of commemoration, in which bodily habit is treated as a form of memory: see P. Connerton, *How Societies Remember* (Cambridge, 1989).

10 N. Gedi and Y. Elam, 'Collective memory – what is it?', in *History and Memory*, 8:1 (1996), p. 40 and 30–50 generally.

11 A. Confino, 'Collective memory and cultural history: problems of method', *American Historical Review* 102 (1997), p. 1386.

12 See D. Draaisma, *Metaphors of Memory: a History of Ideas about the Mind* (Cambridge, 2000), also ch. 4 ('Metaphors of memory') of S. Rose, *The Making of Memory: from Molecules to Mind* (London, 1993); P. Antze

and M. Lambek , 'Introduction: Forecasting memory', in Antze and Lambek (eds), *Tense Past*, pp. xi-xii.

13 A. Leroi-Gourhan, quoted in J. Le Goff, *History and Memory* (New York and Oxford, 1992), p. 53.

14 S. Foot, 'Remembering, forgetting and inventing: attitudes to the past in England at the end of the first Viking age', *Transactions of the Royal Historical Society* 6th series 9 (1999), pp. 187–8.

15 For general introductions to the ideas of social or collective memory, see J. Fentress and C. Wickham, *Social Memory* (Oxford, 1992); I. Irwin-Zarecka, *Frames of Remembrance: the Dynamics of Collective Memory* (New Brunswick, NJ, 1994); B. Misztal, *Theories of Social Remembering* (Maidenhead, 2003).

16 M. Matsuda, *The Memory of the Modern* (Oxford, 1996), p. 15.

17 P. Nora, 'Mémoire collective', in J. Le Goff, R. Chartier and J. Revel (eds), *La nouvelle histoire* (Paris, 1978), p. 398.

18 R. Gildea, *The Past in French History* (New Haven, 1994), p. 10.

19 Misztal, *Theories of Social Remembering*, p. 7.

20 M. Innes, 'Introduction: using the past, interpreting the present, influencing the future', in Y. Hen and M. Innes (eds), *The Uses of the Past in the Early Middle Ages* (Cambridge, 2000), pp. 6–7.

21 E. Shils, *Tradition* (Chicago, 1981), p. 167.

22 M. Schudson, 'Dynamics of distortion in collective memory', in Schacter (ed.), *Memory Distortion*, pp. 346–7.

23 Foot, 'Remembering, forgetting and inventing', p. 186.

24 M. Schudson, *Watergate in American Memory: How We Remember, Forget, and Reconstruct the Past* (n.p., 1992), p. 4.

25 See, for example, A. Landsberg, *Prosthetic Memory: the Transformation of American Remembrance in the Age of Mass Culture* (New York, 2004); C. Locke, 'Digital memory and the problem of forgetting', in S. Radstone (ed.), *Memory and Methodology* (Oxford, 2000), pp. 25–37.

26 For useful efforts to draw distinctions between different understandings of collective memory, see J. Olick, 'Collective memory: the two cultures', *Sociological Theory* 17 (2000), pp. 333–48; J. Wertsch, *Voices of Collective Remembering* (Cambridge, 2002), pp. 20–4.

27 For a case of such apparent interchangeability, see Misztal, *Theories of Social Remembering*.

28 Fentress and Wickham, *Social Memory*, p. ix.

29 D. Paez, N. Basabe, J. L. Gonzalez, 'Social processes and collective memory: a cross-cultural approach to remembering political events', in J. Pennebaker, D. Paez, B. Rimé (eds), *Collective Memory of Political Events: Social Psychological Perspectives* (Mahwah, NJ, 1997), p. 147.

30 M. Bal, 'Introduction', in M. Bal, J. Crewe and L. Spitzer (eds), *Acts of Memory: Cultural Recall in the Present* (Hanover, NH, 1999), p. vii.

31 M-R. Trouillot, *Silencing the Past: Power and the Production of History* (Boston, Mass., 1995), p. 16.

32 J. Olick, 'Introduction', in J. Olick (ed.), *States of Memory: Continuities, Conflicts, and Transformations in National Retrospection* (Durham, NC, 2003), pp. 6–7. For the detection of a drift in this direction in (some) recent memory scholarship, see Olick and Robbins, 'Social memory studies'. For another relevant critical exploration of the possibilities and limitations of collective memory studies, see W. Kansteiner, 'Finding meaning in memory: a methodological critique of collective memory studies', *History and Theory* 41 (2002), pp. 179–97.

33 K. Hodgkin and S. Radstone, 'Introduction: contested pasts', in K. Hodgkin and S. Radstone (eds), *Contested Pasts: the Politics of Memory* (London, 2003), p. 2.

❦ 1 ❦

HISTORY AND MEMORY:
AN IMAGINED RELATIONSHIP

If social memory is the name we give to the processes by which knowledge and awareness of the social past are generated and maintained in human societies, then history, as an intellectual discipline geared to the production and extension of such a knowledge and such an awareness, is obviously part of social memory. And insofar as individual memory also contributes to social memory processes, history has an engagement with individual memory. But 'memory' can also be considered as a discursive term that has been repeatedly, but variously, deployed in the debates that have arisen over history's character as an intellectual activity and over the status of the 'historical knowledge' that is its ostensible product. Here, memory's meanings have often been elusive and ambiguous, but her potency as a rhetorical term has been considerable and sometimes disruptive. One effect of the recent turn to memory in historical studies and in contiguous disciplines has been to bring the issue of history's supposed relationship to memory once again to the forefront of attention. My aim in this chapter, however, will be less to review a current state of debate than to explore the implications of some longer patterns of argument. For if (as Kerwin Lee Klein puts it) 'the emergence of *memory* promises to rework *history*'s boundaries', this is not only because, as he points out, 'history' is a word that always 'finds its meanings in large part through its counter-concepts and synonyms',[1] but also because history and memory have long been terms fashioned in each other's shadows. I want to start with some general remarks about why this may be so.

Past and present

The broader conceptual context within which the twin vocabularies of history and of memory take on meaning is, of course, that of discourse on the relationships of past to present in human societies. The variety and complexity of meanings that have been assigned to these vocabularies reflect the existence of two radically different ways of describing the basic structure of this relationship. In the first of these, the relationship is understood to be cumulative and causal: the past is everything that precedes the present, and that is deemed, through an infinitely complex set of connections and interactions, to have contributed to making the present what it is – making it this present rather than another. The past, defined in this sense, has a substantial existence that is independent of present consciousness: indeed our present consciousness of the past is to be viewed from this angle simply as one of the features of the present that things in the past have combined to produce. Past is linked to present in a continuous flow of development, and the present is thus to be thought of less as a vantage-point from which the past can be summarized and assessed than as simply the latest moment in an inexorably advancing stream of historical happenings and interactions.

In the second understanding, the relationships are reversed: it is not the past that produces the present, but – figuratively at least – the present that produces the past, through an effort of the creative or analytical imagination. The past, in this understanding, is not the totality of all past happenings – for this is a totality we can never hope to apprehend – but the past that we have a 'sense' of, the past as it exists in current awareness, a past constructed through the complex mixture of reflection and recollection, research and imaginative representation, that allows us the feeling of conscious retrospection. The past that is thus constructed may be connected in certain ways to the substantially existing past that the first understanding refers to; at least, the belief that it is connected to such a past is implied by the conviction that what we are registering is a retrospective awareness rather than a fantasy. In its inherent selectiveness, however, and in the kinds of significance that give it meaning, it is to be regarded not as the continuation of the past that has been, but as the past that makes sense for the present.

The central problem for any effort to appreciate the temporal dimension of human existence is to bridge the gap between these two understandings. It seems essential to grasp, on the one hand, the ways in which our retrospective constructions of the past are themselves historically conditioned – shaped, in other words, by the very flow of past events and experiences at which their selective and creative backward gaze is directed. But it seems important, also, to grasp the converse, namely that the development and articulation of 'the sense of the past' makes a contribution to the unfolding historical process that is often crucial. It is here that the discourses of history and of memory, in their prevailing modern forms, come into play. Each of these discourses straddles the gap between the two understandings of the past-present relationship that have just been outlined. Looking at their different ways of doing so gives us a possible clue to what may be significant in debates about the history–memory relationship.

The discourse of history, as it has classically been elaborated in connection with the modern historical discipline, posits a separation of past and present that is overcome through a particular kind of critical encounter. The separation is evident in the two quite different senses that the term 'history' is recognized as bearing, in the first of which history denotes the continuous stream of happenings that constitutes 'the past', and in the second of which it denotes the accounts of the past that historians produce as a result of their critical labours in the present. For the more radical critics of the historical discipline, the relationship which 'history as written' bears to 'history as lived' is intrinsically problematic: since the past is gone for ever, our reconstructions of it are unverifiable and therefore intrinsically arbitrary.[2] For defenders of the discipline, however, a truly significant knowledge of the past is made possible by the historian's regular and repeated application of critical methods to the (usually mainly documentary) objects that are the surviving traces of past events and experiences. Historical knowledge has its foundations in the magic of these critical encounters, in which intellects grounded in the present interrogate the debris that the past has bequeathed. This is how the modern professional discourse of history bridges the cognitive gap that otherwise separates past and present.

Yet, as historians themselves are generally well aware, this is obviously an incomplete account of what contributes to the production of historical knowledge. Focusing on the historian's magic moments of critical interpretation, it ignores the complex longer processes by which these moments have been prepared. Historical sources are not just evidential objects that passively await the historian's critical scrutiny: often, at least, their production and survival reflect earlier efforts either to hold on to elements of a past or present reality that might be in danger of being forgotten, or to influence the retrospective judgements of posterity. Historians, for their part, are not just the critical agents of a present consciousness that seeks to overcome its disconnection from a past that has definitively receded. They, and their skills, and the prior assumptions about the past (and about things and life in general) that guide their application of those skills, are all products of the historical process, caught up in the very flow of events and experiences whose earlier phases they seek to recover and to interpret. We are all relativists now, at least to this extent: we know that our historical knowledge and understanding and curiosity – and indeed our conceptions of historical method – are themselves historically positioned. But once we recognize this, we require a more fluid conception of the production of historical knowledge than the conventional professional discourse of history has tended to offer – a conception that allows us more fully to explore the subtle transformative processes by which 'history as lived' and 'history as written' (or history as understood) influence each other's production.

It is at this point that memory becomes a seductive concept for historians to think about. This is partly because we may see memory itself – the phenomena that the term is commonly used to designate – as playing a significant part in the broader processes that have just been described: historians' approaches to historical study are influenced by what they themselves remember, and memory operates on numerous levels in the transmission both of the information that ends up by being encapsulated in historical source materials and of the ideas that shape the way these materials are interpreted. But it is also because memory as a discursive concept offers a facility for thinking freshly about the process more generally. In its commonest acceptations at least, 'memory' seems to capture a sense of the fluidity that the conventional research-focused discourse of professional history tends to exclude, but that a broader appreciation of the production of historical knowledge seems to require. Where the discourse of history poses the question of how the present can achieve knowledge of a past from which it is separated, the discourse of memory posits a more intimate or continuous connection between past experience and present consciousness. At its most obvious, the continuity is personal: the continuity of the individual mind which retains and later reproduces the memory of its past impressions and experiences. But even where – as in talk of 'collective' or 'social' memory – the concept of memory is less precisely focused on the individual, the implication is of the existence of structures – whether mental or social – that have a power to retain and to transmit, to ensure the persistence of certain impressions, and to impart a moulding to present consciousness through the medium of such survivals. Such an emphasis need not exclude the idea that memory transforms and reconstructs the past that it remembers: such a transformation is presented, however, as the effect not of the focused critical engagements that are the hallmark of historical study, but of an evolving process of reflection rooted in the continuities of human existence. The discourse of memory haunts and shadows the discourse of history, now offering to complete it and reinforce it, to expose its inadequacies and fragile pretensions. It is in this ambiguous relationship that the more concrete arguments that historians and others have used in debating the history–memory relationship are rooted.

History and memory: connections and separations

Two opposing tendencies can be detected in these past debates: on the one hand, a desire to associate the idea of history with that of memory; on the other, a desire to disconnect them or differentiate them. A quick sampling of writings on the nature of history by historians and philosophers produces a host of passages in which the ideas of history and of memory appear closely connected. 'The parts of human learning', wrote Francis Bacon, 'have reference to the three parts of Man's Understanding [. . .]: History to his Memory, Poesy to his Imagination, and Philosophy to his Reason.'[3] Modern authors, without replicating Bacon's general categories, have often seemed to echo his assumption that history is somehow characterized by its relationship to memory – that it is, in effect, the intellectual form under which memory spills over into organized knowledge. 'History is nothing but assisted and recorded memory', wrote the philosopher George Santayana.[4] John Lukacs writes of history as 'the remembered past', Peter Burke of 'history as social memory', Patrick Hutton of 'history as an art of memory'.[5] For Ludmilla Jordanova, 'the writing of history is about the transmission of memories'; indeed, 'the practice of history is, after all, a highly specialized form of commemoration'.[6] Many things separate these authors, but all insist on a rhetorical coupling of history and memory as concepts: history is an extension of memory, or a form of memory, or a codification or arrangement of memory, or at the least is somehow meaningfully similar or analogous to memory.

A similar trawl, however, produces a contrasting string of quotations. For the philosopher Leon Goldstein, 'what we assert on the basis of memory is not asserted as established in the historical way'.[7] For David Lowenthal, 'History differs from memory not only in how knowledge of the past is acquired and validated but also in how it is transmitted, preserved and altered.'[8] For Michael Bentley, the difference amounts to outright opposition: 'history is precisely non-memory, a systematic discipline which seeks to rely on mechanisms and controls quite different from those which memory triggers and often intended to give memory the lie'.[9] For these authors, memory is, so to speak, history's defining 'other' – a contrasting and radically different form of knowledge.

The juxtaposition of these two sets of quotations, taken un-ashamedly out of context, no doubt conceals as much as it reveals: it ignores a host of qualifying nuances and obscures the fact that both key terms have diverse possible meanings, so that ostensibly similar statements coupling them can sometimes turn out to mean quite different things. The juxtaposition does, however, reveal a tension at least at the level of rhetorical formulations, which can alert us to deeper cleavages and ambiguities in the way that history has been thought about.

It is not hard, on one level, to see how such a tension arises. One does not have to think for long about what historians do and about the conditions under which they do it to begin to perceive, on the one hand, ways in which the production of historical knowledge intersects with activities of remembering, and on the other, ways in which it may diverge from those activities. One of the commonest arguments asserting the connectedness of history and memory affirms the fundamentally memory-based character of the (usually documentary) source materials on which historians base their claims to knowledge. History differs from other branches of scholarly inquiry, the argument implies, in having an object of study – the past – that has already gone for ever. Inherently unobservable, past events and circumstances can be approached only through the memories of them that have been encapsulated in documentary source materials. The knowledge that historians are involved in producing is a knowledge at second-hand, to which the memories of others make a decisive contribution. Such an argument contains an element of truth, which will not, however, bear the kind of weight that the bolder exponents of the 'history as memory' view have sometimes sought to place upon it. Historians do depend heavily on documentary sources, and sources of this kind do require memory of some kind for their production. The scribe who records a trial proceeding must possess a procedural memory of the techniques of writing, coupled with the kind of short-term memory that enables him to retain the impressions of each moment for long enough to commit them to record. These requirements are, however, not in themselves sufficient to give to such a source the kind of status as a personal or autobiographical recollection of past events or experiences that would be necessary to support the assertion that history is essentially a reworking of other people's memories. No doubt, sources embodying such recollections – eye-witness accounts, diaries, memoirs, etc. – are often important for historians, but they are seldom the only sources available, and need not always be the ones that do most to influence the historian's perceptions and lines of argument: economic historians may be as interested in account books and industrial archaeology, military historians in manuals of infantry tactics.

Source materials are, in any case, not the only ingredients in the production of historical knowledge and historical under-standing: we must consider also the mental instincts and procedures that are put to work in the use of such materials. The specification of these is, however, another area in which strikingly different emphases have been apparent. These can be approached by briefly contrasting positions adopted by two still influential philosophical thinkers on historical knowledge, R. G. Collingwood and Wilhelm Dilthey.

For Collingwood, history was radically dissimilar from memory. This was so 'because history is a certain kind of organized and inferential knowledge, and memory is not organized, not inferential at all':

> If I say 'I remember writing a letter to So-and-so last week', that is a statement of memory, but it is not an historical statement. But if I can add 'and my memory is not deceiving me; because here is his reply', then I am basing a statement about the past on evidence; I am talking history.[10]

For Collingwood, then, historical knowledge was distinguishable by its obligatory relationship to citable evidence. The inferences that a historian drew from the evidence might be mistaken or contestable, but the possibility of showing the evidence on which they were based brought them into the public arena: historical knowledge was, in principle, shareable and verifiable. Memory, by contrast, was entirely subjective: the knowledge derived from it had no point of reference outside the personal consciousness of the rememberer, who alone could experience its authority. The moment remembered knowledge was justified by reference to external evidence, and thus became admissible as a contributory element in the formulation of historical knowledge, its character was fundamentally changed.

For Collingwood, however, the point was not simply that historical statements about the past differed in their criteria of knowledge from statements of how that past was remembered, but that the kind of overall understanding of past reality that historical scholarship was geared to producing was, in a fundamental sense, one that went beyond the limits of recollection. This was made clear in one of the notes that was not reproduced in the arrangement of Collingwood's writings published posthumously as *The Idea of History*:

> The historian who sketches the economic history of the Roman Empire depicts a state of things which no contemporary ever saw as a whole; and this whole is not built up in the historian's mind out of parts, each separately seen and reported by a contemporary; because the whole which is the object of the historian's thought is not the sum of these parts but the system of relations uniting them, and it is because he grasps this system of relations that he is able to reject certain contemporary statements of alleged fact as inaccurate or misleading, and to interpolate inferences of his own concerning matters on which his own sources are silent.

The 'historical past', Collingwood concluded, is 'not a remembered past, nor a sum of remembered pasts', but an 'ideal past' – a past that has been organized through the workings of a constructive analytical imagination.[11] This imagination, Collingwood implies, is concerned with conceptual issues (ones of causation, for example, or of social structure, or of long-term continuity and change) that derive from the realm of historical thought rather than from remembered experience. The essential achievement of historical reasoning is to rescue us from a slavish dependence on memory's limited and subjective form of consciousness.

Dilthey's starting-point, in the area of his thinking I want to highlight, is quite different. Here the emphasis falls not on a critical method that distances history from memory, but on the central role of autobiographical remembering in the incubation of a historical mode of thinking. For Dilthey, 'the root of all historical comprehension' lies in the individual's mental relationship to his or her own life-experience. 'The power and breadth of our own lives and the energy with which we reflect on them are the foundation of the historical vision. It alone enables us to give life back to the bloodless shadows of the past.' It is by grasping the interactions and conjunctions of forces that shape our own lives that we establish the elements of an understanding that can then be applied to a larger social reality, and it is by identifying a temporal structure in our own experience that we make this understanding a specifically historical one. Here, as Dilthey makes clear in his comments on autobiographical writing, memory plays a vital role, not by indiscriminately preserving the traces of past experience, but by ordering them selectively and interpretatively, in ways which articulate an unfolding sense of life's direction:

> The person who seeks the connecting threads in the history of his life has already, from different points of view, created a coherence in that life which he is now putting into words. He has created it by experiencing values and realizing purposes in his life, making plans for it, seeing his past in terms of development and his future as the shaping of his life and of whatever he values most. He has, in his memory, singled out and accentuated the moments which he experienced as significant; others he has allowed to sink into forgetfulness. The future has corrected his illusions about the significance of certain moments. Thus, the first problem of grasping and presenting historical connections is already half solved by life.

The units are formed by the conceptions of experience in which present and past events are held together by a common meaning. Among these experiences are those which have a special dignity both in themselves and for the course of his life; they have been preserved by memory and lifted out of the endless stream of what has happened and been forgotten. Constantly changing connections have been formed from different standpoints within life itself, so that the task of historical presentation is already half performed by life.[12]

Autobiographical remembering is thus, for Dilthey, integral to the mind's training in historical thinking.

Dilthey's and Collingwood's positions are not strictly incompatible: they are simply very differently focused – in the one case, on the inward mental origins of historical thinking, in the other, on the outwardly applied methods through which historical interpretations are in practice developed. The comparison of them allows us, however, to see how different ways of focusing an account of the mental operations that give rise to historical knowledge can give quite different constructions to the history–memory relationship. The comparison also highlights differences of emphasis in another area. Dilthey's conception of historical understanding is individualistic: such an understanding is seen as an outgrowth of each individual's memory-assisted reflection on his or her life-experience. Collingwood's is essentially a more social conception: if individuals are the formulators of historical interpretations, it is the historian's ability to demonstrate to others the evidential foundations of his or her interpretations that crucially separates history from memory. Critical exchanges between individuals – or, at the very least, the continual possibility of such exchanges – are thus, for Collingwood, a significant part of the process by which historical knowledge is generated.

The comparison of Collingwood and Dilthey thus alerts us to some of the ways in which thinking about history intersects with thinking about memory, both individual and social, and in which different ways of conceptualizing historical production can be reflected in different ways of presenting the history–memory relationship. In exploring these issues further, we need to be aware, not just of the different meanings that the two words 'history' and 'memory' can bear, but of the different values that can be assigned to them in different cultural contexts. For, in our own culture at least, remarks on the history–memory relationship have tended to

.ve: implicitly or explicitly, they have determined the
one of the terms by manipulating its relationship to
er. The intended polemical effects of such manoeuvres have
ᴖ from case to case. Among those who have seen history and
ᴖory as fundamentally different, some have meant to establish
the superiority of historical knowledge (scientific and objective)
over memory (subjective and unreliable); others have intended
the opposite, contrasting memory (an authentic and immediate
form of knowledge) with history (an uncertain compound of
retrospective guesswork and wishful thinking). A more fiercely
political version of the latter opposition has also become common,
in which 'history' stands for oppression by grand narrative – for a
constructed and putatively authoritative view of the past which
serves the interest of an elite by excluding or marginalizing
other experiences – and 'memory' designates the multiple and
disorganized, but always potentially resurgent, voices of the
marginalized or excluded. Among those who have seen history as
closely connected to memory, on the other hand, some have
seen the connection as proof of history's credentials as a socially
useful discipline, others as grounds for questioning its intellectual respectability. Shifting conceptions of the history–memory
relationship form part of broader shifts and contests in cultural
values: the arguments that have prevailed have not necessarily been
those that were logically unassailable, but those which have
resonated most appealingly with larger cultural aspirations or
political perceptions.

Carl Becker's famous and often-cited American Historical
Association presidential address of 1931, entitled 'Everyman his
own historian' is a telling example here. 'History', Becker asserted,
'is the memory of things said and done'; historical knowledge was
'the artificial extension of the social memory'. Considered as a
piece of logical reasoning, Becker's speech left something to be
desired. Starting from a definition of history as the 'knowledge of
events that have occurred in the past', and then observing that
there can be no such knowledge without memory, he then blithely
rephrases the definition so as to equate history with memory,
peremptorily excluding anything of a non-mnemonic or non-
recollective character that might conceivably enter into the
production of historical knowledge.[13] Memory, itself, furthermore,
is handled by Becker in ways which tend to obscure arguably

important distinctions between, for example, the memory that individuals have of their own experience and the knowledge about the past that they derive from other sources. Focusing disapprovingly on such elisions can, however, lead us to overlook the larger strategic point of Becker's argument. The conclusion he draws from his equation of history with memory is that, since everyone has a memory, everyone is in effect a historian. The intellectual processes by which historical knowledge is arrived at are fundamentally continuous with, rather than different from, the processes by which ordinary citizens, taking their own memories as starting-points, develop the kinds of knowledge about the world that enable them to function successfully within it. (This is Dilthey's argument translated into the language of a democratic pragmatism.) The role of historians is therefore not to generate a specialist form of knowledge that stands separate from and above what ordinary people remember, but to be of service to ordinary people in extending and completing at a social level that pragmatically useful sense of the past that has its basic origins in the uses of individual memory. What Becker provided for his audience of professional historians, then, was not a tight-knit philosophical argument defining the relationship of history to memory, but an impassioned plea for historians not to allow their sense of professional and intellectual dignity to separate them from a lively awareness of ordinary people's needs and modes of thought. The term 'memory' was put to work, in this connection, to affirm the priority of the pragmatic and the commonsensical over those aspects of history's disciplinary identity that were rooted in a specialized academic culture.

I want now to proceed to a broader examination of the functions which notions of memory, and of the history–memory connection, have had in the thoughts and arguments that have arisen, not so much over history's precise characteristics as a form of knowledge, but over its significance for society. Two preliminary generalizations may be helpful in orientating this discussion. The first (which the analysis of Becker has already suggested) is that contrasting positions on history's relationship to memory have often been closely connected to different attitudes to the dignity of history as a professional activity. Arguments affirming the radical differences between history and memory have generally formed part of intellectual strategies that have sought to present history as a specialist field – a type of enquiry with its own exacting methodological disciplines, its own class of specially trained (and probably professional) practitioners, its own monitorial systems, and its refined and specialized product (historical knowledge). Arguments of this kind acquired their cultural force as part of the grand offensive by which history established itself, in the nineteenth and early twentieth centuries, as a prestigious branch of knowledge founded on and appealing to the prevailing positivist ideologies. Arguments seeking to establish a close connection between history and memory, on the other hand, have generally been linked to strategies that sought to root historical understanding in some kind of common human experience – either in forms of consciousness conceived to be innate in every human individual, or in the supposedly organic traditions of social life. In the early stages of history's emergence as a modern discipline, the thrust of such strategies was often to enhance that discipline's claims to prestige, by presenting it as the intellectual articulation of deeply-rooted forms of human consciousness and aspiration. Initially at least, such a presentation was not necessarily regarded as being in tension with history's claims to be a critical and 'scientific' discipline. (Leopold von Ranke, for example, often seen as the founder of the modern scientific conception of history, himself drew sustenance from the notion that historical scholarship had the function of assisting the passage of memories from generation to generation.)[14] Later, however, the increasing professionalization of the discipline and the hardening of positivist ideology widened the gap between these two ways of describing history as an intellectual endeavour. As a result, in the twentieth century, arguments linking history and memory were more often intended to 'democratize' or 'popularize' the discipline. Sometimes, as in Becker's case, this has been done cautiously, by gently reminding professional historians of their obligations to a larger public. Sometimes, however, the challenge has been a more radical one, openly critical of professional historians' supposed efforts to affirm a monopoly of historical knowledge. Raphael Samuel's memorable castigation of what he saw as the inbred, blinkered, archive-fetishizing tribalism of the academic historical profession, in the opening pages of his *Theatres of Memory*, is a fine example of this. For Samuel, 'popular memory' is indeed 'the very antithesis of written history', as the latter is currently defined by its professional practitioners:

his plea, however, is for a more inclusive conception of the historical endeavour in which this antithesis would be replaced by fertile interaction.[15]

The second generalization connects with the first. Part of history's pretension to 'scientific' status has conventionally lain in its claim to 'objectivity'. Fundamental to this claim has been the idea that history has its own distinctive object of study – 'the past' (or 'past events' or 'past reality') – which is essentially separate from the minds of those who study it. Assertions of the radical difference between history and memory have been part of the structure of argument by which this notion of separateness has been maintained. They have served, in other words, to promote a conception of historical study as the study of a past that is now over, that is accessible for the purposes of scholarly study only through the material traces it has left behind, and then only through the application to those traces of a rigorous method of scholarly analysis. Arguments linking history closely to memory, on the other hand, have appealed instead to the notion of a past that is never over, never neatly separable from the present in which it is studied, always therefore flowing into our present modes of historical consciousness, and shaping the historian's agendas in ways that go beyond the mere constraints imposed by the available material evidence. Part of the reason why history's relationship to memory has remained contentious is that the tension between these two ways of viewing the past has lain persistently close to the heart of modern thinking on the historical discipline: it has seemed hard to give that discipline a distinctive identity without separating the past as an object of knowledge from the present, but hard to justify it socially without viewing the past as a matrix to which the present is crucially connected.

History and collective memory

For some of history's admirers and practitioners, since its emergence as a modern scholarly discipline, the obvious way to bring this tension under rhetorical control has been effectively to define history itself as the working memory of society. The force of the argument lies in a perceived analogy, between the mental lives of individuals and of societies: the point is not that history relies on memory, or that it incorporates memory, or that it is one of a diversity of cultural vehicles through which social memories are circulated and constructed, but that it does for society what memory (in the sense of individual memory) supposedly does for the individual. The analogy is often tilted into metaphor: history *is* the collective memory, in its developed and efficacious form; it is the form of intellectual discipline, and the type of knowledge, through which a given society is able to remember. Arguments of this kind have their roots in a characteristically nineteenth-century conjunction of ideas, drawing on the one hand on idealist conceptions of the flow of history as the progressive development of self-conscious human reason, and on the other on conceptions of collective identity that envisaged human beings as members of organic communities held together by deep awareness of a common heritage. 'Recollections', wrote the German historian Johann Gustav Droysen in 1868, 'belong to humanity's deepest nature [. . .]. In the highest degree personal as they appear, they yet form a bond between the souls which meet in them. No human community is without them. Each possesses in its previous life and history the image of its being, a common possession of all participants, which makes their relationships so much the firmer and more intimate'.[16] History, for thinkers such as Droysen, was the intellectual vehicle through which, in the modern era, 'the self-consciousness of humanity' reflected on its own development.

The communities that loomed largest in the nineteenth-century imagination were, of course, nations. Ernest Renan, in a famous lecture of 1882, placed memory at the core of nationality: a nation was 'a soul or spiritual principle', which animated a given people by virtue of their 'possession in common of a rich legacy of memories', and of their determination to develop that legacy in the present.[17] Seizing on such a conception of nationhood, historians in many countries readily presented themselves not just as the guardians and transmitters and presenters of this precious national memory, but as its essential interpreters. They asserted, in many cases, a kind of organic connection between their own narratives and the collective traditions of the people to whose past those narratives related. J. R. Green's *Short History of the English People*, to take just one example, was described by his widow not merely as delivering 'the vision of the continuous life of a mighty people', but as being 'the very expression of the people among whom it was conceived and for whom it was written' – history, in effect, by the people, for the people and about the people.[18]

In the twentieth century, such organicist effusions became after a while less common, at least in academic and liberal intellectual circles. Even if toned down, however, the habits of thought and expression honed in the nineteenth century have continued to leave a mark. Even the leading critic of Whiggish historiography, Herbert Butterfield, somewhat against the run of play in his own argument, let slip the suggestion that history might be regarded on one level as 'something like the memory of mankind', representing 'the spirit of man brooding on man's past'.[19] The 'something like' is a nice touch of twentieth-century caution – converting yesterday's philosophical fantasies into today's cautious analogies. What Butterfield suggested with mankind in general in mind, others have suggested for specific nations or societies. 'For a people to be without history, or to be ignorant of its history, is as for a man to be without memory', wrote the American historian Henry Steele Commager,[20] and while such a comment need not necessarily refer to history as a specialized academic form of knowledge, the implication has often been that it is this kind of history in particular that performs this vital social function. For some – for example Hobsbawm, when he states that historians 'compile and constitute the collective memory of the past'[21] – this has perhaps meant only that history is the vehicle through which societies can accumulate the funds of practical knowledge that can assist their present undertakings. For many, however, the implication has been also that history is vital to the maintenance of collective identity. Richard Hofstadter's assertion that 'memory is the thread of personal identity, history of public identity' sets a tone that has frequently been echoed.[22] Hofstadter himself was acutely aware of the possible dangers of the history–memory analogy: too often, he wrote, historians were expected to provide society with a kind of memory 'that is not very different from that we all provide for ourselves – that is, memory that knows how to forget, memory that will rearrange, distort, and omit so much as is needed to make our self-images agreeable'. The provision of this kind of memory was in tension with history's other (and more instrumental) function of analyzing society's past experience 'in such a way as to put into its hands workable tools for the performance of certain tasks'.[23] For many commentators, however, the analogy has seemed straightforward: what memory does for the individual, history does for human societies.

Handled sensitively, the analogical mode of reasoning may conceivably be helpful in exploring the sense in which we can (and the senses in which we cannot) attribute an activity of remembering to human social formations. Treated uncritically, however, functional analogies between history and memory tend to obscure important differences between individuals and societies. If we speak of memory conferring a sense of identity upon the individual, we mean that through memory the individual becomes aware of the continuity of his or her own existence as a thinking, feeling, physically and morally developing person. If we speak of history doing the same for a group or society, what we actually mean is that history helps to foster a sense of transgenerational belonging in which people feel sympathetic connections to other beings from whom they are not just physically and chronologically, but often also culturally and intellectually, removed. In practice, functional analogies between history and individual memory have served, rather too often, to obscure the elements of conflict and contingency in the ways that societies have developed – in effect, to 'naturalize' what are actually politically or culturally constructed identities – and by presenting history as the memory of an organically existing community, to conceal the generally ideological character of historians' contributions to the shaping of these identities.

Though its uses have often been conservative, the description of history as the social equivalent of individual memory embodied, at least originally, a confidently progressivist vision of mankind's intellectual development. In such a vision, history was, in effect, collective memory brought to a point of perfection, through the development of a critical scientific method. The application of this method strengthened rather than weakened the connection which national communities (and perhaps humanity more generally) had to their remembered pasts, allowing the collective tradition to be interpreted even as it was extended. By the mid-twentieth century, however, another – and opposing – way of understanding history's relationship to collective memories began to gain ground. Here, history appeared not as a renewal or continuation of collective memory, but as a radically different form of knowledge whose emergence was linked to memory's weakening hold on human societies. Maurice Halbwachs, whose influential theorization of the 'collective' character of memory will be considered more fully in Chapter 3, was a pioneering exponent of such a view. For Halbwachs, memory (i.e. collective memory) was traditional, group-specific, and predominantly oral. History, by contrast, was essentially a written record of the past, and as such became necessary only when the traditional organization of society into groups that were capable of keeping memory alive began to break down. History arises, then, not as a genuine form of collective memory, but as an artificial substitute. It seeks to repair the effects of memory's breakdown, but can never reproduce the kind of connection to the past that memory itself embodies:

> If the necessary condition for memory is that the subject which remembers, whether individual or group, has the feeling that it goes back to its remembrances [souvenirs] in a continuous movement, how could history be a memory, since there is a breach in continuity between the society which reads this history and the groups in the past which witnessed or acted in the events?[24]

For Halbwachs, memory presupposes continuities of consciousness between past and present; history is founded on the rupture between them. There is, indeed, a kind of tension in Halbwachs's reading of the history–memory relationship. On the one hand, he sees historical writing as, originally at least, a more or less deliberate effort to salvage elements of memory from the ruins of the social frameworks that had previously supported them. (Indeed, he sometimes uses the term 'historical memory' to convey this idea.) On the other hand – and this becomes, in the end, the dominant emphasis – he makes clear that, while the constituent ingredients of historical knowledge may often have originated as ingredients of collective memory, history recombines and reconfigures these elements in ways which transform their significance, by incorporating them into a radically different system of knowledge.

Halbwachs drew attention to what he considered to be two basic differences between the ways in which history and collective memory structure knowledge about the past. Firstly, whereas memory is 'a current of continuous thought', persisting so long as the group which sustains it persists, and organizing its impressions of the past in relation to the basic continuity of that group's experience, history is an intellectual system premised on discontinuity. Memory, in

short, assimilates past to present and present to past; it blurs
distinctions between different phases of past experience, because
it retains from each only what is still felt to be 'alive' – still felt by
members of the group to be part of 'their' collective experience.
History, on the other hand, produces narratives of change that
emphasize (excessively, in Halbwachs's view) discontinuities in
human experience, dividing the past into periods as well as
distancing it from the present. Where memory emphasizes the
organic unity of each group's relationship to its past experience,
history presents a schematic account of human development, in
which the connections between past experience and present
identities are loosened. Secondly, and relatedly, whereas memory,
being always group-specific, is inevitably multiple, history is or
aspires to be unitary and universal. The memories which different
groups have of the past, being the reflection of their different past
experiences, remain essentially separate; they do not fit together
into some overarching framework of 'universal memory'. The
tendency towards a 'universal history', on the other hand, is,
according to Halbwachs, 'the natural orientation of the historical
mind'; even at its most specialized, history always seeks to bring
local detail under the umbrella of a general historical understanding. So long as the French, Germans and Italians exist as
separate groups, their collective memories remain incommensur-
able; the histories of France, Germany and Italy, by contrast,
are always envisaged as capable of being synthesized, with each
other and with other national histories, into a broader historical
account, whose scope is taken to be potentially universal, and whose
composition is governed by interpretative principles that are
assumed to transcend the narrow perspectives of any particular
group. Memory, in short, is always a view from within a group;
history, in theory at least, views groups from the outside. The
construction of historical accounts requires the data of the past to
be abstracted from the socially-grounded mental frameworks within
which memory has arranged them.[25]

Halbwachs's view of the differences between memory and history
lent itself readily to incorporation in narratives of the social
transition from tradition to modernity. In the context of such
narratives, history – as a mode of consciousness even more than
as an intellectual activity – stood as a cultural emblem of the passing
of a traditional order and of the forms of memory that had sustained

it. It might be seen, too, not just as memory's conceptual 'other', but as its antagonist – an active agent or willing accomplice in the processes that eroded it or overthrew it. For some, memory's recession and history's advance might give straightforward grounds for rejoicing. For others (even among professional historians) there might be a greater ambivalence – a sense of regret for the loss of a more organically rooted sense of the past, an anxiety at history's own inadequacy as a social replacement. In a work which charts the unfolding relationships between 'Jewish history' and 'Jewish memory' since the Biblical period, for example, Yosef Hayim Yerushalmi explicitly links the emergence of modern Jewish historical studies to the breakdown of collective Jewish traditions, and hence 'the ever-growing decay of Jewish group memory', that commenced in the early nineteenth century.[26] By historicizing the study of Judaism, he argues, modern historiography participates in the further erosion of traditional modes of consciousness:

> Memory and modern historiography stand, by their very nature, in radically different relations to the past. The latter represents, not an attempt at a restoration of memory, but a truly new kind of recollection. In its quest for understanding it brings to the fore texts, events, processes, that never really became part of Jewish group memory even when it was at its most vigorous. With unprecedented energy it continually recreates an ever more detailed past whose shapes and textures memory does not recognize. But that is not all. The historian does not simply come in to replenish the gaps of memory. He constantly challenges even those memories that have survived intact.

In its aspiration to uncover the totality of a past, Yerushalmi continues, historiography also 'disturbs and reverses' the natural tendency of memory to be drastically selective. Yet, while Yerushalmi defends the dignity of the historical enterprise, he also articulates a sense of history's inadequacy to fill the gap that is left by memory's disintegration. Asking whether, as a result of the historian's critical efforts, 'some genuine catharsis or reintegration is foreseeable', he answers that 'at the present moment the very opposite seems to be the case': the vision of the Jewish past that history offers supplies no new vision of unity on which a sense of collective identity might be founded, but a sense only of 'multiplicity and relativity'.[27]

It is in an influential essay by Pierre Nora that the idea of history
as the nemesis of memory has been most forcefully articulated,
and made central to a general account of history's role in the
broader evolution of modern sensibilities. The opening pages of
Nora's article abound in exuberant formulations of this central
idea. 'What was left of experience, still lived in the warmth of
tradition, in the silence of custom, in the repetition of the ancestral,
has been swept away by a surge of deeply historical sensibility';
there has been 'an uprooting of memory', an 'eradication' of it
'by the conquering force of history'; 'Memory is always suspect in
the eyes of history, whose true mission is to demolish it, to repress
it'. The 'acceleration of history' (a term that seems to cover both
the increasing rate of historical change and the 'surge' of historical
sensibility) brings us face to face, Nora argues, with:

> the enormous distance that separates real memory – the kind of
> inviolate social memory that primitive and archaic societies embodied,
> and whose secret died with them – from history, which is how modern
> societies organize a past they are condemned to forget because they
> are driven by change; the distance between an integrated memory,
> all-powerful, sweeping, un-self-conscious, and inherently present-
> minded – a memory without a past that eternally recycles a heritage,
> relegating ancestral yesterdays to the undifferentiated time of heroes,
> inceptions, and myth – and our form of memory, which is nothing
> but history, a matter of sifting and sorting.[28]

For all the vigour with which he states these oppositions, Nora's
concern is not simply to map two opposing forms of consciousness,
but to suggest the process by which what was originally a latent
tension between history and memory has become an outright
antagonism. Focusing on French experience in particular, Nora
recognizes the centrality of history as a discipline to the building
of national traditions. History's intended object, in the earlier
phases of its development, was not the destruction of memory and
tradition, but their development and consolidation within the
frameworks of modern nationality. In this sense, he argues,
'France's entire historical tradition [. . .] developed as a disciplined
exercise of the mnemonic faculty, an instinctive delving into
memory in order to reconstruct the past seamlessly and in its
entirety.' Even in the twentieth century, 'every major revision of
historical method has been intended to broaden the base of collective memory'. Over time, however, the development of history's

critical practices begins to subvert the mnemonic purposes which these practices were originally intended to serve. Decisive here, in Nora's view, is the development of the historiographical instinct, by which history starts to reflect critically on its own conditions of production:

> when history begins to write its own history, a fundamental change takes place. Historiography begins when history sets itself the task of uncovering that in itself which is not history, of showing itself to be the victim of memory and seeking to free itself from memory's grip.

History then turns critically on the traditions that memory has bequeathed, deconstructing their legends and symbols: 'historiography sows doubt; it runs the blade of a knife between the heartwood of memory and the bark of history'. As history enters this historiographic phase of its development, its 'divorce from memory' is consummated: it becomes an accomplice – or even a central agent – in the erosion of memory's hold on human societies.[29] A final phase is reached, in Nora's narrative, when history becomes aware of the irony of this position, and turns its critical and retrospective gaze on the debris and traces of the once living traditions that it has been instrumental in undermining. It is here that Nora's influential formulation of the notion of *lieux de mémoire* (sites of memory) becomes relevant – a term which evolved in his thinking to cover not just symbolically significant places or monuments, but 'any significant entity, whether material or non-material in nature, which by dint of human will or the work of time has become a symbolic element of the material heritage of any community'.[30] The point about *lieux de mémoire* as objects of historians' interest is that they are quintessentially residual: what they bring into focus is not the existence of still living communities of memory, but merely the lingering awareness of memories and traditions that once had social meaning. A history focused on *lieux de mémoire* is no longer a history at the service of memory, but a history for which memory has become the emblem of loss and social rupture. 'Memory is constantly on our lips because it no longer exists'.[31]

Nora's postmodernist handling of the history–memory relationship presents us with a slightly fatalistic vision of history in the present – a discipline shaped by an awareness on the one hand of its earlier history as a mnemonic enterprise, and on the other of its now chronic mnemonic incapacity; a discipline for which memory may be an intellectual preoccupation (or even obsession), but for which it can no longer be a living phenomenon to which historians themselves contribute. Such formulations of the issue have prompted others, however, to reaffirm a basic belief in history's mnemonic potential, even under contemporary conditions. For Patrick Hutton, for example, history's way forward lies in recognizing and reviving its status and vocation as 'an art of memory'. Doing this requires, in Hutton's view, a recognition of the part that historical thinking plays in mediating the relationship between two aspects of memory processes (or 'moments of memory'): repetition and recollection.

> Repetition concerns the presence of the past. It is the moment of memory through which we bear forward images of the past that continue to shape our present understanding in unreflective ways. One might call them habits of mind; they are the stuff of the collective memories that we associate with living traditions. Recollection concerns our present efforts to evoke the past. It is the moment of memory with which we consciously reconstruct images of the past in the selective way that meets the needs of our present situation. It is the opening between these two moments that makes historical thinking possible.[32]

Though history's emergence as a discipline in the eighteenth and nineteenth centuries was characterized on one level by a sympathetic engagement with received traditions, the rhetoric of scientific objectivity in which the discipline came to clothe itself has tended to emphasize its essential affinities to the moment of 'recollection' – to see history not as the reproduction of a received pattern, but as an essentially critical labour of reconstruction. In reality, though, Hutton argues, history always 'draws on both sides of the memory puzzle': it seeks to reconstruct the past, but it is prompted to do so by understandings that are rooted in 'oft-repeated habits of mind'.[33] Historians do not, in other words, come to the past as a *tabula rasa*: the past on whose evidences they go to work is a past already structured for them by earlier perceptions: historical thinking is always, in this sense, both critical and traditional; recollection is always grounded in repetition. A proper appreciation of history's social and cultural functions depends, Hutton implies, on restoring our awareness of this duality. In a pluralist post-modern world, historians cannot, of course, hope to 'renew their vocation'

by making themselves, as their nineteenth-century predecessors
sought to be, the privileged interpreters of a single unitary tradition.
Rather, in Hutton's view, they must seek to rediscover the multiple
buried strands of tradition that lie beneath life's surface:

> Historians may feel beleaguered by the variety of traditions that vie
> for their favour, yet they are privileged in their capacity to survey the
> historiographical scene as if it were a vast landscape of memory,
> whose topographical features highlight the many traditions that may
> be investigated. The popular consensus about the nature of our
> culture may be gone. But the richness of the resources of tradition
> are as profound as the depths of human experience. The end of a
> consensus about what is worth remembering in our present situation
> paradoxically has opened up to us once more history's hidden roots
> in tradition, covered over in modern historiography in the name of
> positivist science.[34]

As this passage makes clear, historiography, which for Nora was
the critical impulse that drove a wedge between history and
collective memory, is for Hutton the impulse which allows history
to probe the multiple traditions of memory that have shaped its
own development. The purpose of the exercise in the end, however,
is to go beyond a post-modernist emphasis on representations,
and to replenish the sense of history as the recovery of lived
experience.[35]

History and memorialization

For Nora, the contemporary historian stands, a trifle wistfully, at
the point in history where memory seems to have run out; for
Hutton, the historian remains in the flow of memory, shaped by
it and reflecting on it. The two positions illustrate the continuing
variety of thinking that focuses on history's fluctuating relationship
to the patterns of memory that contribute to social identity.
Alongside the debates which arise on this issue, and sometimes
entangled with them, there runs a second strand of thinking about
history and memory that has its roots in a slightly different
conceptualization. Here, the focus falls on history's function as a
preservative against oblivion – its role as a potential arbitrator of
what is to be remembered and what can be forgotten. Ever since
Herodotus, in the fifth century BC, wrote his *Histories* 'so that
human achievements may not become forgotten in time, and great

and marvellous deeds [. . .] may not be without their glory', people have assigned to historical writing a memorializing function – the function of keeping things alive in memory.[36] Belief in such a function has, of course, often been closely linked to conceptions of a 'memory' that is the property of a particular group – a nation, for example – but it is possible to consider it also from a more general angle, in which the emphasis falls less on the social entities to whose 'collective memory' history is deemed to contribute than on the actual business of mnemonic preservation. The twelfth-century Byzantine writer Anna Comnena captured this idea in a powerful image:

> Time in its irresistible and ceaseless flow carries along on its flood all created things, and drowns them in the depths of obscurity, no matter if they be quite unworthy of mention, or most noteworthy and important [. . .]. But the tale of history forms a very strong bulwark against the stream of time, and to some extent checks its irresistible flow, and, of all things done in it, as many as history has taken over, it secures and binds together, and does not allow them to slip away into the abyss of oblivion.

It was in order to prevent the deeds of her father, the Emperor Alexius, from being 'swept away [. . .] on the current of time into the sea of forgetfulness', that Anna herself resorted to the writing of history.[37] The things which ancient and medieval writers sought to preserve from oblivion varied from case to case: the characters of great men, their virtuous actions and wise sayings, their heroic achievements, the wrathful or benevolent interventions of the deity in the lives of individuals or of peoples, the acts by which political institutions were founded or rights to property established. But the basic idea, that the purpose of writing about the past (whether a past in recent or in remoter memory) was to fix things in lasting memory – the kind of memory that could endure from generation to generation – seems consistent. In largely illiterate societies, the fact of committing something to writing seemed vitally significant – more so, perhaps, than the question of precisely when and how this commission to writing occurred, whether by participants or witnesses at the time of the events that were recorded, or by others long afterwards.

In our print-ridden and bureaucratic age, our perceptions are somewhat different. Writing as such seems less special than it once did, and the different relationships that different kinds of written document have to a remembered reality – the differences, for example, between 'primary' and 'secondary' written evidence – perhaps therefore seem more significant. Accustomed to being swamped in far more written and printed material than we can ever hope to read, we have less faith than our predecessors may have had in the capacity of writing to 'keep things in mind': we (academic historians especially) know all too well how books and documents can achieve an instant obsolescence, even when scrupulously preserved in libraries and archives. We are less persuaded, also, of the capacity of written text, even when read and treasured, to transmit fixed and stable meanings from one generation to another: where our predecessors contrasted the fixity and durability of the written word with the fluidity and insecurity of the oral, we are more struck by the susceptibility of even the written to contestation and reinterpretation. Partly for these reasons, our conceptions of history as a form of knowledge have come to focus less on the power of historical writing, to preserve or perpetuate, than on the power of historical research, to rediscover, reconstruct or reinterpret – less on history's modes of expression (the writing in which it is embodied) than on its modes of critical analysis (the researches that precede the writing). Such a way of thinking has tended, in the modern era, to overshadow the notion of history as a form of memorialization.

This contrast should not, however, be too sharply drawn. The very period – the nineteenth and early twentieth centuries – that saw the establishment of the modern historical discipline with its emphasis on the critical analysis of documentary evidence, was also marked by a powerful belief among historians in the capacity of these 'scientific' methods to deliver a kind of historical knowledge that was fixed and definitive. It was true, wrote Lord Acton in a famous report to the Syndics of the Cambridge University Press as editor of the Cambridge Modern History in 1896, that a 'universal history' was not realizable in the present generation, but its achievement could be clearly foreseen 'now that all information is within reach, and every problem has become capable of solution'.[38] Acton's vision was, effectively, of a history that would fix and articulate what humanity needed to remember. Modern historical method would confer the same benefits of mnemonic stability that in a less literate age had been assumed to flow from the fact of writing. Such a vision of definitiveness has, of course, substantially receded since Acton wrote: traumatic historical experiences and post-modern epistemologies have combined to undermine the articles of faith – in progress, in science, in the nation, in the very concept of historical objectivity – that underpinned it. Yet historians still congratulate each other, from time to time, on producing a contribution that is 'definitive' (if only in some small corner) and durable: the assumption that history ought to be built to last, rather than merely to meet the needs of the present moment, remains appealing.

More importantly, although present-day historical writing, at least in liberal democratic countries, no longer generally proclaims an intention of safeguarding the memory of great men or noble deeds, recent historical scholarship, in a variety of fields, has not fought shy of announcing memorializing or commemorative intentions of another kind. Historical writing on the Holocaust, for example, is frequently intended, on one level at least, as a instrument of remembering – a way of holding on to people and events that are in danger of being forgotten or misremembered. In the final pages of their oral history of the Armenian genocide of the early twentieth century, Donald and Lorna Miller contrast their impression of the orderly rows of lovingly tended graves in a present-day Armenian cemetery with the knowledge which their interviews have bequeathed of how such a burial was not the lot of those burnt alive or shot and left to rot three-quarters of a century ago: the final paragraph of the book deepens the memorializing perspective by recording the authors' participation in the procession to the Martyrs' Memorial on the anniversary of the genocide.[39] Histories of genocide are no doubt, for obvious reasons, particular susceptible to a memorializing inflection, but the idea that the keeping alive of particular kinds of memory should be regarded as one of history's primary functions is certainly not confined to this area of historiography: practitioners of oral history, of women's history, of the histories of slavery and of colonialism, of gay and lesbian history, of working-class history are only some of those who have expressed and recognized the motivational force of such an idea.

It may be, in fact, that recent historical writing is marked less by any straightforward rejection of the memorializing or commemorative purpose that ancient and medieval historians assigned to history, than by a more complex understanding of the social dynamics of remembering and forgetting. For Anna Comnena (and others like her), it was time that produced forgetting; historical writing forestalled it, selectively but fairly straightforwardly. Modern historians, when they explore the memorializing potential of their discipline, attach a less prominent agency to time, and a more ambiguous one to historical writing. Rather than seeing collective forgetting as the effect of time's general tendency to sweep out of consciousness whatever is not stably anchored in writing (or in other commemorative devices such as monumental sculpture), they see it as at least partially the outcome of political choices, of power differences, of cultural preferences. They see history, furthermore, not as an automatic agent of preservation, but as a discipline whose strategies and procedures can work to procure forgetting as well as remembering. They draw attention to the fact that any historical narrative is based on selection – that in retaining some things, it represses others; that in focusing on the development or the interests of certain groups, it implicitly (if not explicitly) excludes or marginalizes other perspectives; that in promoting one kind of memory, it obstructs other ways of remembering. They see in history, therefore, a powerful political instrument – a potential vehicle for emancipation and enlightenment, but also for repression and domination. In short, when historians nowadays set themselves up to preserve or rescue certain episodes, groups, viewpoints or experiences from being forgotten, they have in mind an oblivion that is ideologically constructed, and in the construction of which other schools of historical writing may well have played a part. Commonly, therefore, there is a historiographical aspect – an element of historical revisionism or counter-revisionism – to the act of rescue. Preserving the memory of the Holocaust means not just fixing it in writing in a form that can survive the passing of the generation that personally witnessed or experienced it, but defending it as an object of memory against the pernicious alternative understandings of history fostered by Holocaust deniers.[40] For oral historians, the task has been not only to renew contact, through the gathering and analysis of oral testimony, with currents of memory that might otherwise be lost, but to show how such memories – those of workers, women or of oppressed ethnic groups, for example – have been marginalized or excluded by the strategies and orientations of conventional historical writing.

An example may help to illustrate, a little more fully, some of the ways in which the language of remembering and forgetting may articulate a concern with such issues. By its author's own account, Iris Chang's *The Rape of Nanking* has memory and the denial of memory at the core of its being. Chang's own initial awareness of the atrocities which the invading Japanese forces perpetrated in Nanking in 1937 came from family memories of the Sino-Japanese conflict passed on to her by her parents, first-generation immigrants from China to the United States. Her interest in the Nanking events as a historian was strengthened by the resurfacing of memories and information relating to it within the Chinese diaspora as part of the reaction to the Tiananmen Square massacre of 1989.[41] Her original intention in writing a book on the subject was partly an explicitly memorializing one – 'to provide my own epitaph for the hundreds upon thousands of unmarked graves in Nanking'. But her desire to offer such an epitaph did not flow only from the expressions of memory to which she had been exposed, but also from her shock at the extent to which such memories, and the events to which they referred, had been suppressed by the prevailing political cultures and historiographical traditions of the post-war world, and of Japan especially. The final chapter of her book is an attempt at once to denounce and to analyse the mechanisms of this suppression; the book as a whole seeks to draw lessons both from the events that can now be remembered and from the way they have been forgotten.[42]

In a work such as Chang's the notion of 'forgetting' carries a powerful emotional charge. Its precise meaning is actually often elusive. Chang calls the rape of Nanking 'the forgotten holocaust of World War II', but in fact her own book makes heavy use of the testimonies of people for whom the events of 1937 are clearly still very much a living memory. The 'forgetting' that is referred to is a deficiency of public recognition – a failure to accord these events and those who were their victims their due place in the stories of the past that politicians refer to in their speeches, that textbooks impart to schoolchildren, that public monuments evoke, and that historians compose. It is not a lapsing of awareness, such as might arise by accident or through the simple passage of time, but a form or expression of injustice that cries out to be rectified. Recognition of the moral claims of those whose experiences have been forgotten may take many forms – monetary compensation, restitution of property, public acts of apology or atonement, punishment of those considered responsible for past atrocities – but for the historian, it means, first and foremost, the enactment of justice in the historical record.

Truth, justice and memory (or the prevention of forgetting) have long been closely interwoven concepts. Retribution and punishment depend on remembering; even amnesty and 'forgiving and forgetting' depend on first remembering. And even where justice may no longer be able (or willing) to visit punishment on the criminal, what it seems minimally to require is the effort at recollection that prevents wrongs and injuries from being ushered into oblivion as if they had never happened. From one standpoint at least, what is damaged if such things are forgotten is truth itself: 'If the victims of mass crime are left faceless and nameless, if the hour, manner, and place of their last moments are unknown, then they are outside the light of truth, lost to forgetting. The world is left incomplete; its integrity broken; its reality undermined', writes James Booth in an analysis of such perceptions.[43] To give a truthful account of the past, in which such things are not forgotten, may be understood not just as a requirement of abstract justice, but as the fulfilment of a more human kind of moral obligation: 'Those who are alive receive a mandate from those who are dead and silent forever: to preserve the truth about the past', Czeslaw Milosz has written.[44] Such perceptions have been deepened in the twentieth-century by an awareness of the determination with which totalitarian regimes have pursued what Tzvetan Todorov has called 'the blotting out of memory',[45] sometimes on at least three levels: deletion of the memory of the states of affairs that preceded them, deletion of the memory of their own crimes, deletion of the memory of those who were the victims of those crimes. In an era of war-crimes trials and truth commissions, the rhetorical and conceptual connections between memory, justice and historical truth have again been repeatedly brought to the surface of public discourse, and it is not surprising that they have left a potent mark on the way some historians talk about their own discipline, and about its social functions. Some commentators, on the other hand, have alluded to the possible 'pitfalls of an ethics of remembrance' whose commitment to a particular understanding of what must be remembered may in some circumstances actually be in tension with the requirements of historical accuracy or justice in the present.[46]

One of the problems with the equation of justice and memory lies in the fact that memory is, in practice, always selective. We can make a deliberate decision not to allow certain episodes of suffering or injustice, and the people who were the victims of those episodes, to be forgotten, and we can, if we wish, structure our historical practice to secure that end, but in taking this decision for some we are inevitably not taking it for others. Todorov argues, indeed, that what is involved in contemporary appeals to 'the duty of memory' (in relation to France's wartime past, for example) is not an aspiration to establish the facts of the past as fully as possible, but rather 'the defense of a particular selection from among these facts, one that assures its protagonists of maintaining the roles of hero or victim when faced with any other selection that might assign them less glorious roles'.[47] The conception of remembering as a moral duty is always, in other words, partial in its application, and geared to fixing not only what is to be remembered, but how it is to be remembered.

Tensions can arise at this point between the idea of history as memorialization or witness and other conceptions of what history ought to be about. The rhetoric of memory struggles, sometimes, to contain such tensions. One example may illustrate this. In an acceptance speech which she gave in the mid-1990s for a historical prize named in honour of an Austrian social democratic and feminist activist killed in Ravensbruck concentration camp, the historian Gerder Lerner spoke movingly of the 'obligation of remembering' the atrocities of the Nazi period that lay as a 'heavy burden' on those such as herself who had witnessed those atrocities: 'One cannot forget and one must not forget and one must be a witness'. While she looked to history – as 'our collective memory' – to maintain a recognition of such experiences once the generation of direct witnesses had passed away, Lerner worried that such a collective memory was prone to be selective. Its tendency to forget 'the dark side of events' was hurtful, she argued, not just to those whose painful experiences were thus allowed to slide into oblivion but also to society as a whole, 'because one cannot heal nor can one make better decisions in the future, if one evades responsibility for the consequences of past actions'. But Lerner's intention was not simply to affirm the need for history to maintain a moral engagement with the inhumanities perpetrated under the Nazi regime, for she went on instantly to draw attention, on a more general level, to the ways in which the experiences of women especially, but also of slaves, proletarians and colonized peoples were 'selectively forgotten and historically marginalized' in the conventional historiography generated by ruling male elites. She praised feminist historians for taking the lead in 'seeking a holistic worldview in which differences among people are recognized and respected and which records the commonality of human striving in all its variety and complexity'. Her conclusion was couched again in the language of memory: 'In remembering wholly, without selective forgetting, one can fight the system of distortions and half-truths out of which sexism, classism, racism and anti-semitism grow like poisonous weeds.'[48]

The problem here lies not with Lerner's impeccably liberal agenda, but with knowing what 'remembering wholly' can really mean, as a general prescription for historical practice. No doubt it means writing histories that include 'the dark side', that give recognition to the historically disadvantaged as well as to the elites, to the oppressed as well as the oppressors. But can we really conceive of a practice – either of history or of memory – that omits or marginalizes nothing and nobody? And how far can the notions of recognition and respect that Lerner evokes be carried when the memory we are dealing with is of deeply divisive experiences? Restoring women, slaves and proletarians to their rightful place in the historical record presumably means not only remembering that they existed but according a kind of moral recognition to their interests and perspectives, so that they can be classed as full participants in history, rather than as irredeemably subordinate actors. But can we, within the same frame of historical conscious-ness, accord the same kind and degree of moral recognition to the interests and perspectives of Gestapo agents? If we cannot, then there is still a kind of selectiveness in our supposedly holistic historical remembering. Nor is it easy to see how the conflicting experiences of Jews and anti-Semites, for example, can really be encompassed within a holistic gesture of remembrance that 'records the commonality of human striving in all its variety and complexity', since an essential feature of much of their striving was the murderous antipathy of one group for the other. Two differently focused conceptions of history as memory – the one stressing the need for societies comprehensively to process their past collective experiences, the other a duty to accord moral recognition to the victims of past inequalities and injustices – merge uncertainly together in Lerner's rhetoric of historical recollection.

Continuations

The strands of thought and argument about history and memory that I have just been tracing have many of their roots long before the recent turn to memory in historical studies, but they constitute powerful elements in the rhetorical exchanges that the turn has inspired, both among its enthusiasts and among its critics. The turn to memory is a composite phenomenon, which many different agendas have contributed to generating, and from which many different approaches both to memory as subject matter and to history as mode of enquiry have emerged. It would be naïve to expect such a complex interweaving of intellectual currents magically to stabilize the discursive terrain on which history's relationship to memory has been debated, or to produce, like a rabbit from the hat, a neat and tidy resolution of these debates on which those with an interest in issues of memory might agree – and certainly this is not what has happened.

Contradictory formulations of the history–memory relationship persist, and a deeper ambivalence can often be detected. On the one hand, memory is heralded as the new thematic focus and subject matter of historical study with a kind of insistence which, by seeming to imply the supercession of more traditional themes and subjects, may seem to promise a reconceptualization in which history's exchanges and interactions with memory would become a central defining feature. On the other hand, discourses of memory sometimes seem to require a defining 'other', and history, envisaged as a self-proclaimedly objective, would-be authoritative, homogenizing narrative of the collective past, is still the commonest candidate for this role. Scholars who agree that an engagement with memory is important are less clearly agreed on what they mean by memory or on whether they expect the engagement with it to dissolve the boundaries of the historical discipline, to reconfigure them, or to reaffirm them. Indeed, some of the most interesting explorations of themes of memory by historians in recent years seem geared less to a reconfiguration of conceptual relationships than to their creative destabilization, probing experimentally around the elusive intersections of history with other investigative modes (e.g. psychoanalysis) and with other literary genres (e.g. autobiography), in ways which always resist conclusion. Thus, in Ronald Fraser's *In Search of A Past*, the methods of oral history (practised on the servants) and of psychoanalysis (which Fraser himself underwent) are used to explore the social and psychic tensions that ran both through Fraser's upper-class childhood and through his later efforts to compose a satisfactory account of it. Yet a resolution of the quest remains elusive: what is offered is 'a book in search of an author [. . .]: an assemblage of raw materials waiting for the subject who can make something of them'.[49] In Carolyn Steedman's *Landscape For a Good Woman*, the author undercuts conventional historical narrativizations of working-class experiences through a simultaneous analysis and evocation of what her own memories of childhood and of family relationships conceal and reveal. Yet Steedman resists the idea of a history – a sense-making central story of the past – that can simply incorporate, or refound itself upon, the recollected stories it has previously excluded: 'I refuse to say that my mother's story, or my father's, or mine are perfectly valid stories, existing in their own right, merely hidden from history, now revealed. [. . .] I think that the central stories are maintained *by* the marginality of others, but that these marginal stories *will not do* to construct a future by.'[50] In practice, her book explores the unsettling contacts of the historical and the autobiographical, perpetually moving between the impulses of a historical sensibility which strives implicitly to relate personal experiences to structures of historical understanding, and the urge to give prominence to the mental experiences of fantasy and denial, of resentment and deprivation, that are integral to lives and to relationships and to the ways these things are remembered, but whose meanings can find no stable place in historical narratives.

If the turn to memory does not produce a stable new reading of the history–memory problem, and if its effect is in some ways simply to refocus attention on issues – of the present's relationship to the past under conditions of rapid historical change, of the historical discipline's relationship to society under conditions of professionalization, and of history's status in relation to truth and justice – that have a longer provenance, these issues have taken on new layers of significance from the fact that both history and memory have been perceived by many commentators to be in crisis.

In the case of history, the crisis arises from the radical challenging of the credentials of historical knowledge by post-modernist and post-structuralist criticism in its various guises. In questioning the very possibility of meaningful knowledge about the past as it really was, criticism of this kind implicitly questions the utility – and indeed the respectability – of history as an intellectual pursuit, and of the historical profession as a social institution. It thus agitates, in a peculiarly polemical way, some of the issues that have often been at stake when history's relationship to memory has been evoked or debated. Critical commentators on the dramatic emergence of memory as a category in historical studies have tended to link it, either implicitly or explicitly, to the crisis of confidence that this assault, and its partial acceptance within the historical profession, is felt to have produced. The link has been made in different ways: for some, the turn to memory marks the moment of history's own bracingly creative engagement with new intellectual agendas, for others a nervous and disorientated withdrawal, for others a rhetorical reinflation of history's essentialist pretentions. Nor have these critics always been focusing on precisely the same thing: in some cases what has been analysed has been a perceived shift in history's subject matter, in others a shift in scholarly method, in others a shift in the use of vocabulary in which things once described otherwise are relabelled as 'memory', in others an increasing tendency to use this vocabulary to describe the historical endeavour itself. In most cases, the suggestion seems to be that the turn to memory marks or confirms a retreat from history's former claims to mastery. Thus, for Ankersmit, the redescription of history as memory is 'a sure sign of a personal-ization or privatization of our relationship to the past', and is thus a significant moment in the disintegration of the once proud project of a general historical understanding to be realized through the collective efforts of an organized historical profession.[51] For Kerwin Lee Klein, on the other hand, the infatuation with the language of memory betokens an attempt, disguised by being combined with a surface acceptance of post-modernist agendas, to 're-enchant our relation to the world and pour presence into the past', by couching history's projects in a vocabulary that resonates subliminally with traditional and religious meanings.[52]

A history that is in crisis may seek to reground itself by reforging an older rhetorical connection to memory. But the effort to do so is complicated if memory itself is perceived to be in a state of insecurity or even disintegration. The notion of a contemporary 'crisis of memory' will be explored in greater detail in the final section of Chapter 5. The crisis in question is conceived to be complex and cumulative, rooted in the breakdown of 'traditional' social structures and in a later undermining of faith in the nation-state as a moral project, but brought to an escalating pitch of acuteness by the disorientating effects of modern mass culture and communications technology – a combination of developments which is felt to be rapidly depriving the inhabitants of modern societies of stable frameworks within which to construct meaning-ful mnemonic relationships to any kind of collective past. The relationship of history's crisis to memory's is ambiguous: for some (such as Nora), historicism is a major vehicle of memory's erosion; for others, the crisis in confidence in history is simply part of the larger mnemonic collapse. But whether history and memory are seen as allies or antagonists, a situation in which both are felt to be dissolving into possibly fatal fragility makes a fixing of their relationship seem further away than ever.

It should be clear by now that the history–memory problem is not one that is likely to be settled – either in the sense of being resolved or in that of being gently reduced to quiescence – by incisive rational debate. What is at issue is not the relationship between two well-bounded entities, whose positioning in relation to each other may change but is always in principle definable, nor is it one between two evolving substances whose elusive mutations and interpenetrations we have at least an agreed basis for observing. It is not even, in the end, the relationship between concepts whose various possible formulations can have their heuristic utility debated and tested in an atmosphere of relative scholarly neutrality. Rather, it is the relationship between two discursive terms, each of which has acquired a multiplicity of sometimes contradictory rhetorical uses, and each of which comes into play already overcharged with a complex array of shifting emotional resonances and symbolic meanings. In short, the terms 'history' and memory' are not mere descriptors, but indicators of tension and instruments of contes-tation – sometimes stakes, sometimes catalysts and sometimes weapons in a range of overlapping disputations, both within the historical profession (or academia more generally) and within society at large. Different ways of deploying these terms carry different contentious messages, not just about the nature of historical knowledge, but about the historian's social positioning and social responsibility, about the politics of culture, and about the problematic nature of modern societies. Disagreements over the history–memory relationship are therefore to be understood, on one level at least, as manifestations less of uncertainties over the appropriate framing of precisely applicable analytical concepts, than of struggles to control – to modify or extend, or perhaps to stabilize or contain or restrict – the symbolic resonances, and therefore the possible uses, of key discursive terms. This is not to say that every intervention in debates on history and memory is to be construed as a bid for power, or as a *prise de position* in an essentially binary kind of ideological conflict. As I have sought to show, the ways in which the terms 'history' and 'memory' are coupled and uncoupled are complex in their significance, partly because the terms can carry multiple meanings simultaneously, but also because these meanings are apt to resonate not within a fixed and single framework of debate but within a variety of frameworks, whose interrelationships are complex and sometimes elusive. The argument advanced here is simply that 'history' and 'memory' are terms which have become so multiply significant, so overburdened with contestable meaning, so caught up in the complex politics and emotionalism both of academic discourse and of public discourse more generally, that cutting through all this to establish stable conceptual relationships has become a misconceived objective.

The significance of the present wave of interest in memory among historians must lie, not in this direction, but in the way it helps us to explore and to analyse the complex processes by which the past invests the consciousness of the present in human societies.

Notes

1 Klein, 'On the emergence of *memory* in historical discourse', p. 128.
2 See, for example, K. Jenkins, *Re-thinking History* (London, 1991), esp. p. 5.
3 F. Bacon, *The Advancement of Learning*, in B. Vickers (ed.), *Francis Bacon: a Critical Edition of the Major Works* (Oxford, 1996), p. 175.
4 G. Santayana, *The Life of Reason: or the Phases of Human Progress* (New York, 1954), p. 394.
5 J. Lukacs, *Historical Consciousness, or the Remembered Past* (New York, 1968); P. Burke, 'History as social memory', in T. Butler (ed.), *Memory:*

History, Culture and the Mind (New York, 1989); P. Hutton, *History as an Art of Memory* (Hanover NH, 1993).

6 L. Jordanova, *History in Practice* (London, 2000), p. 138.

7 L. Goldstein, *Historical Knowing* (Austin, 1976), p. 146.

8 D. Lowenthal, *The Past is a Foreign Country* (Cambridge, 1985), p. 212.

9 M. Bentley, *Modern Historiography: an Introduction* (London, 1999), p. 155.

10 R. G. Collingwood, *The Idea of History* (Oxford, 1961 [original edn. 1946]), pp. 252–3.

11 R. G. Collingwood, 'Notes towards a metaphysic', in R. G. Collingwood, *The Principles of History and Other Writings in Philosophy of History*, W. Dray and W. van der Dussen (eds) (Oxford, 1999), p. 136.

12 H. P. Rickman (ed.), *Meaning in History: W. Dilthey's Thoughts on History and Society* (London, 1961), pp. 86–7. The passages cited here are taken by Rickman from the 'Drafts towards a critique of historical reason', included as 'Plan for the continuation of the Construction of the Historical World in the Human Studies' in volume VII, part II (ed. B. Groethuysen) of Dilthey's collected works, and probably date from 1907–10.

13 C. Becker, 'Everyman his own historian', *American Historical Review* 37:2 (1932), pp. 221–4.

14 L. von Ranke, Preface to his *Universal History* (1880), in L. von Ranke, *The Theory and Practice of History*, G. Iggers and K. von Moltke (eds) (New York, 1983), p. 164.

15 R. Samuel, *Theatres of Memory, vol. I: Past and Present in Contemporary Culture* (London and New York, 1994), pp. 3–6.

16 Extract from J. G. Droysen, *Outline of the Principles of History* (1868), reproduced in F. Stern (ed.), *The Varieties of History, From Voltaire to the Present* (2nd edn., New York, 1972), p. 137.

17 Renan, 'What is a nation?', p. 52.

18 A. S. Green, Preface to J. R. Green, *A Short History of the English People* (illustrated edn., 4 vols, London, 1892) I, p. vi.

19 H. Butterfield, *The Whig Interpretation of History* (London, 1931), p. 3.

20 H. S. Commager, *The Nature and the Study of History* (Columbus, Ohio, 1965), p. 2.

21 Hobsbawm, 'What can history tell us about contemporary society', in E. Hobsbawm, *On History* (London, 1997), p. 33.

22 R. Hofstadter, *The Progressive Historians: Turner, Beard, Parrington* (New York, 1968), p. 3.

23 R. Hofstadter, 'History and the social sciences', in Stern (ed.), *The Varieties of History*, pp. 359–60.

24 Halbwachs, *La mémoire collective*, pp. 130–1.

25 Ibid., pp. 130–42.

26 Y. H. Yerushalmi, *Zakhor: Jewish History and Jewish Memory* (2nd edn., Seattle, 1996), p. 86. For a critique of Yerushalmi's stark distinction between Jewish history and Jewish memory, see A. Funkenstein, 'Collective memory and historical consciousness', *History and Memory* 1(1989), pp. 5–26; for further discussion, which examines the historical production of this opposition, see J. Hess, 'Memory, history, and the Jewish question: universal citizenship and the colonization of Jewish memory', in A. Confino and P. Fritzsche (eds), *The Work of Memory: New Directions in the Study of German Society and Culture* (Urbana and Chicago, 2002), pp. 39–61.

27 Yerushalmi, *Zakhor*, pp. 94–6.

28 Nora, 'General introduction: Between memory and history', P. Nora (ed.), *Realms of Memory: Rethinking the French Past*, vol. I: Conflicts and Divisions (ed. L. Kritzman) (New York, 1996), pp. 1–3.

29 Ibid., pp. 3–4.

30 P. Nora, 'From *Lieux de mémoire* to *Realms of Memory*': in Nora (ed.), *Realms of Memory*, vol. I, p. xvi.

31 Nora, 'General introduction', pp. 1 (quotation), 6.

32 Hutton, *History as an Art of Memory*, pp. xx–xxi.

33 Ibid., pp. xxii–xxiii, xxv.

34 Ibid., pp. 166–7.

35 Ibid., pp. xxiv–xxv: 'Historians neglect the moment of repetition at their peril, for living memory ultimately remains the ground of their interest in the past, just as it was once the foundation of the historical actors they seek to understand. [. . .] The past as it was experienced, not just the past as it has subsequently been used, is a moment of memory we should strive to recover.'

36 Herodotus, *The Histories* (Harmondsworth, 1996), p. 3.

37 Anna Comnena, *The Alexiad* (London, 1967), p. 1.

38 Lord Acton, *Longitude 30 West: a Confidential Report to the Syndics of the Cambridge University Press* (New York, 1969).

39 D. Miller and L. Miller, *Survivors: an Oral History of the Armenian Genocide* (Berkeley, 1999), pp. 191–2.

40 See, for example, P. Vidal-Naquet, *Assassins of Memory: Essays on the Denial of the Holocaust* (New York, 1992); D. Lipstadt, *Denying the Holocaust: the Growing Assault on Truth and Memory* (new edn., London, 1993); also, for comparison, R. Hovannisian (ed.), *Remembrance and Denial: the Case of the Armenian Genocide* (Detroit, 1998).

41 I. Chang, *The Rape of Nanking: the Forgotten Holocaust of World War II* (Harmondsworth, 1997), pp. 7–11.

42 Ibid., 11–16, 119–225 (quotation, p. 220). For further discussion, see J. Fogel (ed.), *The Nanjing Massacre in History and Historiography* (Berkeley, 2000).

43 W. J. Booth, 'The unforgotten: memories of justice', *American Political Science Review* 95:4 (2001), pp. 777–91 (quotation, p. 781).

44 C. Milosz, *Beginning With My Streets* (New York, 1991), p. 281, quoted in Booth, 'The unforgotten', p. 782.

45 T. Todorov, 'The uses and abuses of memory', in H. Marchitello (ed.), *What Happens to History: the Renewal of Ethics in Contemporary Thought* (New York, 2001), p. 11.

46 R. Golsan, 'History and the "duty to memory" in postwar France: the pitfalls of an ethics of remembrance', in Marchitello, *What Happens to History*, pp. 23–39. Todorov similarly warns of the dangers of an ethical practice which allows itself to be based on 'unconditionally praising memory and discrediting forgetting' ('The uses and abuses of memory', p. 12).

47 Ibid., p. 21.

48 G. Lerner, 'Of history and memory', in G. Lerner, *Why History Matters: Life and Thought* (New York and Oxford, 1997), pp. 52–4.

49 'Review Discussion: In search of the past: a dialogue with Ronald Fraser', *History Workshop* 20 (1985), p. 181; R. Fraser, *In Search of a Past: The Manor House, Amnersfield 1933–1945* (London, 1984), p. 185.

50 C. Steedman, 'History and autobiography: different pasts', in C. Steedman, *Past Tenses: Essays on Writing, Autobiography and History* (London, 1992), p. 46; C. Steedman, *Landscape For a Good Woman* (London, 1986). For discussion of Steedman's and Fraser's books, see ch. 2 of N. King, *Memory, Narrative, Identity: Remembering the Self* (Edinburgh, 2000).

51 F. R. Ankersmit, *Historical Representation* (Stanford, 2001), p. 154.

52 Klein, 'On the emergence of *memory* in historical discourse' (quotations, pp. 145, 134).

✳ 2 ✳

MEMORY AND
THE INDIVIDUAL

In everyday life, if not always in scholarly discourse, when we speak of memory and remembering, we tend to mean something that we take to be personal and attributable to individuals. We all know what it feels like to have a memory of something, to strive to remember, to be aware of having forgotten, and we regard these experiences as ones that are at once part of the common human condition and yet innate, for each of us, in our existence as separate and self-conscious individual beings. Our memories seem (in Fentress and Wickham's words) 'indissolubly ours', so much 'a part of us' that to deprive us of them would be to jeopardize our sense of personal identity.[1] No doubt, we also speak familiarly of sharing memories with others, or of joining with others in remembrance or commemoration, but these ways of speaking do not, for the most part, undermine our residual conviction that memories are, in the final analysis, a private property of the individual remembering mind, and that something in them is always lost in translation from one such mind to another. We cannot, as in one of Borges's fictions, meet a man in a bar who can give us Shakespeare's memory;[2] we cannot sit by the fireside with friends 'swapping memories' till each of us has a full and identical collection. The thing that must go missing in such exchanges is, we suppose, the sense of intimate personal involvement that makes memory a matter not just of what we know, but of who we are.

These assumptions about memory are, of course, themselves culturally and historically conditioned. The implicitness with which we accept them is no doubt a reflection both of the general individualizing tendency of post-Enlightenment thought, and of the extent to which the processes of social change which have disrupted and dissolved many relatively static and traditional forms of community in western societies have thereby placed (in Antze and Lambek's words) an 'increasing burden . . . upon the individual body to serve as the sole site of memory'.[3] One contribution that historians and anthropologists may make to thinking about memory is no doubt to explore the understandings that have been attached to it in societies that are less generally inclined to take individuality and selfhood as basic points of reference.[4] One does not, however, have to be all that deeply committed to a cultural fascination with the supposedly autonomous individual to feel that human beings have minds that are at least ostensibly separate, that remembering is an activity of these minds, and that any understanding of what memory may mean for and in society must at least incorporate some understanding of how it operates and is experienced at a personal level. This is the standpoint from which the present chapter and parts of the next one are developed.

Definitions and approaches

Even when we confine our initial horizons to a discussion of memory that is deemed to have the mind of the individual as its essential location, however, the terms 'memory' and 'remembering' still have a bewildering variety of applications. Both in scholarly and in everyday parlance, 'memory' may refer either to the mind's general systems for the retention and retrieval of data derived from past experience, or to the specific data that are thus retrieved; either to the general awareness an individual may have of having a past dimension to his or her existence (what the philosopher Michael Oakeshott called 'a remembered past'), or to the more detailed recollection he or she may have of particular past experiences (in Oakeshott's terms, 'a recollected or a consulted past').[5] 'Remembering', for its part, is a term that is used to cover a host of superficially different kinds of mental performance: remembering a particular event, remembering a person or a place, remembering a piece of factual information, remembering to do something, and remembering how to do something are types of activity that share a verbal description, but whose phenomenology and whose implications may seem quite dissimilar. Whether (and how) these different kinds of remembering may be connected at the level of basic mental processes is something philosophers and psychologists continue to debate: how exactly it comes about that

minds process some of the inputs they receive as 'objective' knowledge about the world, some as a kind of 'procedural' knowledge
of how to do things, and some as 'subjective' recollection of a
personal past is a mysterious and complex question, which the
present book makes no pretence of addressing. In practice, the
kinds of discussion of individual memory that have an impact on
historical research and writing seldom embrace the full range of
phenomena that the term 'remembering' may be taken to cover.
A first task, then, is to define slightly more clearly the provisional
focus of this chapter's discussion.

Psychologists working on memory have developed a number of
conceptual distinctions.[6] While these are rooted in a specific set
of disciplinary concerns, and may not always be the most fruitful
ones for framing investigations of memory that arise from different
intellectual preoccupations, they can help to give at least a preliminary definition of the kinds of memory that the present chapter,
and parts of the next, seek to engage with. Most basically,
contemporary psychological discourse distinguishes *short-term* or
working memory (the kind that retains information just received
for the brief period that permits an immediate response) from
long-term memory (which permits some of that information to be
retained over longer periods and incorporated into larger structures
of knowledge). Within long-term memory, a second distinction is
commonly drawn, between *declarative* (or *explicit*) and *non-declarative*
(or *implicit* or *procedural*) forms of memory, the former involving
the conscious retention or retrieval of data in the form of information that can be articulated, the latter the maintenance of the
essentially unconscious forms of procedural knowledge that are
involved in such forms of instinctive practice as riding a bicycle or
speaking one's native language. Finally, and for present purposes
most significantly, declarative memory itself is often divided further,
into *semantic* memory (memory for factual or conceptual information, of a kind that can be abstracted from the circumstances
of its acquisition) and *episodic* memory (the individual's conscious
memory of events and experiences in which he or she has been
personally involved).[7]

From a historian's point of view, short-term memory as defined
by psychologists is scarcely distinguishable from the immediate
action that is based on it: it is only when memory is banked up
into something that shapes behaviour over longer periods – months

or years or decades – that it becomes potentially meaningful as a category in historical analysis. Nor do historians possess obvious means of studying non-declarative memory, other (again) than by observing the behaviours that are presumed to incorporate it: it is only to the extent that memory is capable of being consciously articulated, and therefore of being approached through an analysis of its expressions in speech or text, that we can hope to make it a distinguishable focus of historical study. The psychologists' category of semantic memory, by contrast, does indeed cover matters that may be of interest to historians – the kinds of factual and conceptual knowledge that people possess and their ways of acquiring and organizing it – but historians who explore such matters at the level of the individual are still generally more inclined to conceptualize their field of interest as the study of those individuals' thought or ideas, rather than as the investigation of the mnemonic processes by which thought, ideas or knowledge are underpinned. In practice, the type of memory that is envisaged in most recent discussions of individual memory as an object of historical enquiry – and the type that this chapter will be principally concerned with – is the memory by which individuals recall their own previous experience of events and situations.

The psychologists' term 'episodic memory' should not mislead us at this point, for the memory we are talking about need not always be focused on particular episodes (in the sense of discrete experiential moments): it may be a more general memory of people or places or past experiential phases. What distinguishes it from other forms of memory is simply the fact that it involves a significant element of *autonoetic* (self-knowing) as well as merely *noetic* (knowing) awareness – the sense of being personally implicated in whatever experiences are being remembered, and in the ways that these are remembered.[8] But autonoetic awareness has varying degrees of intensity. Sometimes, an individual who participates in an event feels, or comes subsequently to feel, that this event, and his or her participation in it, are closely connected to his or her identity or destiny as a person, and this conviction may strongly affect how the event is remembered. On other occasions, the personal investment is less obvious, and the remembering of the event may be more heavily influenced by other factors. In what follows, I shall use the term *personal memory* broadly, to refer to any recollection of past events or circumstances that carries a trace of autonoetic awareness, and the term *autobiographical memory* more narrowly, to refer to cases where the remembering of events or experiences relates them, at least implicitly, to larger conceptions of the individual's identity or development as a person.[9] Taken together, these two terms cover the memories that historians find embodied in memoirs, diaries, eye-witness testimonies, oral reminiscences and the like – the memories whose intricacies they must learn to interrogate if they wish to use such productions of the individual mind either as sources of factual information or as bases from which to launch enquiries into the character of historical experience, the shaping of subjectivity, or the elusive but significant operations of memory itself.

Most historians have to deal, at least some of the time, with sources that incorporate or articulate this kind of memory, and the issues that the present chapter will be addressing are therefore certainly not the exclusive preoccupation of specialists in any particular period or branch of historical enquiry. Important contributions to thinking about the significance of individual memory for historians, and about the conceptual and methodological issues that the study of memory may pose, can certainly be made by, for example, medievalists or legal historians or historians of ideas. However, one group of historical practitioners in particular – oral historians – have, by virtue partly of their peculiar relationship to such sources and partly of the range of interdisciplinary connections that this has given them, been especially active in bringing memory to the forefront of historical agendas, and in using the encounter with it to bend historical thought in new directions. Oral history's 'special relationship' to the study of memory derives from the fact that its practitioners do not simply (as other historians do) seek to discover and to analyse sources that incorporate or embody personal memory, but themselves intervene, actively and purposefully and on several levels, in the bringing into existence of such sources, and in the prompting and moulding of the recollective processes of which they are the outcome. The circumstances of oral historians' research are, in other words, ones which repeatedly prompt them to think about memory less as a process accomplished in the past that has bequeathed products, in the form of documentary evidence, that are there to be critically scrutinized than as a process whose outcomes are always fluid, mutable, provisional, responsive to changing conditions and to human interventions, and therefore open not just to textual scrutiny but to probing and interrogation – though also, of course, to concealment and inhibition. Viewed from such an angle, memory becomes less a precondition for the development of historical knowledge than an integral and endlessly intriguing element in the historical process, and one which historians must discover new ways of approaching. In the early phases of oral history's emergence as a movement and as a disciplinary field, its agendas remained fairly close to those of other forms of social history: oral historians looked to the memories of their informants for the means of reconstructing the past's more intimate experiential textures, or for access to kinds of information (relating, for example, to the histories of subordinate or marginal groups) that were excluded from the elite-generated documentary record and from the mainstream historical scholarship that took that record as its essential foundation. The need to reflect on the methodological and conceptual difficulties of the enterprise – to think constructively about memory's elusive relationship to past experience, about the conclusions to be drawn from the sometimes undeniable gap between past occurrences and the way they are subsequently remembered, about the influence of culture on the ways in which individuals remember, and about the ways in which the production and articulation of memories may be affected by the social dynamics of the oral history interview – has, however, drawn many oral historians towards new formulations of their objectives, in which the radical commitment to investigate the consciousness and experience of non-elite sections of society is by no means abandoned, but in which a sophisticated engagement with memory's forms and functions and meanings is increasingly defined as a vital concern.[10] The shift of focus is well captured by the leading oral historian Luisa Passerini, in speaking of her interviews with members of the Italian generation of 1968:

> Memory narrates with the vivid tones of actual experience. But what interests me is neither the liveliness of the accounts nor their faithfulness to reality, both of which would make these stories a secondary source for a good social history of Italy after 1945. Rather, what attracts me is memory's insistence on creating a history of itself, which is much less and perhaps somewhat more than a shared social history.[11]

When oral historians or other historians fix their attention on individual memory, they enter a field of thought that is already partially shaped by existing approaches. The intellectual space within which most recent discussions of individual memory in the humanities and social sciences have taken place is one that we may think of as being structured by the tensions and interactions (and in some cases the repugnances) between three contrasting general approaches. Though these approaches may be said to have their most obvious points of origin in different disciplinary camps (or groups of camps), exchanges of some kind or other between them have become a feature of work on memory in almost all of the disciplines that the turn to memory has affected, so that assigning them neat disciplinary labels is liable to be misleading. I shall call them the *cognitivist*, the *subjectivist* and the *socio-cultural* approaches. The account of them that follows is wilfully schematic, and certainly inadequately captures the interweavings of different intellectual currents and multiple nuances of opinion that each of these labels conceals, but it may help to set some guidelines for the discussions of particular aspects of individual memory that follow.

The *cognitivist* approach (most fully elaborated in the work of cognitive psychologists) views memory essentially as a vital part of the mental equipment that individuals use to register and process information about the world around them. Memory is viewed as pragmatic – geared to allowing us to orientate ourselves in the world and to get on with the business of living – rather than introspective. The approach is individualizing, in the sense that it tends to treat individuals as self-sufficient mnemonic agents, but it is not especially preoccupied with the inner psychic dynamics of selfhood and subjectivity. (Indeed, as we have seen, autonoetic remembering is only one of the much wider range of mnemonic activities that cognitive psychologists are interested in.) Cognitivist methodology tends to assume that the appropriate criteria for evaluating memory are ones of cognitive efficiency: how speedily, how accurately, and how consistently can information to which the mind has been exposed at one moment be retrieved from memory at later moments? Memory's omissions or alterations of detail are viewed, from this perspective, either as instances of cognitive malfunctioning – 'lapses' or 'distortion' or 'misremembering' – or as part of the mind's larger strategies for improving overall efficiency, rather than as possible indicators of functions that may

not be purely cognitive in character. Emotions and social relationships and cultural influences tend to be viewed as external variables
that may disrupt or enhance cognitive performance, rather than
as things which may be somehow integral to the very business of
remembering.

In the *subjectivist* approach, the central cognitivist emphasis is
reversed: memory is treated not as an instrument for forming
knowledge of the external world, but as the central vehicle of
subjectivity, crucially engaged in fabricating the inner meanings
that we give to our psychic experience. Memory, in this view, is
important chiefly as the primary locus of our sense of self and is
assumed to be geared to maintaining that sense of self in the face
of life's disruptive vicissitudes. Where cognitivists gauge cognitive
efficiency, subjectivists read or probe memory for its symbolic
connections and hidden fantasies and secret constructions, whether
through literary analysis of narrative texts in which remembered
experience is presented, or through psychoanalytical enquiries.
Memory's meanings, according to this view, do not emerge
straightforwardly; rather, in the psychoanalytical vision at least,
'memory is conceptualized as a force in conflict with the counter-
force of repression and as highly compromised in the encounter',
and specific memories are understood as 'highly condensed symbols
of hidden preoccupations'.[12]

The *socio-cultural* approach has many forms, spun in disciplinary
corners such as sociology and anthropology, constructionist
psychology and literary studies. What they have in common is a
disposition to view the mnemonic life of individuals as something
not just casually influenced but framed and structured by those
individuals' positioning within society and within culture. Some
versions of this approach develop this idea through the concept
of a group-specific 'collective memory', which is held to condition
the structures of individual recollection; others stress the socially
interactive character of mnemonic activity; others allude to the
ways in which selfhood may be seen as a 'relational' rather than a
purely individualized phenomenon, or is modeled through the
implicit use of elements (myths, stereotypes, narrative forms) drawn
from the cultures in which the individual is embedded. There are
important differences between these positions, but what runs
through them all is the suggestion that individuals always remember
in social contexts, and that the ways in which they remember cannot

be coherently understood unless the influences that govern those contexts and the terms of their engagement in them are thoroughly examined.

If developed in a narrow and exclusive spirit, each of the three approaches just outlined surely produces a one-dimensional account of what goes on when individuals remember; insights of the kind that historians can build on seem most likely to come when efforts are made to negotiate exchanges between them. In practice, historians have usually been keenest to integrate the second and third approaches: oral historians, in particular, have striven to produce analyses that are focused on individual subjectivities, but which seek to relate these not simply to the general historical experiences (war, revolution, class conflict, etc.), which are the inevitable contexts of their formation, but to the formative effects of culture and of social relationships. The cognitive aspects of remembering usually receive less explicit attention, whether through the assumption that they are too commonsensically obvious to need serious conceptual discussion, or through a feeling that a focus on them is somehow linked to an outmoded belief that memory is of interest for the access it can give us to 'how things really were' in the past. But our labours of subjectivity surely arise in the context of larger efforts to make sense of the world around us, and are interwoven with them, as is the use we make of cultural resources,[13] and it seems therefore unwise to downplay cognitivity completely. Historians have grown used to affirming that memory is a reconstructive process, less used as yet to thinking through what they mean by this (beyond perhaps a vague notion that what it means is that remembered events are always remembered 'from a present standpoint'). Cognitive psychologists have no monopoly of wisdom in this area (any more than historians have an exclusive right to talk about historical processes of historical change). But their efforts to conceptualize remembering as a cognitive process in individual minds do yield models that can help historians to formulate their own, probably more socially focused, conceptions of mnemonic processes. In the later stages of this chapter and in the next, I shall move from general discussion of memory as a reconstructive mental activity, through to discussion of issues of selfhood and narrativity, and then to a consideration of memory's social and cultural aspects. Such a sequence will bring the three approaches to personal memory that I have outlined successively into focus; the overall aim, however, is not to affirm the priority of any of these approaches over any other, but to show how elements in them can be blended together.

Memory as reconstruction

From the standpoint of the remembering individual, remembering seems to be at once a mental activity (something one does) and a mental experience (something one feels). Any conscious mental activity has its experiential dimension, of course, but in the case of remembering the point is not merely banal, for the term is used to cover two actually very different kinds of mental experience, one of which feels more 'active' than the other. Aristotle famously distinguished *memoria* from *anamnesis*.[14] The first of these terms denoted the kind of remembering that takes the apparent form of retention or preservation: the persistence within the mind of impressions formed at an earlier moment. The second denoted the kind of remembering that is experienced as a deliberate action of retrieval or recovery: the effortful bringing to the surface of the mind of things otherwise latent or seemingly forgotten. For Aristotle, *anamnesis* presupposed *memoria*, since no amount of effort could bring to consciousness things of which the mind had previously retained no trace whatever. Some such distinction between two presumably connected but phenomenologically different modes of remembering – the one ostensibly continuous and passively retentive, the other intermittent and effortfully geared to retrieval – has been a common feature of theorizing about memory since Aristotle wrote. Saint Augustine, for example, developed the metaphor of memory as a storehouse, in which the sensory and intellectual impressions of past experience are preserved awaiting future use. There follows a comical account of the vagaries of *anamnesis*:

> When I go into this storehouse, I ask that what I want should be brought forth. Some things appear immediately, but others require to be searched for longer, and then dragged out, as it were, from some hidden recess. Other things hurry forth in crowds, on the other hand, and while something else is sought and inquired for, they leap into view as if to say, 'Is it not we, perhaps?' These I brush away with the hand of my heart from the face of my memory, until finally the thing I want makes its appearance out of its secret cell.[15]

Alongside memory as a latent persistence of mental impressions, and remembering as a deliberate mental effort at bringing particular impressions to consciousness, Augustine offers us this importunate bubbling up of unsolicited memories. For him, these are a by-product of the deliberate effort to remember. Other writers, however, have focused on the more inadvertent appearance of such memories – in cases where they catch us unawares, in response perhaps to some accidental external stimulus (Proust's *madeleine* is the most famous literary example). Aristotle's *memoria* could be seen as a persistent bedrock of things latently remembered, available to be reactivated through deliberate efforts at recollection; memory as it is often thought of today seems more of a fluid medium, bringing different things into prominence at different moments, in ways that are shaped not just by our own deliberate efforts to recall them, but by the varied stimuli of our physical, social and cultural environment, as well perhaps as by the inner impulses of our own psychic development and need for equilibrium.

However we view it, remembering seems indissolubly coupled with forgetting. Past experience is not a tape that memory can rewind, tracking backwards through a continuous series of remembered events until everything has been neatly recapitulated: remembering is always a somewhat speculative navigational labour, a quest for points of recognition across a territory of the more or less forgotten whose features we never succeed in bringing into stable focus. To be sure, the significance of forgetting remains contentious. 'Memories are crafted by oblivion as the outlines of the shore are crafted by the sea', the anthropologist Marc Augé poetically remarks[16] – but one man's marine 'crafting' is another's mundane coastal erosion, and forgetting may likewise strike some as a mere lapsing or degeneration, others as a subtler contribution to the shaping of what is remembered. For some, it is a form of natural wastage – something inevitable as a general phenomenon, but more or less haphazard in its occurrence (though affected by such factors as old age, brain damage or failures of concentration), and in the end neither obviously purposeful nor deeply meaningful. For others, it is simply the effect of the selectiveness that is necessary to memory's cognitive efficiency – a functionally purposeful jettisoning of data in the interests of avoiding the cognitive overloading that would otherwise prevent the mind from making usable sense of anything. For others, following thinkers such as Freud or Bergson, the mind's past experiences are never fundamentally erased: even those that are superficially forgotten leave their traces in the subconscious levels of our mental functioning, and continue to exert an influence not just on our behaviour, but on our patterns of conscious recollection.

Our sense of what memory is, then, is marked by unstable oscillations between the latent and the explicit, the persistent and the momentary, the purposeful and the inadvertent, the remembered and the forgotten. The exploration of any of these polarities brings to the surface another conceptual tension – between memory as survival and memory as reconstruction. Viewed from one angle, memory is marked by persistence – a maintenance and carrying forwards in time of residues, traces, impressions or relics of earlier experience. Viewed from another, it is marked by retrospection – a present-based effort to recompose a picture of past reality, guided and motivated less by aspects of the past that is being reconstructed than by the present's needs for meaning and categories of understanding. It is difficult to think about memory without feeling a need somehow to balance and reconcile these two perspectives – to understand, in effect, how a something or other that persists is subjected to continuous reconstruction, and how its persistence may shape and influence the reconstruction by which it is itself transformed.

The prevailing tendency of much recent scholarly thinking has been to dwell on the 'reconstructive' end of this polarity – to focus less on what endures in memory than on how the memory of the past is repeatedly adjusted to present needs and ways of thinking. The argument for such an emphasis is a powerful one. The past does not, as a complete and immediate experiential reality, survive in the present, and few people nowadays would suggest that what memory gives us is somehow an immutable image of things past, quasi-photographic in its accuracy. The conditions and occurrences of one moment do not, once that moment is passed, go into a kind of retirement (as Sartre once claimed)[17], in which they can be visited or from which they can be retrieved by later mental effort; they are surpassed and can never be precisely recaptured. To remember them, we must reconstruct them, not in the sense of reassembling something that has been taken to pieces and carefully stored, but in the sense of imaginatively configuring something that can no longer have the character of actuality.

Everything that happens when we remember the past happens in a present from which the past is absent, not in the past itself, or in some limbo region between the two.

Pushed to extremes, however, such an argument risks reducing memory to the status of an imaginative projection, so heavily determined by present need as to be no longer in any meaningful sense related to past experiences. Memory, thus defined, would be a representation of the past only superficially different from those offered by fantasy or fiction. Retaining a notion of memory as something distinctive seems to involve taking seriously (if not necessarily at face value) the sense of a quasi-umbilical connection between past experience and present recollection that seems inseparable from the actual personal experience of remembering. Philosophers have argued at length – though inconclusively – over whether the connection between experiences and the memories that refer to them is properly describable as a 'causal' connection.[18] What matters, for our present purposes, is simply the conviction that we have, as part of the sensation of remembering, that particular past experiences are not just the object, but in some vital sense the source, of our present recollections. We feel, in other words, not just that what we are remembering is something we really did experience, but that something in that experience, and not just something in our present circumstances, shapes (and perhaps motivates) the way we now remember it, and that this anchoring of memories in past experiences somehow testifies to our own essential continuity as conscious individuals.

All of this might, of course, be so much illusion. There are, however, other more concrete reasons for seeking to incorporate at least some notion of 'survival' or 'persistence' into our notion of memory as a retrospective reconstruction. Moments, in themselves, are inherently fleeting: if memory is to capture them, it can only be by reconstructing them. But things – objects, texts, environmental features, even people – have a greater durability, and their survival exerts an influence on how and what we remember. This influence may be more or less accidental (as when a visit to a place we once frequented triggers memories of people or events that we connect with it), or it may be deliberately produced (as when we turn to a photograph album that we have previously compiled for reminders of people or episodes from earlier stages in our existence). The role of people and places and objects in procuring and guiding recollection will be returned to in later sections of this book: the point for the moment is simply that the reconstructive activity of recollection is conducted within environments that are more durable than the fleeting moments that memory is often striving to recover, and that are littered with markers and reminders that have been deposited at earlier moments. Though the features of these environments are themselves susceptible to evolving interpretations, their structural persistence must, in some measure, exert an influence on the ways in which the past is reconstructively remembered.

For a more detailed account of what a 'reconstructivist' view of memory may entail, we may turn to one of the pioneering exponents of such a view, the psychologist Sir Frederic Bartlett:

> Remembering is not the re-excitation of innumerable fixed, lifeless and fragmentary traces. It is an imaginative reconstruction, or construction, built out of the relation of our attitude towards a whole active mass of organised past reactions or experience, and to a little outstanding detail which commonly appears in image or in language form.[19]

Memories, according to this understanding, are not mental copies of things previously witnessed; nor are they traces which can somehow be reactivated to give a mental duplication of the previous experience. Rather, to remember something is to rework it mentally, within the present's habitual structures of thought and assumption. What is remembered is always reconfigured, and thus implicitly reinterpreted, never merely resuscitated or reproduced. Memory, in Bartlett's view, is not designed to provide us with a completely accurate depiction of our past experiences: its purpose is to provide the kind of selective and organized appreciation of those experiences that is serviceable as a foundation for purposeful action in the present: remembering, he observed, 'is hardly ever really exact, [. . .] and it is not at all important that it should be so'.[20]

This basic 'reconstructivist' view of memory has two general implications. The first is that remembering is not a discrete and self-contained branch of mental activity – as Bartlett put it, 'not a completely independent function, entirely distinct from perceiving, imaging, or even from constructive thinking'[21] – but is, rather, integrally connected to our more general processes of understanding. It is true that remembering former experience tends to feel like a distinctive kind of mental performance – different from merely knowing things, or imagining them, or deducing them from other information. Yet the boundaries are not always easy to locate: we are not always sure whether we have remembered something or merely imagined it, or dreamt it, or been told it, or even merely assumed it on the basis of other knowledge. We sometimes 'remember' episodes that turn out never to have occurred, or 'remember' as our own experiences things that are actually the narrated experiences of others. (The philosopher Elizabeth Anscombe even coined a special verb – to 'rember' – to describe such illusory recollections.)[22] Such misidentifications perhaps alert us to the fluidity of memory's relationships to other types of mental construction. In remembering an event, the 'reconstructivist' view implies, we do not simply conjure up a set of images or impressions that derive from our immediate experience of that event in particular; rather, we make sense of that event, and read meaning into our perceptions of it, by combining such data with information drawn from other sources – from our general culture, from other areas of our experience, and from the environment within which we are situated at the time of remembering.[23] Our ability to remember the event also depends on our ability in some measure to interpret it, by connecting it to the networks of ideas and the systems of meaning that form the current conceptual scaffolding of our general understanding. Aspects of the event that can be readily connected to these frameworks are easily retained; ones that cannot may be either amended or simply forgotten.

The second implication of the 'reconstructivist' view, following on from this, is that memory, for all the sometimes striking apparent fixity of its images, is essentially prone to mutation, both in the impressions it yields of particular moments in past experience, and in the way it connects these together. To be sure, memory cannot be of much use to us, either as a strictly cognitive instrument or as part of our working-out of selfhood, unless it possesses a degree of stability: if our memories of past events changed radically from day to day, we would have little basis for purposeful action, and little foundation for personal identity. Evolutions in memory are, however, from a 'reconstructivist' standpoint, a natural outcome of the processes that constitute remembering. Efforts to recall the same event on two separate occasions are unlikely to produce identical results, firstly because the immediate circumstances of recall will be different, suggesting different mental connections to the rememberer; and secondly, because further experiences that the rememberer may had in the interval between the two occasions will have modified the interpretative apparatus that is brought to bear.

One of the models that psychologists have often used to describe how memory works, and how it changes over time, uses the language of 'encoding' and 'retrieval'.[24] According to this model, the impressions that constitute an event or experience for the individual do not pass directly into memory, but are encoded, more or less at the moment of occurrence, through the application of one or several working mental templates, or schemata.[25] These schemata, which already form part of the mind's equipment prior to the moment of the experience in question, effectively determine what in that experience will be forgotten, and what will be at least potentially available for later recollection. Encoding by means of such schemata imposes a certain organization on the data that are retained, and this initial organization of data in turn influences future possibilities of recollection. When an event or experience is remembered, the process by which data are retrieved from memory again involves the application of schemata, which may or may not coincide closely with those that were involved in the initial process of encoding. Where the two sets of schemata coincide closely, events or experiences will be remembered roughly as they were originally perceived; where the two are significantly different, the memories thrown up by the process of recollection will be differently configured, detail that was previously registered may be lost, and there may in some cases be a difficulty in forming any coherent memories at all. What is more, since retrieval is itself an exercise in the application of schemata that are formally similar to those used in the original process of encoding, every moment of retrieval is, in itself, also a moment of 're-encoding', which exerts its own influence on the possibilities of recollection on subsequent occasions. (How far such re-encodings automatically override and destroy the traces of the original or earlier encodings remains a moot point.) Events that are repeatedly remembered are likely, therefore, to undergo a certain evolution in the remembering. How they are remembered at any given moment will be influenced not just by the circumstances of the original event (and by the way it was then encoded) and by the circumstances that prompt the latest effort at recollection, but also by a history of earlier recollections.

'Encoding and retrieval' models of memory are founded on a textual metaphor, and this makes them relatively accessible to historians, to literary scholars and practitioners of other disciplines that habitually deal with texts, with visual or verbal representations, and the problems of meaning and interpretation that are associated with them.[26] Arguably less accessible, but still important for what they can suggest, are the more 'connectionist' models some psychologists have recently developed. James L. McClelland, for example, views remembering as a pattern of activity within a mental system consisting of numerous 'simple but massively interconnected processing units'. The initial 'memory trace' of a particular event of experience – the pattern of connective activity that it initially generates – is heavily influenced by the event or experience itself, but also by the pre-existing pattern of connections between the units. In effect, the memory trace is best understood not as a discrete image of the event in question, or even as an encoded message, but as a modification of the pre-existing pattern of connections, strengthening the connections between units that have been jointly involved in making sense of the event, weakening connections that have not been drawn on as part of this process. Remembering is prompted when one or more features of the original event reoccur as part of a present situation. The pattern of activity which this reoccurrence triggers off is not, however, necessarily confined to those units which were involved in the original representation of the event, and which are therefore directly mobilized by the reappearance of some of its elements, for the activation of these units may in turn generate activity in further units to which these first ones have weighted connections as a result of other experience. The pattern of activity that is thus constructed – and that the mind experiences as a 'memory' – will thus be influenced by the pattern of connections that was established at the time when the original experience was registered, and to this extent the way the event is remembered will be close to the way it was originally experienced. But it will be influenced also by the further modifications to that pattern of connections that have been generated through subsequent experiences and, to this extent, the memory of events will always in practice offer an adjusted version of the original experience.[27]

Part of the value of this way of thinking about memory lies in the encouragement to think holistically – to view memory in general not as a set of one-to-one correspondences between particular events and the particular memories that represent or re-encode those events, but as a larger network of mental connections, developments in any part of which can have effects elsewhere in the network. This in turn may encourage us to reconsider the automatic centrality that events (as supposedly discrete units of experience) and event-focused memories have sometimes been assumed to have in human processes of remembering. Events, we need to remind ourselves, are not automatically evident features of our experience: they are mental constructions – products of the organizational mental labour by which we impose order and meaning on what would otherwise be the ceaseless, seamless and bewildering flow of our impressions and perceptions. As such, events are not stable; their boundaries are always susceptible to revision, their coherence always a coherence from one point of view, that may dissolve if the angle of vision is adjusted. Psychologists have coined the term 'memory binding' to refer to that maintenance of connectedness between the different elements in our perception of an event that holds them together as a discrete bundle of impressions – as constituents of this event in particular, defined by their relationships to each other, rather than by whatever connections they may have to other tracts of our experience. But memory binding is always to some extent fragile and provisional. Evolutions in our experience, acquisition of further information, shifts in our general frameworks of understanding can all produce changes in the kinds of connections that the mind draws both within events and between them, and in the extent to which it distinguishes one event from another.

For, in truth, memory is not as good at keeping the events of the past separate as those who look to it for a faithful reproduction of past experiences might like it to be. Much of what cognitive psychology labels memory distortion stems, in one way or another, from the mind's tendency to transfer or conflate, assimilating detail that has its origins in one experiential context into the memory of another (errors of 'source attribution', in psychologists' language), or combining detail drawn from different contexts into synthetic 'memories' of events that never actually happened ('memory conjunction' errors). Studies geared to assessing the likely reliability of eye-witness testimony in the context of police enquiries and judicial proceedings has shown how people's memories of events they have personally witnessed can be distorted through the inclusion in those memories either of 'post-event information' (i.e. information that has been fed to the witness subsequent to the event they are being asked to remember but prior to the moment when the testimony is delivered) or of ideas suggested in the course of questioning at the moment of delivery. Controversies over alleged 'recovered memories' of episodes of sexual abuse in childhood have generated studies which suggest that apparent memories even of events which, if real, would be deeply personal and highly traumatic, can, under certain conditions, be synthetically induced.[28] Judged by criteria of representational accuracy, memory in such cases appears obviously dysfunctional. Some psychologists have suggested, however, that memory's liability to this kind of distortion may be (in Daniel Schacter's words) 'a price we pay for processes and functions that serve us well in many respects'[29] – evidence, in fact, less of memory's fallible inadequacy than of its deeper effectiveness, and systemic ruthlessness, as an instrument for the cognitive management of experience. What matters in memory, this view implies, may be less the ability to provide us with perfectly accurate detail on a succession of neatly separate events, than the ability to synthesize, to generalize, to prioritize, to select – to give us the kind of simplified digest of experience that allows us to frame and pursue coherent courses of action. Viewed from such an angle, the potential for distortion is implicit in the function of interpretative simplification: memory that is generally serviceable may carry as its risk memory that is sometimes mistaken. Such an approach encourages us – historians included – to view memory's instances of 'unreliability' less as simple manifestations of defectiveness than as part of the more general – and always both necessary and problematic – process by which the mind creatively and pragmatically interprets and engages with its stream of experience. It encourages historians to move beyond a simple methodological concern with gauging the accuracy of specific recollections, and to develop techniques that are geared instead to comprehending the place which 'erroneous' detail occupies in larger patterns of recollection, and to exploring the meanings that memories of past experience, including 'distorted' ones, may embody or articulate.

One possible line of approach to such questions was developed by the psychologist Ulric Neisser in a seminal article analysing the testimony which one of President Nixon's White House staff gave to the Senate Investigating Committee on the Watergate affair in the early 1970s. John Dean's testimony related to conversations with Nixon and other White House personnel that he had been party to during the Watergate cover-up. Comparing Dean's account of these conversations with the transcripts of tape-recordings of the meetings in question, Neisser showed how Dean's apparently vivid and detailed recollections of particular conversations were at odds with what the tapes showed had actually occurred on the occasions referred to. Dean's memories were skewed both by hindsight and by a tendency to exaggerate the centrality and significance of his own role in the conversations recalled. Though he recalled some passages of conversation fairly accurately, his account both of the details and of the general gist of particular exchanges was often inaccurate. Sometimes details were transplanted from one conversation to another; at other times, Dean's memory supplied presidential interjections, giving answers or expressions of approval where none had actually been forthcoming. Neisser's purpose in documenting these distortions was, however, to push beyond a simple conception of memory's cognitive inaccuracy. Dean's recollections, he argued, should be understood less as what they purported to be – precise 'episodic' memories each relating to a specific conversational exchange – than as memories whose real character and functions were (in Neisser's own newly coined term) 'repisodic'. What such memories really articulated were Dean's impressions, not of individual meetings envisaged as isolated episodes, but of a series of conversational episodes that his mind had classified as structurally similar and as thematically connected, and that it therefore tended to blur together. It was the cumulative and repetitive impact of this series of conversational encounters, and of his own mental preparations for them and reflections on them afterwards, that shaped the memories that Dean attached to the specific episodes his interrogators asked him to focus on. Where he remembered the detail of a particular conversation accurately, it was because that detail conformed fairly closely to his overall impressions, or involved features that were typical of the series of conversations more generally, or related to contributions of his own that he had rehearsed in advance or repeatedly mulled over; where the detail was inaccurate, it was generally because it had been adjusted to bring the memory of the particular episode more closely into line with Dean's overall impressions. For Neisser, this analysis of the apparent inaccuracies of Dean's memory revealed important truths about memory more generally. Much of what we think of as memory of specific events may in fact be at least partially 'repisodic' in character; it may be focused, in other words, less on the distinctive features that make a particular event stand out from others, than on the generic, recurrent or typical elements that make it part of a more general experience. Attention to 'inaccuracies' in the way particular events are recollected needs to be coupled to a sensitivity for the broader (and, in Neisser's view, possibly broadly accurate) perceptions such memories may articulate.[30]

Neisser's analysis of Dean's memories was still shaped by a cognitive psychologist's basic concern with the accuracy of re-collection. The essential thrust of his argument was that although Dean's memories were inaccurate as memories of specific events, they actually gave a correct impression, at a more general level, of what was going on in the Nixon White House; once the memories were reconceptualized as 'repisodic', their relationship to an objective past reality became apparent. Scholars working in other disciplines – literary studies, psychoanalysis, anthropology, oral history – have approached the issue of memory's distortions from a different angle, attaching less importance to the idea of objective accuracy or truthfulness, and more to memory's role in the symbolic construction of a past that is adapted to present (not necessarily basically cognitive) needs and perceptions. To the extent that memories of specific events offer a seemingly concrete point of focus for perceptions which often actually derive from broader sweeps of experience, their significance is always partly symbolic, as are the connections that memory establishes both within and between different remembered events. When we 'misremember' specific features of the events, it may be argued, we may be doing so less (as is implied in Neisser's conception of 'repisodic' memory) because our remembering is actually focused on the general features of some objectively existing phase of past reality in which the specific event is embedded, than because our minds are using the event to forge or sustain symbolic connections that are integral either to our sense of self or to our present ways of viewing things. This kind of interpretation has been developed, for example, by the oral historian and literary scholar Alessandro Portelli, in an influential article focused on memories of the killing of an Italian steelworker, Luigi Trastulli, in a clash with police during a demonstration in the town of Terni in 1949.[31] Portelli shows how the episode of Trastulli's death was symbolically structured and connected to other aspects of post-war experience in the memories of the working-class Terni inhabitants whom he, as an oral historian, interviewed roughly twenty years after the event. In recollecting and narrating the episode, these informants did not merely accentuate some of its potential symbolic connections to other meaningful narratives (playing, for example, on Crucifixion imagery and other motifs evocative of Christ's Passion); they actually relocated the episode historically, transplanting it in memory from its original context – that of the protests occasioned by the Italian government's ratification of the North Atlantic Treaty in 1949 – to the different setting of protests against layoffs and dismissals in the Terni steelworks in 1953. For Portelli, the discovery of such striking inaccuracies is the occasion not for gloomy reflections on the factual unreliability of oral sources, but for the proclamation of a methodological opportunity. 'The discrepancy between fact and memory', he affirms, 'ultimately enhances the value of the oral sources as historical documents', for it is this discrepancy that gives us clues to the mental strategies by which those who are caught up in history make sense of their own experience and of the political and social conflicts that have moulded it. To understand this, according to Portelli, we need to recognize that memory's departures from historical fact in relation to episodes such as the Trastulli killing are not a matter of 'faulty recollections' – of defective cognition, pure and simple – but are rather 'actively and creatively generated by memory and imagination in an effort to make sense of crucial events and of history in general'.[32] For those he interviewed in the 1960s and 1970s, Portelli argued, the mental links connecting Trastulli's death to the specific protest against NATO had far less resonance than those that connected it to the longer and wider history of their own collective struggle against the agencies of capitalism and the capitalist state, a struggle of which the events of 1952–3 rather than of 1949 had been the obvious culmination. The transposition of Trastulli's death to this later but (in terms of their present concerns) more significant moment was part and parcel of its incorporation into consciousness as an episode of 'martyrdom' whose symbolic meanings were rooted in the generality of their post-war experience. The feelings of impotence and humiliation that may originally have been attached to their failure to react forcefully to the killing in 1949 may also, Portelli speculates, have been alleviated by blending the recollection of Trastulli's death with memories of the more determined militancy of the later industrial conflicts. The retention of Trastulli's death as an episode in the memories of his fellow workers and fellow citizens depended on memory's capacity for adjusting detail to meet changing symbolic and psychological requirements.

In their different ways, Neisser and Portelli both highlight the impossibility of separating memories of particular events from the broader contexts and longer histories to which those events may be related. Events are porous; meaning seeps across their boundaries. The memories we have of them are always, therefore, freighted with meanings that go beyond their immediate and obvious points of reference. However precisely focused particular memories may appear to be, they are always an adjustable part of the mind's more general efforts to order and interpret the continuous flow of its experience. Indeed, since Neisser first formulated his concept of 'repisodic memory', he and other psychologists working on autobiographical memory have gone a stage further in demolishing the conception of memory as something that is always primarily geared to recapturing the specific lineaments of particular episodic moments in past experience.

In Neisser's more recent formulation of the issue, 'individual episodes have no privileged status in memory; it is at least as natural to remember extended situations or typical patterns'.[33] In one influential development of this idea, Martin A. Conway has sketched a model of autobiographical remembering in which memories are 'compilations' of data drawn from three interconnecting strata of knowledge. On the first level, knowledge relating to *lifetime periods* records the 'goals, plans, and themes of the self' that were operative, at a general level, during particular phases – usually of at least a few years – of the individual's existence. Such knowledge may include, for example, 'knowledge of significant others, records of goal attainment, and general knowledge of actors, actions and locations' that were important for the individual during the period in question. On the second level, knowledge relating to *general events* consists of 'records of extended and repeated events', usually occurring over a matter of weeks or months rather than years. (John Dean's 'repisodic' memories of his repeated meetings with Nixon would fit this description.) Only on the third level – that of *event-specific* knowledge – however, do we reach a level at which knowledge has to do with the actual experiential detail (the 'images, sensations, smells and other sensory-perceptual features') of specific events. In Conway's model, the recollection of particular events is a structured process of retrieval, in which we home in on the event-specific detail only by mentally traversing layers of more generalized autobiographical knowledge. Much of the actual work of remembering goes on at these more general levels, and is geared less to the production of precisely focused impressions of specific past events, than to the cultivation of a general sense of the chronologies and of the spatial and social contexts that are the structuring containers of the individual's past experience.[34] These containers, we may add, should perhaps be regarded not as objective features of life's experience – features that are 'out there' in the past, simply waiting for memory to refer to them – but as part of the apparatus that the mind constructs for making sense of things – an apparatus that is always symbolic in character, influenced by the categories of a larger culture, and prone to evolution as life continues.

Once we see memory not as a collection of one-to-one representations of discrete and specific moments in past experience, but as a continuous interpretative reconstruction of that experience, oscillating between general and particular levels of perception, and mobilizing a wide variety of mental resources, it becomes harder to think of memory as something always separate from and manifestly posterior to the experience from which it derives. Obviously, events – as specific and discrete occurrences – cannot be remembered until they have happened. But events are made sense of, and are constituted, in relation to broader and longer flows of experience, into which a continuous practice and experience of remembering is interwoven. Indeed, from one angle, we might argue that memories should be seen not as straightforwardly posterior reconstructions of experiences that are past, but as temporal extensions of experience – extensions which testify, however, to the inherent mutability of experiences, the meanings of which are never fixed definitively by the sensations of an original moment of 'happening', but are always evolving as these moments become subsumed in longer developments, or are refracted through the prism of later events.

Memory, selfhood and narrativity

Memory, in reconstructing past events and experiences, does so from the standpoint of a particular individual. But this standpoint cannot simply be taken for granted, for there is a sense in which the remembering individual is himself or herself constituted by the experiences that are remembered, and by the experience of remembering. In effect, autobiographical remembering is a doubly constructive activity: in mentally reconstructing the past events and conditions that are the ingredients of personal experience, we simultaneously construct and maintain ourselves as remembering subjects – that is to say, as subjects each of whom is aware of being the possessor of – and therefore the only person truly capable of recollecting a particular and distinctive record of personal experience. Evolutions in the way we remember that experience are, in this sense, simultaneously evolutions in our sense of personal identity – our sense of 'self'. Yet the relationship between the psychic phenomena of memory and of selfhood remains elusive and controversial. For John Stuart Mill, they were 'two sides of the same fact': it was one's consciousness, through memory, of 'a long and uninterrupted succession of past feelings' that sustained one's sense of self:

> Myself is the person who had that series of feelings, and I know nothing of myself, by direct knowledge, except that I had them. But there is a bond of some sort among all the parts of the series, which makes me say that they were the feelings of a person who was the same person throughout [. . .].[35]

Yet this view may seem problematic, when we consider how fragmentary a knowledge of our 'succession of past feelings' memory seems really to retain: far from being evidenced by the seamlessness of our recollection, the remembered self (in the literary critic Daniel Albright's phrase) 'begins and ends in a state of nothingness, and from beginning to end is riddled with nothingness'. [36] Chiefly in the context of larger conceptual debates over whether it is continuity of body or continuity of mind (i.e. of consciousness) that is the decisive criterion in determining continuity or discontinuity in the existence of a human 'person', philosophers have keenly debated the question of whether memory is the foundation of a sense of personal identity, or vice versa. [37] (Is it because I am able to remember episodes from previous experience that I have a sense of myself as a continuously existing person, or is it only because I have such a sense of my own continuous existence that I am able to distinguish some of my mental impressions as memories – i.e. as impressions that relate to past rather than to present experience?) To the non-philosophical observer, such disputes may occasionally call to mind the comparable priority disputes about chickens and eggs: we may prefer to rest content with assertions that 'memory and identity serve to mutually validate each other' or that 'memory and the development of the self are concurrent processes'. [38] It is important, however, to recognize the problematic character of a relationship that is sometimes too glibly taken for granted. No doubt a sense of selfhood does not depend on memory supplying us with a continuous blow-by-blow record of our past experiences. (From a psychoanalytic perspective, indeed, it may depend on precisely the opposite – our ability to repress the memory of elements of experience that are hard to assimilate to our self-conception.) No doubt, indeed, there is a level on which a sense of personal identity depends less on memory's ability to summon up particular details than on the familiarity we have as individuals with the general sensation of remembering. If the sense of selfhood is to have active influence on our behaviour – if it is to amount to something more than a philosophical abstraction – it needs, however, to have a gritty content of some kind or other: one needs to have not just a general sentiment of continuity, but the sense of having been shaped by a particular course of experience, or of having maintained one's particular cast of self across a certain set of vicissitudes. While memory can contribute materials for the composition of such an active sense of selfhood, it is less clear that the simple registration of a succession of past experiences would be sufficient to generate it.

Rather than viewing a sense of self as something that is occasioned – i.e. created – by the process of remembering, recent psychological thinking has generally preferred to include conceptions of selfhood among the operative 'schemata' that structure that process (but which are, of course, susceptible to gradual modification in the course of it). In Jerome Bruner's view, 'the crucial cognitive activities involved in Self-construction seem much more like "thinking" than "memory"'.[39] From this interpretative standpoint, 'selves' are not things that we know by remembering them: they are things we mentally construct out of a range of available materials, including memories, but also narrative conventions, cultural stereotypes, myths, collective expectations. They are operative conceptions, not remembered realities. As such, they may be flexible, even in a sense provisional, but can also be demanding. 'Self is a perpetually rewritten story', Bruner writes. 'What we remember from the past is what is necessary to keep that story satisfactorily well formed.'[40] Scholars more influenced by the psychoanalytical tradition give the psychic development of the self a more central place in the general economy of remembering and forgetting, and understand it somewhat differently: for them, the self is less a piece of cognitive software – a mental construction in need of maintenance, whose function is to frame and organize a certain area of human recollection – than an expression of the human psyche's perpetual, and not always entirely successful, struggle to achieve and maintain the composure and integrity that the flow of difficult experience often threatens to disrupt.

Neither of these schools of thought supposes selfhood to be effortlessly unitary. What Antze and Lambek call 'the ideal of an unambiguous, limpid self' is, they argue, seldom realized: 'ambiguity is the rule' – with the result that memory, rather than simply sustaining 'the dominant view of our identity', instead 'always threatens to undermine it, whether by obvious gaps, by uncertainties, or by glimpses of a past that no longer seems to be ours'.[41] While the emphasis here, and in most psychoanalytically-inspired discussions, is on the threatening aspects of ambiguity and division (most graphically reflected in cases of 'multiple personality disorder'), those who are more inclined to see the self as a piece of constructed mental equipment sometimes stress the elements of alternation, and even maybe of choice and experimentation, that may be at work in self-construction: individuals may, according to such a view, dispose of several different self-conceptions, adapted to the requirements of different kinds of occasion, or deployed for different audiences or in the processing of different kinds of experience. (How far there needs still in such cases be what the philosopher Jonathan Glover calls an 'inner story' of the self, somehow mediating between different self-presentations, remains a moot point.)[42] But whether unitary or multiple, crisis-ridden or experimental, the self is, for most contemporary theorists, always in the process of construction or of revision: it never, in this sense, quite becomes a stable object of memory, but always remains a kind of project, through which memory itself is structured and interpreted. The oral historian Alastair Thomson summarizes the connection:

> Remembering is one of the vital ways in which we identify ourselves in storytelling. In our storytelling we identify what we think we have been, who we think we are now and what we want to become. The stories that we remember will not be exact representations of our past, but will draw upon aspects of that past and mould them to fit current identities and aspirations. [. . .]. Memories are 'significant pasts' that we compose to make a more comfortable sense of our life over time, and in which past and current identities are brought more into line.[43]

For oral historians such as Thomson, the analysis of these mutually constitutive interactions between constructed selfhood and personal memory is a central scholarly objective.

Scholars in different disciplines have used a number of different conceptual languages in seeking to understand the impact of self-construction on memory and its expressive articulations. In the 1950s, for example, the psychoanalyst Ernst Kris suggested that autobiographical remembering is shaped by the 'personal myth' of the individual concerned. Such 'myths', which may be applied either to the whole of the individual's remembered past, or to particular parts of it, are rooted, according to Kris, in the psychological experience of early childhood, when fantasy and reality are not yet clearly separated in the child's perceptions. In effect, the myth is an element of fantasy that remains interwoven with perceptions of reality as the latter evolve in the course of the individual's development, and whose effect is to skew auto-biographical remembering towards the maintenance of a certain narrative or self-conception.[44] Other scholars have placed a similar emphasis on 'myth' as an element in autobiographical remembering, but have been concerned less to probe the origins of mythical formations in the early evolution of the individual psyche than to explore the materials for mythical self-construction that are supplied by the cultures in which individuals are implicated. Any culture is likely to generate a range of stereotypical images that individuals may make use of in structuring their projections of self and framing autobiographical recollections: Christian culture, for example, offers images of the martyr, of the repentant sinner, of the born-again believer; capitalist culture, ones of the heroic entrepreneur, the self-made man, the purposeful consumer.[45] The sociologist-cum-psychoanalyst Jeffrey Prager has explored the way in which patients undergoing psychoanalysis make use of culturally available 'categories of experience' (or 'frames of meaning'), which allow them to understand their problems by casting themselves as victims or sufferers of a recognizable kind (e.g. homosexuals, African-Americans, victims of sexual abuse). The individual's appropriation of such a category is accompanied by the weaving of 'elaborated narratives of experience, in which personal history is interwoven with tales of suffering that include themes of estrangement or discrimination, recognition or redemption'. Such narratives, Prager argues, 'are not solely of the individual's own making, but reflect substantial borrowing from a culture that has perfected various tales of victimization'.[46] Somewhat similarly, in her oral history of the Turin working-class's experience of Fascism, Luisa Passerini has stressed the role of 'recurring self-representations' in structuring the autobiographical accounts given to her by her elderly informants. Rooted either in the familiar narrative forms of working-class culture or in those generated by political or religious ideologies, these essentially stereotypical representations cast the individual as, for example, 'a natural rebel' or a 'born socialist' or a 'hard worker' or a 'joker', or simply as 'always lucky' or as having always led a 'miserable existence'. By applying them, the individuals Passerini interviewed gave a kind of consistency and intelligibility (both for themselves and for others raised in the same culture) to existences which had often in fact been difficult and disrupted.[47] The anthropologist Maurice Bloch, finally, has drawn attention to the ways in which the mental reactions of individuals to certain kinds of experience (for example, revolutions, migrations or colonial oppressions), including the ways in which they personally remember these experiences, may be moulded by culturally embedded conceptions of collective

identity which describe the essential character of a group's relationship to historical experience. Thus the Sadah of the northern
Yemen, whose proclaimed descent from the Prophet Mohammed
makes them, in their own eyes, the vessels of a timeless holy wisdom,
feel themselves to be 'only in history as a rock is in the middle of
a stream', always ultimately unchanged by whatever waves of
adversity may afflict them, while the Bicolanos of the central
Philippines view themselves as a people 'who have nothing' and
whose destiny is therefore always to be malleable, always moulded
by their contacts with more powerful outsiders. Such collective self-
representations impart, Bloch argues, an inflection to experience
and to memory that human scientists ought not to ignore.[48]

These examples, drawn from different disciplinary fields,
illustrate the variety of ways in which cultural stereotypes or frames
of meaning may have an impact on the ways in which memories
are framed and presented. Culturally generated but personally
appropriated, such devices of the mind may be either liberating
or restricting: at one end of a spectrum they may be crucial in
stabilizing a sense of personal identity that would otherwise be
threatened by life's disruptions and fluctuations; at the other, they
may be cultural impositions – 'enforced narratives', in Carolyn
Steedman's phrase[49] – whose adoption reflects not so much an
individual's search for meaning as his or her painful entrapment
in a social world in which the terms of personal identity are set by
other people. Sometimes, the frames or stereotypes that individuals
make use of are more or less given by a larger culture, while at
others, a more variegated culture supplies a range of models that
individuals can choose from and experiment with; sometimes such
choices and experimentations are heavily constrained by social
conditions and power relationships, sometimes less so.

But whether the individual's use of such devices is coloured with
alienation or with a more comforting sense of enabling self-
composure, their incorporation as structuring elements in the
articulation of individual recollections is seldom completely artless
and smoothly automatic. In focusing on her Turin informants' use
of stereotypical self-representations, Passerini suggests that it
involves an element of conscious narrative performance, from
which a sense of the discrepancy between experience and narration
is not entirely absent: 'The subjects realise that there are two levels,
that is, that their story does not entirely tally with real life. But

precisely because they are telling a story, they resort knowingly to the stereotypes which story-telling in their culture requires'.[50] But where Passerini highlights this disparity, Prager, in discussing his patients' somewhat similar narrative practice, highlights the practical difficulty of disentangling personal memory from appropriated narrative convention: 'It becomes nearly impossible to parse out memories of the past from the categories of experience available in the present, the narratives offered to link the present to a story of its origins in the past, and the consequences of these particular forms of self-understanding for the rememberer in the present.'[51]

We are confronted here with the larger issue of memory and narrativity. When historians or others (psychologists, sociologists, literary scholars, etc.) set out to study memories, what they in practice observe and analyse is not memory as an inner mental condition, but the outward articulations of memory, usually in verbal or textual form. To suppose that the study of these articulations can give us an unmediated access either to memory's inner mental textures or to the original experiences of the individual that the memories that are being articulated ostensibly refer to, is obviously naïve: things, no doubt, are not remembered precisely as they were originally experienced, and are not narrated to others precisely as they are inwardly remembered. Yet such a statement itself seems to imply a three-phase model (experience, memory, narration) that is obviously problematic, for when we view them from a different angle – as continuous or repetitive processes rather than one-off performances – experiencing and remembering and narrating are not separate and consecutive, but simultaneous and interconnected. We do not, in other words, run through the whole of life as experience before we begin to remember it, and finish remembering it before we begin narratively to arrange what we remember: rather, experience and memory and narrativity are aspects of consciousness that unfold together, penetrating each other, nourishing each other and modifying each other, as human beings strive continuously to maintain and develop and articulate their working understandings of a changing world and of their own changing place within it. The ways in which we experience a particular occurrence may be influenced by memories of earlier experiences; the ways in which that occurrence is later remembered and narrated may be influenced both by memories of intervening experiences, and by the conditioning effects of earlier narrative arrangements. If the history of our remembering cannot be simply identified with the history of its narrative arrangements, nor can it easily be separated from it.

In his own discussions of the methodological problems posed by the analysis of autobiographical memory in clinical settings, the psychoanalytical theorist Donald Spence has probed the issue of narrativity further. For Spence, patients narrating their past experience are in effect 'translators', struggling to convert 'the private sensations of experience' (as present to them in memory) into 'the common language of speech'.[52] Memories, in their pure state, are (he argues) non-verbal: they consist of images or sensations, which may be clear and precise, but which are often in fact somewhat vague and uncertain. Putting these images or sensations into words, for the purpose of communicating them to a psychoanalyst (or to anyone else), is a descriptive action which, like all such actions, actually modifies the impression that it purports simply to represent. This is so in two ways. Firstly, the choice of words and terms to describe the initial image inevitably highlights certain aspects or ingredients of that image at the expense of others: since no verbal description can capture every aspect of what is often a rather unco-ordinated jumble of impressions, every attempt to narrativize remembered experience involves a distortion or misrepresentation. Secondly, since the terms that are employed in describing a memory are bound also to be the carriers of other mental associations, meanings will be imported through the act of narration which were not part of the original memory impression.[53] For Spence, these effects of narrativization are sufficient actually to destroy, and to replace, the original memory:

> The point is this: once expressed in a particular set of sentences, the memory itself has changed, and the patient will probably never again have quite the same vague, nonspecific and unspoiled impression. Thus, the very act of talking about the past tends to crystallize it in specific but somewhat arbitrary language, and this language serves, in turn, to distort the early memory. More precisely, the new description *becomes* the early memory.[54]

Narrativity, according to this view, obscures – or radically trans-forms – the memory that it strives to articulate. The way in which memories are first verbally articulated conditions their subsequent shape: there can be no return to a pre-narrative condition. The point is contestable: drawing on examples from his anthropological fieldwork, in which the same informants provide differently focused narrative accounts of a given remembered episode on different kinds of occasion, Maurice Bloch has suggested that memories themselves are not, in fact, wholly absorbed and radically modified as soon as they are narrated. Rather, he argues, memories are stored in forms that are not essentially linguistic, and can supply the materials for a range of different narrations, triggered by different kinds of environmental or social cuing. Where Spence sees narrations as second-phase memories – memories irretrievably converted into narrative form – Bloch sees them simply as state-ments about what is remembered, shaped by the requirements of particular kinds of occasion, but always leaving scope for other possible narrations, in which memory will be equally though differently implicated.[55] Whichever view we take on this, however, it seems reasonable to concur with Spence's basic suggestion that there is always an unfathomable discrepancy between memory as an inner set of psychological impressions and the narrative compositions of memory that psychoanalysts – but also historians – are largely forced to deal with, and that the narrative patterns into which memories are fitted at particular moments may exert a significant, if not a completely defining, influence on the way those memories are later made sense of and re-narrated.

If we accept it thus far, Spence's argument has three significant implications for how historians should approach the accounts of memory that they encounter in oral and written sources. Firstly, it suggests that their handling of these accounts must be sensitive to their verbal and narrative character – to narrative structures and strategies, to the tricks and resonances of language, and to the cultural provenance and symbolic significance of the forms adopted.

Secondly, Spence's emphasis on the ways in which earlier moments of narrativization influence later patterns must remind us that, as historians, we are rarely privileged to witness the moments at which memories first acquire a narrative form. Samuel Schrager has rightly cautioned oral historians against the naïve assumption that the memories thrown up in oral history interviews have somehow lain dormant until the moment when the dynamics of the interview awakens them. Rather, he argues, the oral historian is usually 'an intervener in a process that is already highly devel-oped', for 'as in most circumstances of storytelling, most of what is told has been said before in a related form', quite likely on numerous occasions. 'In the form that the oral historian is likely to encounter it, the story has already undergone the progressive structuring of detail that accompanies retellings', and the oral historian's most obvious contribution may be simply to provide a fresh context to which an already much-rehearsed tale has to be adapted.[56] Other oral historians have, admittedly, placed more faith in the capacity of sensitively conducted oral history interviews to refocus and refresh their informants' efforts at recollection, but this does not invalidate the reminder that most memory narratives that are told to oral historians (or that historians encounter in documentary form) will incorporate elements that have a significant history of previous rehearsal. Evaluating such narratives requires us to consider the effects not just of narrativization in general, but of a specific history of previous narrative arrangements.

Thirdly, Spence's insistence that narrativization involves both a severing of certain mental connections and an establishment of new ones suggests the need for our analysis of memory narratives to be focused not just on what has ostensibly been articulated but on what has been excluded, not just on what remains constant as we move from an earlier to a later narration but on what has been modified or displaced, not just on the symbolic connections that give the narrations their apparent meaning, but on the alternative connections that those narrations may be instrumental in disrupting or preventing. In effect, Spence's emphasis on memory's trans-formation through narrativization adds a further layer to the issues that are already implicit in much of psychoanalytic practice – namely that memory itself is always crafted by forms of repression, whose effects are felt not just as silence and forgetting, but in displace-ments and rearrangements of what is remembered. Oral historians (along with students of autobiographical writing) have been increasingly eager to fashion their modes of enquiry in the light of these suggestions. They do so sometimes through detailed engage-ments with particular styles of psychoanalytic theory (whether Freudian, Lacanian or Kleinian) or simply through a more general use of vaguely psychoanalytic language to describe agendas whose governing assumption is no longer that oral testimony straight-forwardly articulates a popular consciousness of the past, but rather that it offers oral historians an opening for probing the hidden threads of anguish that run both through and beneath the surface layers of memory and narration.

Thus, for example, Selma Leydesdorff, in her work on the Jewish proletariat of early twentieth-century Amsterdam, describes herself as 'searching for untold stories lurking in the gaps of the stories that are told overtly' – an exercise whose character is further evoked through a telling combination of textual and archaeological metaphors: the 'real story' is to be found 'only by reading between the lines' of her informants' testimony; 'the researcher, like an archaeologist, is continually digging up new layers of the person, both in the memory and in the personality'.[57] In less overtly psychoanalytical vein, Alastair Thomson speaks of the need, in dealing with memories of certain kinds of wartime experience, 'to peel away the layers of meaning that have been constructed around that experience over time and in different social contexts', working back 'through earlier articulations of the same experience', and thus exposing memory's 'sedimentary layers'.[58]

Narrativity enters into the articulation of memory even when this articulation is limited to the recollection of specific occurrences. When we shift our attention to the ways in which such recollections are incorporated into larger structures of autobiographical self-presentation – life-stories – analyzing the relationships of memory and narrativity becomes even more pressing. Linking the events of a life together is inescapably an act of narrative construction. At least in its more developed forms, autobiographical consciousness hinges not just on a sense of personal duration – the sense of there having been a continuously existing being (oneself) on which a succession of experiences have been visited – but on the sense that these experiences have come in a meaningful order, and that part of their significance lies in their sequential and cumulative effect on the individual self in question. The time in which the remembered self is located is a structured and punctuated time – not a seamless flow, but a time with 'befores' and 'afters', longer and shorter durations, moments of immobility and phases of accelerated movement, cyclical rhythms and progressive advances and deteriorative descents. This narrative structuring of autobiographical time typically operates on a number of levels. Firstly, it may deploy any of the various standard and conventional systems of temporal measurement and regulation that are available within a given society – cycles of day and night, of weeks and months, and seasons; the habitual divisions of the day by mealtimes or working tasks; the divisions of the liturgical or the financial or the academic calendar; the charting of progressive time in years and decades and centuries, or in royal reigns, or in relation to birthdays and anniversaries; and so on. Such systems provide useful tools for marking the flow of time in autobiographical narratives, but are seldom sufficient in themselves to give events and experiences a powerful autobiographical significance. For this, a more personal-ized kind of temporality is generally necessary, and again this is a narrative conception: we give a temporal structure to our recollec-tions by connecting them to an implicit (or sometimes explicit) story of personal development. Here again, we draw on mental frameworks that are familiar in our culture. Culture may give us, for example, the concept of the 'life cycle' (with its standard procession from childhood, via youth and mature adulthood to eventual old age), or that of the 'career', which those pursuing a particular walk of life are deemed to follow. Frameworks of this kind may be so commonly accepted as to seem banal, yet they provide important scaffolding for autobiographical recollections and narrations, allowing individuals to assign particular memories to particular phases in a recognizable scheme of development.

The temporal divisions thus imposed can often be reinforced, and perhaps developed further, by reference to other kinds of mnemonic marker, for example ones to do with place (as when our memories focus on the physical settings with which we were familiar during certain phases of our existence) or with social group (as when they relate to the particular people with whom we worked at a particular stage of our career). Thus enriched with detail, different phases of the individual's experience may come to be invested in memory with different affective textures or emotional colourings, allowing a kind of narrative patterning to be developed that can seem almost independent of more explicit styles of narrative emplotment. Thus, for example, in the memoirs of the Victorian lady Elizabeth Grant of Rothiemurchus, successive phases in the author's childhood (as remembered in middle age) are mapped in terms of the physical locations to which they relate, and of the social relationships associated with those settings. Out of her fragmented recollections of life as a three- or four-year old in the Scottish Highlands, Grant forges an idyllic image of childhood freedom linked to the fondly remembered figure of her nanny Betty:

> She washed us well, dressed us after a fashion and then set off out of doors, where she kept us all day. We were a great deal in the fields with John Campbell the grieve and we talked to every body we met, and Betty sang to us and told us fairy tales, and made rush crowns for us, and kept us happy as I wish all children were.

What gives this account its force, however, is the detailed contrast that is almost immediately established between it and the next remembered phase of Grant's childhood:

> In the winter of 1802, after a season of all blank, I wake up in a gloomy house in Bury Place. There are no aunts, no Betty, a cross nurse, Mrs Day, who took us to walk somewhere where there was gravel, and nothing and nobody to play with; the few objects around us new and disagreeable. William and Jane were kept in great order by Mrs Day. William she bullied. Jane she was fond of, she was always so good. Me she did not like. I was so selfwilled.

A further move, the following year, to an airier abode in Lincoln's Inn Fields, again relaxes the regime:

> We had the Square to play in, were allowed to run about there without a maid, and soon made acquaintance with plenty of children as well pleased with new companions as ourselves. From this time our town life was never an unhappy one.

From these oscillations between lightness and gloom, freedom and constraint, social mixing and social separation, relaxation and discipline, Grant's reminiscences of childhood derive a kind of narrative tension, rooted in textural contrast rather than in explicit dramatic detail, that contributes powerfully to her retrospective sense of personal development.[59]

Individuals may also, of course, assign a more explicitly dramatic kind of narrative structure to their remembered existences. Equipping ourselves once again from a variety of cultural sources – folklore, fictional literature, epic poetry, religious mythology – we endow our past experience, in whole or in part, with the imaginative structure of a heroic quest, of a spiritual (or a rake's) progress, of a drama of conversion, of a pastoral idyll; we fashion it narratively as comedy or tragedy, confessional revelation or moral tale, romantic melodrama or farce. In doing so, we confer on it a kind of dramatic unity and a degree of narrative coherence that may scarcely have been present in the daily flow of our existence. In the more developed forms of autobiographical writing, shaped by modern culture's enduring preoccupation with the concept of 'self', this dramatic structuring of the individual existence finds a peculiarly formal expression. As the literary scholar Georges Gusdorf put it in an influential essay, the autobiographer seeks 'to reassemble the scattered elements of his individual life and to regroup them in a comprehensive sketch', straining 'toward a complete and coherent expression of his entire destiny'. Such writing assumes not just a unity, but a kind of closure to the existence it describes: if life is not precisely at an end (most autobiographers do, after all, hope to survive the completion of their autobiography), the implication is nevertheless that a kind of vantage point has been reached from which the essential features of the life can be reviewed and summarized, in a process which is, in effect, a mixture of remembering and conscious interpretation. What results is a polished representation of the life in question: a literary product whose narrative coherence as text stands for the assumed unity of the existence that is being described. To be sure, recent students of autobiographical writing, especially ones approaching it from a feminist perspective, have undermined many assumptions about the genre, exposing its inner tensions and ideological functions, and challenging its heroic mythology of affirmative and autonomous selfhood in the name of a more complex intellectual and social history of subjectivities.[60] My suggestion here is not that the pretensions of autobiography in its classical forms should be taken at face value, but simply that, as pretensions, they have had an influence on how the memory-narrative connection is perceived.

Plainly, it would be a mistake to take the highly fashioned literary products of high autobiographical art for simple expressions of the way things were originally experienced, or even of the way those things are held onto in memory. Partly for this reason, literary scholars have often not only distanced the study of autobiography from the idea of memory (preferring to speak of subjectivity or self-narration), but have also often been insistent on the gap that separates the activity of narrating from the experience of living. In Louis O. Mink's succinct formulation, 'stories are not lived but told'.[61] The flow of an individual's immediate experiences does not, according to this view, resolve itself automatically into a coherent and unitary story, which the individual in question has only to remember and then to tell. Such a story, if it emerges at all, does so only in the course of the remembering and telling: it is not a fact of life, but a mental achievement. If we take this to mean that the stories which get told (and especially those which get told in formal autobiographical literature) often have a tenuous relationship to the way things are experienced in the everyday business of living, and that one aspect of this tenuousness has to do with the air of narrative certainty and the masterly drive and coherence such retrospective stories seem often to possess, the point seems valid. If it is taken to mean that experience and narrativity are somehow mutually exclusive, it seems less so. When we remember things, we tend already to relate them to schemata or frames of meaning that are at least partly narrative in character, classifying our impressions, for example, as memories of childhood rather than of adulthood, or as relating to an earlier rather than a later stage in the development of a career or a marital relationship. It seems plausible to suppose that schemata of this kind are instrumental in determining the kinds of things we tend to remember: moments of beginning and ending, moments of transition from one phase to another, people and places and things that serve to typify or to define the phases in question. And while the schemata themselves are no doubt susceptible to modification, it seems unlikely that they are entirely different in their general character from the ways in which we experience life as it unfolds. Narrativity – to put it differently – is not purely retrospective: rather, stories (in their general outline as opposed to their specific content) are imaginative constructions that we can use for envisaging the future as well as the past, and thus for making sense of what is happening at any given moment – by relating it to past experiences, to ongoing projects, to speculative future possibilities. Thus, we may perceive aspects of present experience as forming part of our progress along the path of a chosen career, or as marking the onset of old age, or as being part of the hardship that must be endured now in order to secure certain benefits later, or as constituting an unjust deprivation of what was due to us as a reward for earlier efforts. All of these ways of understanding things are implicitly based on narrative conceptions. It seems, therefore, legitimate to join with the philosopher David Carr in perceiving not a fundamental disparity but 'a certain community of form between "life" and written narratives'.[62] In remembering and narrating past experience, we are seldom imposing narrative form on a terrain from which it was previously entirely absent.

It is probably best, anyway, not to model our thinking about the interrelationships of experience, memory and narrativity on assumptions drawn from the contemplation of the more polished and developed forms of autobiographical literature.[63] Even in modern 'self'-obsessed cultures, formal written autobiography is the exception rather than the norm: few people have either the occasion or the inclination (or indeed the leisure and the self-confidence) to construct a detailed 'definitive' version of their life's story. Far more often, autobiographical narration occurs in the context of conversation: its forms are oral rather than literary; it is piecemeal, tentative, often rehearsed and repeated, but often reworked, often adjusted to meet the needs of new occasions or expectations of different audiences. It remains, as Portelli puts it, 'a living thing', and 'always a work in progress'.[64] Oral historians and others have become increasingly sensitive in recent years to the narrative rhythms and discursive patterns of this kind of autobiographical composition. Portelli has written illuminatingly of the kind of narrative production that takes place in the context of oral history interviews, as the production of a 'text' that is always still 'in the making' – always seeking form and stability, yet always composing itself from multiple sources, always still exploring its own narrative possibilities:

> There will be gradual approaches in search of a theme, not unlike musical glissando; conversational repairs and after-the-fact corrections, for the sake either of accuracy or of pragmatic effectiveness; incremental repetitions for the sake of completeness and accuracy, or of dramatic effect. This personal effort at composition in performance is supported by the use of socialized linguistic matter (clichés, formulas, folklore, frozen anecdotes, commonplaces) and by the example of genres derived from writing (the novel, auto-biography, history books) or mass media. These established blocks of discourse define secure paths in the uncharted territory of discourse, much like the invisible but rigid airways that guide airplanes in the fluid territory of the sky [. . .].
>
> Between the fluid textual experiments and the frozen formulaic material, the 'achieved' discourse breaks free and floats like a moving island, the tip of an iceberg. In order to understand how the narrative

is shaped, we must not limit ourselves to these moments of fulfillment; we need to consider also the formulaic materials, the apparently formless connecting and supporting matter, and the dialogic and directive role of the historian.[65]

Elsewhere, Portelli has focused on the practices of temporality that are at work in this kind of autobiographical expression. He contrasts the oral historian's own preoccupation with precise dating and the tidy arrangement of episodes along a unitary time-line with the more variable and flexible temporal arrangements of events and experiences that are deployed by those recollecting their life's experience for the historian and for others. In the latter, the connections are thematic as much as sequential, and are constructed not within a single temporal framework, but within a number of overlapping systems, each with its own conventions of periodization and temporal measurement. Thus events and experiences are grouped differently, depending on whether the narrator's implicit focus is on developments in national politics, or on the life of the local community, or on a more intimate personal and domestic history. Sometimes, one of these perspectives exercises a dominant structuring influence on the way things are remembered and narrated; more often, narrators oscillate between the different perspectives, weaving them together in a tissue of verbalized recollection whose modes of connection and points of focus are perpetually shifting. A similar volatility is evident in the narrative practice that Portelli calls 'shuttlework'. Here the narrator's focus switches backwards and forwards in time (between past and present or between different phases in the remembered past), articulating life's experience less as a sequential narrative than as a perceived disparity – a perpetually alluded to gap between 'then' and 'now' (between the world of one's youth and the world of one's old age; between the experience of one's own generation and the experience of those which have replaced it, etc.).[66] In oral testimonies of this kind, the processes of remembering and of narrating seem inextricably entangled: narrative organization may be more directly influenced than it is in the more literary forms of autobiography by the mental associations that are thrown up in the immediate activity of remembering; in return, the immediate pressures to tell a story of some kind or other may be part of what stirs memory into activity, and gives shape to what we remember.

Each of us, Jerome Bruner maintains, carries in his or her mind 'the rough and perpetually changing draft' of his or her autobiography.[67] The draft remains unfinished for two related reasons: first, because the life itself is not yet over, and second, because we are never through with testing out the ways in which we might narrate it. Telling our life's story involves connecting our past and present being not just to each other, but to futures we confidently or hopefully or speculatively anticipate: it involves projection as well as retrospection. As we move through life, some of our earlier expectations are fulfilled (or retain the prospect of possible future fulfilment); others are frustrated or simply abandoned. Fresh waves of experience force us to revise our anticipations of the future, and in so doing – since modifying our vision of the future means modifying our sense of where our past actions and past experience have been leading us – may affect the ways in which earlier phases of our existence are remembered. Youthful hopes are remembered through the lens of later disillusionment; the abandonment of earlier assumptions gets recast in memory as part of a necessary process of 'growing up'. Divergences in later experience produce differences in the way originally similar experiences are remembered. Interviewing Parisian bakers on their experience of apprenticeship, the sociologist and oral historian Isabelle Bertaux-Wiame found, for example, that those who in their later careers had fulfilled their aspirations to become masters and employers remembered the hardships of their apprentice years as part of the hard grind that was inseparable from eventual achievement, while those who had never risen to this level of independence and respectability tended, in recalling their presumably originally similar experiences, to dwell on the harshly exploited nature of the apprentice's condition.[68] Such a difference is scarcely surprising, but it highlights some important aspects of what is involved in autobiographical recollection.

Since autobiographical remembering reflects our need to comprehend and to adjust to the shifts and disjunctures and discrepancies that are part of life's experience, it is often both an emotionally charged and an emotionally complex business. The past we are connected to by memory is at once the past we keep with us and the past we have left behind. Viewed from one angle, it is what has made us, what has brought us to our present condition and our current possibilities of future development – something inseparable from our sense of self and of personal identity. Viewed from another, it is, for better or worse, a past we can no longer hang on to, replete with horizons that have receded, prospects that never materialized, circumstances and relationships that did not endure. It is a past peopled with lost selves: the selves we once were but no longer are, the more shadowy selves we once might have gone on to become but never did. Sometimes, memory is dominated by the continuities between past and present, or at least the discrepancies between the two are not distressing; sometimes, on the other hand, remembering carries a sense of regret, of nostalgic yearning, of loss or disruption. The emotional meanings that particular memories carry with them are never simply anchored in the past episodes that are being recalled; nor are they simply rooted in the circumstances that prevail at the moment of recollection. They are rooted rather in the mind's continuous efforts to maintain and to police the connections between past and present, prospect and retrospect, identity and possibility. Nor is this always done in the same way. In analyzing the interview materials on which she drew in her work on women in the Second World War, Penny Summerfield identifies two different modes of recollection among her elderly informants. In the first – the 'life review' – the informant deliberately seeks an integrated understanding of her life as a whole, taking the emotional risk of confronting its painful episodes in the hope – not always fully realized – of making a balanced sense of the whole. In the second, these risks are avoided by a strategy whose implicit overriding objective is a 'maintenance of self-esteem', achieved through a reiteration of stories tending to confirm the individual's worth and the value of her past experience.[69] Individuals may oscillate between these modes, depending on which phases of their lives they are recollecting, and on changes in their present circumstances.

The intimate and emotional connections between memory and personal identity are most vividly highlighted when we consider how autobiographical remembering can be disrupted by types of traumatic experience.[70] (Indeed, the emergence and refinement of 'trauma' as an analytical term has itself been influenced by studies of how remembering is affected by such experiences.) Experiences that brutally disrupt people's expectations and relationships do not merely generate memories that are painful in themselves; the difficulty of assimilating these memories to conventional narratives of personal experience can make them more profoundly disruptive. As Leydesdorff remarks, 'a trauma is not an isolated event in a life story but may [. . .] often play a decisive role in a person's perception of life afterwards, interpretations of subsequent events, and [. . .] memories of preceding experiences'.[71] Sometimes minds deal with traumatic threats by struggling to repress the memory of disturbing experience; in other cases, there may be an uncontrollable recurrence of impressions whose horrifically vivid immediacy can find no place in the carefully stabilized structures of autobiographical recollection. In some cases, a selective reworking of remembered detail may allow disturbing experiences to be coped with more effectively. In his sensitive study of the wartime experiences of a young Jewish woman living in hiding from the Nazis, for example, Mark Roseman has shown how, in Marianne Ellenbogen's later recollections, her accounts of the moments of separation or loss that were the most obviously traumatic features of her wartime experience were subtly adjusted, through minor exaggerations or alterations of detail (for example, in the account of her own escape from the Gestapo who arrested the rest of her family), in ways which allowed a possible alleviation of the sense of guilt that may have attached to an earlier understanding of the same experiences.[72] Such an example testifies, perhaps, to the essential toughness of autobiographical remembering – its power to protect itself against dissolution. So, in a different way, does the case of Latvians whose lives were devastated first by Nazi and then by Soviet invasion and occupation during and after the Second World War, whose techniques of psychological survival Vieda Skultans has analysed. Skultans argues powerfully that 'the breakdown of the everyday structures of living creates a need to reconstitute meaning in story telling', and that individuals confronted with such challenges are forced to dig deeply in the cultural resources they have available.[73] Faced with the devastation of their own lives and of the destruction of the social conditions that had supported conventional modes of autobiographical remembering, Latvians drew on the resources of literature and folklore to generate narratives 'constructed of an interweaving of personal lived experience and textual recollections', which allowed them to salvage a meaning for their own existences[74] – and in doing so, also to maintain some of the elements of a distinctive national culture in the face of Soviet oppression.

It would be wrong, plainly, to suppose too automatic a connection between traumatic experience and narrative breakdown. In other cases, however, whether because the violation of individual lives is in some way more profound or because a more wholesale accompanying destruction of social and cultural structures prevents individuals from marshalling the cultural and human resources that might be supportive, traumatic experiences can produce a genuine and perhaps enduring crisis in the organization of biographical remembering. Studies of memories of the Holocaust – a massively expanded field in recent decades – have highlighted various forms of this. Lawrence Langer, for example, highlights the distinction first drawn by an Auschwitz survivor, Charlotte Delbo, between the 'common memory' (mémoire ordinaire) by which the Holocaust survivor seeks to bind Holocaust experience into some kind of structure of normal perceptions (thus making it possible to distance it, to narrate it, to communicate it) and the 'deep memory' (mémoire profonde) that repeatedly interrupts these efforts by bringing that experience to the surface with the brutal immediacy of something that is relived rather than recollected.[75] Elsewhere, Langer speaks of the 'durational persistence' of a Holocaust that is constantly 're-experienced' by those who have lived it, thus disrupting the normal 'chronology of experienced time', in which past experiences find their place in orderly narrative arrangements.[76] The psychologist Henry Greenspan, while emphasizing the efforts that survivors make to turn experience into narration, also stresses the radically problematic nature of the attempt. Survivors' stories and narrative voices emerge, Greenspan writes, 'from two sets of memories: salient themes and identifications salvaged from what survivors themselves often call "the normal circumstances of life" (and which they share with all of us) and memories of the reduction and finally dissolution of those meanings (and much more) within the Holocaust itself'. Efforts to hold these two orders of memory together are always, according to Greenspan, 'a failed compromise': 'Meanings that are salvaged are eventually reduced again; analogies are introduced and then negated and abandoned; stories are cut short or are insistently repeated.' In some cases, survivors achieve a measure of narrative order by displacing the focus of their remembering, shifting it from the Holocaust experience itself to their post-war efforts at recounting the untellable. In other cases, narrative dissolves into 'a pressured

staccato of snapshot images', couched in 'the language of immediacy and simultaneity rather than remembrance and duration'.
It is by analysing the abortiveness of survivors' efforts at recounting,
rather than by studying completed narrative constructions,
Greenspan argues, that we can begin to grasp the real significance
of Holocaust memory.[77]

What makes traumatic experiences, such as those of the
Holocaust, so hard to assimilate to stable structures of recollection
is only partly the psychological damage inflicted by extremes of
personal suffering. It is also the brutal disruption of the social
settings on which memory concentrates – the impossibility, in the
case of Holocaust memories, of building viable mnemonic bridges
between the world of pre-Holocaust experiences, now completely
demolished, and the post-war world in which the survivor now lives,
in which his or her relationships are with people who have no links
of their own either to the survivor's pre-war social circle or to
the social conditions of the Holocaust experience itself. Even
momentous changes of a less intensely devastating kind than those
of the Holocaust – for example, the social, political and cultural
dislocations that followed the breakdown of the Eastern Bloc in
the final years of the twentieth century – can bring problems in
memory, either by breaking or discrediting the conceptual frames
that have previously governed people's autobiographical remembering, or by making a host of memories which had previously
guided people in the routines of everyday life suddenly redundant.[78]

Reflections on such processes necessitate a broader discussion
of memory's social connections. One strand of such a discussion,
relating to the ways in which individuals relate to larger narratives
of the collective past, can be picked up again in section (iv) of
Chapter 5; others can now be pursued through the following
chapter.

Notes

1 J. Fentress and C. Wickham, *Social Memory* (Oxford, 1992), pp. 4–5.
2 J. L. Borges, 'Shakespeare's memory' (1983), in J. L. Borges, *The Book of Sand and Shakespeare's Memory* (Harmondsworth, 2001).
3 Antze and Lambek (eds), 'Introduction', p. xiii.
4 See, for example, M. Lambek, 'Memory in a Maussian universe', in S. Radstone and K. Hodgkin (eds), *Regimes of Memory* (London, 2004), pp. 202–16.

5 M. Oakeshott, 'Present, future and past', in his *On History and Other Essays* (Oxford, 1983), pp. 15–16. For an illuminating clarificatory survey of the different ways in which the term 'memory' has been used in recent psychological writing, see E. Tulving, 'Concepts of memory', in E. Tulving and F. Craik (eds), *The Oxford Handbook of Memory* (Oxford, 2000), pp. 33–42.

6 The mapping of terminology presented here is a synthesis based on a variety of readings, but see helpful discussions in D. Schacter, A. Wagner and R. Buckner, 'Memory systems of 1999', in Tulving and Craik (eds), *The Oxford Handbook of Memory*, pp. 627–43, and in pp. 395–8 of D. Balota, P. Dolan and M. Duchek, 'Memory changes in healthy older adults', in the same volume.

7 The term 'episodic memory' has been somewhat vitiated by inconsistent use. While most psychologists have used it, as here, to refer essentially to forms of declarative memory that are focused on the individual's own conscious experience, others have applied it to the ability of individuals to recall specific items of information (e.g. facts or strings of words) that have been presented to them on a specific previous occasion.

8 See M. Wheeler, 'Episodic memory and autonoetic awareness', in Tulving and Craik (eds), *The Oxford Handbook of Memory*, pp. 597–609.

9 'Autobiographical memory' is another term whose meanings in psychological literature have not been entirely uniform. My understanding of it roughly coincides with the definitions offered by authors such as U. Neisser, 'What is ordinary memory the memory of?', in U. Neisser and E. Winograd (eds), *Remembering Reconsidered: Ecological and Traditional Approaches to the Study of Memory* (Cambridge, 1988), p. 361 and W. Brewer, 'What is autobiographical memory?', in D. Rubin (ed.), *Autobiographical Memory* (Cambridge, 1986), p. 26. See also, besides Rubin's collection, B. Ross, *Remembering the Personal Past: Descriptions of Autobiographical Memory* (Oxford, 1991); U. Neisser and R. Fivush (eds), *The Remembering Self: Construction and Accuracy in the Self-Narrative* (New York, 1994).

10 For indicators of some of these issues, see A. Portelli, 'On the peculiarities of oral history', *History Workshop Journal*, 12 (1981), pp. 96–107; P. Thompson, *Voice of the Past: Oral History* (3rd edn., Oxford, 2000).

11 L. Passerini, *Autobiography of a Generation: Italy, 1968* (Hanover, NH and London, 1996), p. 23.

12 Antze and Lambek (eds), 'Introduction', p. xii.

13 Such interconnections are elegantly handled in Graham Dawson's influential formulation of the notion of narrative 'composure', which highlights the ways in which stories of remembered experience simultaneously 'compose' a cognitively viable narrative of events and

a subjectively viable conception of the self who experiences them, in ways which are also dependent on social recognition. G. Dawson, *Soldier Heroes: British Adventure, Empire, and the Imagining of Masculinities* (London, 1994), pp. 22–3.

14 R. Sorabji (ed.), *Aristotle on Memory* (2nd edn., London, 2004). Modern translators often render the first of these terms as 'memory' and the second as 'recollection' or 'reminiscence'; both, however, refer to things which in everyday speech are commonly referred to as 'memory' or 'remembering'.

15 Augustine, *Confessions*, in *Augustine: Confessions and Enchiridion*, A. Outler (ed.) (Library of Christian Classics Vol. VII) (Philadelphia, 1955), p. 208.

16 M. Augé, *Oblivion* (Minneapolis, 2004), p. 20.

17 J.-P. Sartre, *The Psychology of Imagination* (London, 1972), p. 210.

18 On such debates, see M. Warnock, *Memory* (London, 1987), ch. 3.

19 F. Bartlett, *Remembering: a Study in Experimental and Social Psychology* (Cambridge, 1995 [originally 1932]), p. 213.

20 Ibid.

21 Ibid., p. 13.

22 G. E. M. Anscombe, 'Memory, "experience" and causation', in H. D. Lewis (ed.), *Contemporary British Philosophy*, 4th series (London, 1976), p. 17.

23 Neuroscientific research tends to support such a view, by showing that the neural activity which corresponds to the sensation of remembering is spread across a variety of cortical sites.

24 For a recent introduction to encoding/retrieval models, see S. Brown and F. Craik, 'Encoding and retrieval of information', in E. Tulving and F. Craik (eds), *The Oxford Handbook of Memory*, pp. 93–108.

25 The classic formulation of the concept of schemata (though not of the language of encoding) is in Bartlett, *Remembering*, pp. 199–214. Scholars working in different disciplinary traditions use different terminology, for example that of 'frames of reference', to similar effect; see, for example, M. Michielsens, 'Memory frames: the role of concepts and cognition in telling life-stories', in T. Cosslett, C. Lury and P. Summerfield (eds), *Feminism and Autobiography: Texts, Theories, Methods* (London, 2000), esp. pp. 183–4.

26 For a good example of a historical case study which explicitly applies such models, see R. McGlone, 'Deciphering memory: John Adams and the authorship of the Declaration of Independence', *Journal of American History* 85:2 (1998), pp. 411–38.

27 J. F. McClelland, 'Constructive memory and memory distortions: a parallel-distributed processing approach', in D. Schacter (ed.), *Memory Distortion*, pp. 69–70.

28 On distortion generally, see D. Schacter, *The Seven Sins of Memory: How the Mind Forgets and Remembers* (Boston, Mass., 2001); Schacter (ed.), *Memory Distortion*; H. Roediger and K. McDermott, 'Distortions of memory', in Tulving and Craik (eds) *The Oxford Handbook of Memory*, pp. 149–62. On eyewitness testimony, see also G. Wells and E. Loftus (eds), *Eyewitness Testimony: Psychological Perspectives* (Cambridge, 1984); on induced memory, see, for example, E. Loftus, J. Feldman, R. Dashiell, 'The reality of illusory memories', in Schacter (ed.), *Memory Distortion*, pp. 47–67.

29 Schacter, *The Seven Sins of Memory*, p. 184.

30 U. Neisser, 'John Dean's memory: a case study', in U. Neisser (ed.), *Memory Observed: Remembering in Natural Contexts* (San Francisco, 1982), pp. 139–59.

31 A. Portelli, 'The death of Luigi Trastulli: memory and the event', in his *The Death of Luigi Trastulli and Other Stories: Form and Meaning in Oral History* (Albany, 1991), pp. 1–26.

32 Ibid., p. 26.

33 Neisser, 'What is ordinary memory the memory of?', p. 362.

34 M. Conway, 'The inventory of experience: memory and identity', in Pennebaker, Paez, Rimé (eds), *Collective Memory of Political Events*, pp. 22–8. For a parallel discussion of the ways in which oral history narrators weave their references to specific occasions together with various kinds of generalizing description, shifting focus repeatedly across these levels of reference, see S. Schrager, 'What is social in oral history', reproduced in R. Perks and A. Thomson (eds), *The Oral History Reader* (London, 1998), p. 295.

35 J. S. Mill, note in his edition of James Mill's *Analysis of the Phenomena of the Human Mind*, in *Collected Works of John Stuart Mill*, vol. XXXVI: 'Miscellaneous Writings' (Toronto, 1989), pp. 212–3.

36 D. Albright, 'Literary and psychological models of the self', in Neisser and Fivush (eds), *The Remembering Self*, p. 22.

37 For discussion of such debates, see Warnock, *Memory*, ch. 4.

38 M. Lambek, 'The past imperfect: remembering as moral practice', in Antze and Lambek (eds), *Tense Past*, pp. 243–4; J. Prager, *Presenting the Past: Psychoanalysis and the Sociology of Misremembering* (Cambridge, Mass., 1998), p. 123.

39 J. Bruner, 'The "remembered" self', in Neisser and Fivush (eds), *The Remembering Self*, p. 43.

40 Ibid., p. 53.

41 Antze and Lambek (eds), 'Introduction', p. xvi.

42 J. Glover, *I: the Philosophy and Psychology of Personal Identity* (Harmondsworth, 1988), pp. 139–53.

43 A. Thomson, *Anzac Memories: Living with the Legend* (Melbourne, 1994), p. 10.

44 E. Kris, 'The personal myth: a problem in psychoanalytical technique' (1956), in *The Selected Papers of Ernst Kris* (New Haven, 1975), pp. 129–43.

45 For general discussion, see J. Peneff, 'Myths in life stories', in R. Samuel and P. Thompson (eds), *The Myths We Live By* (London and New York, 1990), pp. 36–48; for more on capitalist models, C. Clark, '"Martyrs to a nice sense of honor": exemplars of commercial morality in the mid-nineteenth-century United States', in G. Cubitt and A. Warren (eds), *Heroic Reputations and Exemplary Lives* (Manchester, 2000), pp. 204–10; O. Löfgren, 'My life as consumer: narratives from the world of goods', in M. Chamberlain and P. Thompson (eds), *Narrative and Genre* (London, 1998), pp. 114–25.

46 Prager, *Presenting the Past*, pp. 4–5.

47 L. Passerini, *Fascism in Popular Memory: the Cultural Experience of the Turin Working Class* (Cambridge, 1987), pp. 17–63.

48 M. Bloch, 'Internal and external memory: different ways of being in history', in Antze and Lambek (eds), *Tense Past*, pp. 215–31 (esp. 222–3, 230).

49 C. Steedman, 'Enforced narratives: stories of another self', in Cosslett, Lury and Summerfield (eds), *Feminism and Autobiography*, pp. 25–39. Steedman draws attention, for example, to the ways in which certain kinds of formulaic self-narration were imposed on applicants for poor relief in England between 1660 and 1900; her conclusion (p. 36) is that, for these plebeian narrators, 'autobiography was not a straightforward telling of a self', but was rather a response to the demands of others – ' a thing that could be fashioned according to requirement, told and sold, alienated and expropriated'.

50 Passerini, *Fascism in Popular Memory*, p. 60.

51 Prager, *Presenting the Past*, p. 5.

52 D. Spence, *Narrative Truth and Historical Truth: Meaning and Interpretation in Psychoanalysis* (New York and London, 1982), p. 86, also pp. 55–61.

53 Ibid., pp. 56–7.

54 Ibid., p. 92.

55 M. Bloch, 'Autobiographical memory and the historical memory of the more distant past', in M. Bloch, *How We Think They Think: Anthropological Approaches to Cognition, Memory, and Literacy* (Oxford, 1998), pp. 117–9.

56 Schrager, 'What is social in oral history?', pp. 284–5.

57 S. Leydesdorff, *We Lived With Dignity: the Jewish Proletariat of Amsterdam, 1900–1940* (Detroit, 1994), p. 32.

58 Thomson, *Anzac Memories*, p. 239. This is one of two methods Thomson claims to have practised in his oral interviews with former Australian soldiers; the other works in the other direction, tracing 'the

construction of memory over time, as new layers of meaning are added and old identities are re-worked or shed.

59 E. Grant, *Memoirs of a Highland Lady* (ed. A. Tod) (Edinburgh, 1988), pp. 9–10, 15. For another discussion of this kind of affective 'texturing' of autobiographical narrative, this time focusing on oral materials, see R. Grele, 'Listen to their voices: two case studies in the interpretation of oral history interviews', in R. Grele, in *Envelopes of Sound: the Art of Oral History* (2nd edn., New York, 1991), pp. 212–41.

60 See, for example, the essays in Cosslett, Lury and Summerfield (eds), *Feminism and Autobiography*.

61 L. O. Mink, 'History and fiction as modes of comprehension', in L. O. Mink, *Historical Understanding* (Ithaca, NY, 1987), p. 60.

62 D. Carr, *Time, Narrative, and History* (Bloomington, 1986), p. 16. See also P. J. Eakin, *How Our Lives Become Stories: Making Selves* (Ithaca, 1999), p. 100, for whom 'narrative is not merely a literary form but a mode of phenomenological and cognitive self-experience'.

63 To say this is not to deny that oral autobiographical accounts can have a subtlety of narrative construction that makes them an appropriate subject for a 'literary' type of critical analysis: for an example, see T. G. Ashplant, 'Anecdote as narrative resource in working-class life stories: parody, dramatization and sequence', in Chamberlain and Thompson (eds), *Narrative and Genre*, pp. 99–113.

64 A. Portelli, '"The time of my life": functions of time in oral history', in A. Portelli, *The Death of Luigi Trastulli*, p. 61.

65 A. Portelli, 'Oral history as genre', in A. Portelli, *The Battle of Valle Giulia: Oral History and the Art of Dialogue* (Madison, 1997), pp. 4–5.

66 Portelli, '"The time of my life"', esp. pp. 63–73.

67 J. Bruner, *Acts of Meaning* (Cambridge, Mass., 1990), p. 33.

68 I. Bertaux-Wiame, 'Life stories in the baker's trade', in D. Bertaux (ed.), *Biography and Society: the Life History Approach in the Social Sciences* (Beverley Hills, 1981).

69 P. Summerfield, *Reconstructing Women's Lives: Discourse and Subjectivity in Oral Histories of the Second World War* (Manchester, 1998), pp. 18–20, drawing on categories formulated by P. Coleman, 'Ageing and life history: the meaning of reminiscence in late life', in S. Dex (ed.), *Life and Work History Analyses: Qualitative and Quantitative Developments* (London, 1991), pp. 120–43.

70 For broader discussion of memory and trauma, see, for example, C. Caruth (ed.), *Trauma; Explorations in Memory* (Baltimore, 1995); K. Rogers, S. Leydesdorff, G. Dawson (eds), *Trauma: Life Stories of Survivors* (New York and London, 1999); Antze and Lambek, *Tense Past*; S. Felman and D. Laub, *Testimony: Crises of Witnessing in Literature, Psychoanalysis and History* (New York, 1992).

71 Leydesdorff, *We Lived With Dignity*, p. 15.
72 M. Roseman, *The Past in Hiding* (Harmondsworth, 2000), pp. 474–9 and passim.
73 V. Skultans, *The Testimony of Lives: Narrative and Memory in Post-Soviet Latvia* (London and New York, 1998), pp. 25–6.
74 Ibid., p. 47, and 46–66 generally.
75 L. Langer, *Holocaust Testimonies: the Ruins of Memory* (New Haven and London, 1991), pp. 5–9. The rest of Langer's book analyses the disjunctures and 'mutilated' forms of Holocaust remembering in further detail.
76 L. Langer, 'Memory's time: chronology and duration in Holocaust testimonies', in L. Langer, *Admitting the Holocaust: Collected Essays* (New York, 1995), pp. 13–23.
77 H. Greenspan, *On Listening to Holocaust Survivors: Recounting and Life History* (Westport, CT, 1998), pp. xviii, 13, 20.
78 On these themes, see M. Michielsens, 'Memory frames: the role of concepts and cognition in telling life-stories', in Cosslett, Lury and Summerfield (eds), *Feminism and Autobiography*, pp. 183–200; E. Ten Dyke, 'Memory and existence: implications of the *Wende*', in Confino and Fritzsche (eds), *The Work of Memory*, pp. 154–69.

❦ 3 ❦

REMEMBERING
IN SOCIETY

If remembering is fundamentally an activity engaged in by individual minds, it equally fundamentally possesses a social dimension. To say this is not to say that social units – groups or societies – are themselves to be considered as mnemonic agents, possessed of a capacity for remembering that is conceptually distinguishable from that exhibited by their individual members. It is to say only that the individuals who remember do so not as isolated agents, but as social beings, constantly engaged in interactions with other such beings, enmeshed in networks of social relationship, implicated in various kinds of social or cultural community. The very contents of memory reflect this: our memories are rarely of moments of isolation or of purely inward reflection; more often, they relate to moments and experiences involving interaction with others. Even memories of loneliness are memories of social deprivation; they assume the normality of sociable exchanges. Samuel Schrager has drawn attention to the way in which people narrating their past experience to oral historians tend to interweave what is strictly personal to them with things that pertain to others with whom they feel closely associated, and whose viewpoints and experiences they implicitly assume a responsibility for representing.[1] (Paul John Eakin speaks similarly of the 'large component of "we"-experience in the "I" narrative' of autobiographical writing.)[2] In practice, it is largely from impressions relating to social experience that memory weaves that sense of continuous selfhood to which the previous chapter paid attention.

When we remember, furthermore, we draw, as has already been seen, on cultural resources that we have access to as members of particular groups or societies, and that permit us to articulate our memories in forms that are comprehensible to others who have a similar cultural endowment. Much of our remembering is, indeed, obviously socially motivated – prompted by social occasions, geared to social exchanges. We remember in the context of conversation, in response to interrogation, under the impulse of some need to contribute to joint activities, or to forge mutual understandings, or to justify ourselves in the eyes of others: the nature of these social occasions shapes the ways in which we remember. Memory, in short, is 'embedded' (culturally and socially) as well as 'embodied' (physically and individually).[3] If it is a constituent of what we consider to be our individuality, it is also a vital part of our social equipment – part of what enables us to position ourselves in relation to others, and to function effectively in social settings.

The point may be turned round. If memory is necessary to individuals in society, this is at least partly because it is necessary to the functioning of society itself. Social formations cannot subsist unless people within them have a certain capacity to remember things that have happened previously. Again, what is being said here is not something grand, about the need for societies to have a kind of 'collective memory' of their past as a community, but – in the first instance at least – something more prosaic: people cannot secure, or even envisage, the benefits of social exchange and social co-operation, and therefore cannot be brought to engage in these things in more than a very occasional and momentary way, unless they can place some faith in their own and in other people's ability to recall previous experience and agreements previously entered on. Social operations depend on a capacity for deferred action: the functioning of society at any given moment depends, firstly, on people allowing their present conduct to be guided by an awareness of what they and others have said or done previously, and secondly, on their being willing to act now in ways which will make sense only on the assumption that this action will be remembered and taken account of in framing later courses of action. Without this memory-dependent capacity for deferred action, there can be no formal planning of collaborative enterprises, no collective debate on the implications of previous experience, no concept of rules or of normative principles, no notion of making and keeping promises or of entering into binding contracts, no system of rewards or punishments, no sense of entitlement based on prior possession or previous agreement – no custom, no law, no property, no established trade, no framing of common policy. All of these things depend, not just on people having a certain memory for information, but on their having the kind of sense of continuous identity (whether focused on an individualistic concept of self or on a broader notion of social participation) that memory is vital in supporting. Ultimately, it is memory that underpins all our possibilities of social activity and social construction.

Two further points must be made, however. The first is that society depends not just on memory, but on the capacity to communicate it. It depends on people being able to exchange remembered information, to produce it publicly at appropriate moments, to compare their own memories with those of others – to contribute, in fact, to socially available pools of remembered knowledge, from which members of society, individually and collectively, can draw the elements of information that help them to construct identities, and to plan and pursue courses of socially significant action. Reflecting on this social need for communication reinforces the feeling that it is misleading to separate the concept of memory as an internal activity of mind from a consideration of its modes of external expression.

Secondly, the social functions of memory go beyond those that are strictly generated by the need to enable people who are each other's contemporaries to do effective business one with another. Social exchanges between contemporaries take place within, and are regulated and facilitated by, social and institutional structures and frameworks of customary action that may persist over generations. It is thanks to the relative stability of such structures that projects or programmes of action can be sustained beyond the lifetimes of individuals, thus rescuing each generation from the need to do the social equivalent of re-inventing the wheel. But a society's ability to develop such structures itself depends on its capacity to organize the retention of ideas and information, so that each successive moment does not simply obliterate the impressions which previous ones have generated. As Marc Bloch once remarked, 'a society that could be completely molded by its immediately preceding period would have to have a structure so malleable as to be virtually invertebrate'.[4] Societies, like individuals, function best if their members (individually and collectively) are able to meet the challenge of fresh experience with a response that is grounded in structures of knowledge and action that have been matured and adjusted over a longer period. Societies need, therefore, to structure the passage of ideas and information in ways which permit a purposeful retention of certain kinds of experiential data, and the transgenerational consolidation of certain bodies of knowledge and practice. This is one of the essential functions of social institutions. In performing it, such institutions tend also, in practice, to promote the organization of at least some of the information that passes between generations into more or less narrative assemblages which give an account of the past of the institutions themselves, or of the groups associated with them. In short, they participate, and invite those who are involved with them to participate, in the formation not just of bodies of knowledge derived from past experiences, but of a sense of the past as a collective experience.

Individual memory is crucially involved in generating the information that passes between generations: nothing enters the social food-chain of transmission unless someone or other has at some time remembered it on the basis of personal experience and communicated this memory to others. In societies whose culture is fundamentally oral, the maintenance of data in individual memory is also a continuous requirement for transmission: any detail that is not continuously held in some remembering mind or other is lost irretrievably, and transmission therefore consists of the relaying of data through direct oral encounters between different individual remembering minds. In most societies, however, the transmission of data is effected at least partially (and in many modern societies, predominantly) through processes of 'externalization' – ones in which the data to be communicated are somehow encapsulated in objects or artefacts (texts, pictorial images, physical monuments, architectural features, electronic patterns, etc.) that are visible or tangible, durable, and in many cases replicable or transportable. Externalization introduces retrievability: once the techniques that procure it have been mastered, data can be stored for future use, and can be circulated socially and geographically, without having to be continually 'kept in mind' by individuals. Individual memory is still important in the process of transmission, but its importance is displaced: what has to be continually sustained is less the detailed personal memory of the data that are being transmitted than the operational memory that gives access to the systems of storage – the remembered knowledge of written languages, of symbolic codes, of archival systems, and so on.

Information that passes across generations, especially through external conveyances, tends over time to drift from being cast as personal recollection to being cast as something that psychologists would call semantic knowledge. Memories of personal experience are not, on the face of it, built to withstand transmission: the fact of passing from one mind to another strips them of their defining autonoetic sensation. Listening to an old man's reminiscences of wartime experience can develop my knowledge of the war and give me a knowledge of his participation, but this is not the kind of knowledge that he himself carries in memory, or that memory gives me of the things that I myself have experienced. The externalizing of memories as written texts can offer shortcuts across the generations, by allowing memories narrated in one generation to pass to readers several generations later without having to pass through a whole chain of intermediaries, but in another sense it merely renders the process of depersonalization more obvious. One generation's vivid or traumatic memories of personal experience become, in the end, later generations' general historical knowledge.

But, while this plainly means that any developed understanding of social memory processes must extend beyond a simple concern with the more personal and autobiographical forms of remembering, we should not be too quick to cut the individual's personal investment in the way the past is remembered out of the picture. A sense of the past means little if people have no way of finding it relevantly connected to their own lived experience, and while connections to a remoter past can sometimes be supplied by perceptions of cause and effect (as when people born and brought up in the aftermath of a war become conscious of ways in which that war has generated the conditions that are a crucial part of their own experience), they can also be established in ways which depend more directly on autobiographical recollection. It may be, for example, that individuals associate their acquisition of a particular view of the past with a particular formative moment or phase in their existence; or that their knowledge of certain stories or pieces of information is connected to their memory of individuals by whom they were influenced or emotionally affected; or that their initiation into a social group to which they are powerfully attached has involved the acquisition of fluency in that group's understanding either of its own past or of the larger past of the society that contains it. Thinking about social memory may lead us, in fact, to re-examine the sharp distinction that is sometimes posed between semantic knowledge and knowledge that is the bearer of self-awareness. Who we think we are need not be wholly determined by what we are aware of personally remembering. The most resolutely 'semantic' forms of knowledge – scientific knowledge, for example – can be 'taken personally' by those who possess them, if effort has been involved in their acquisition, or if prestige or social status is entailed in it. (One has only to consider the possessiveness that academics sometimes display towards their fields of expertise to see this.) Nor should we underestimate the kinds of mark that witnessing other people's efforts at remembering or forgetting can leave on the witnesses, especially when the efforts are themselves painful or emotionally laden, or when the witnesses are closely bonded to the rememberers, for example as friends or relatives. To say that the full subjective content of an autobiographical memory is not transmissible is not to say that it can leave no impact in the personal memories of others. Marianne Hirsch has used the term 'postmemory' to describe cases like that of the children of Holocaust survivors, whose memories and whose sense of identity may be deeply and problematically marked by an unavoidable – if sometimes deeply ambivalent – awareness of the memories that their parents struggle either to articulate or to suppress. For Hirsch, 'postmemory characterizes the experience of those who grow up dominated by narratives that preceded their birth, whose own belated stories are evacuated by the stories of the previous generation shaped by traumatic events that can be neither understood nor recreated'.[5] Focusing more broadly, the sociologist Eviatar Zerubavel proposes the term 'sociobiographical memory' to describe the 'existential fusion of one's own biography with the history of the groups or communities to which one belongs'.[6] The term covers a multitude of conditions: there is a world of difference, for example, between the kinds of 'postmemory' that have just been referred to, where the devastatingly traumatic effects of a still very recent experience are passed across one or two generations, and the case of, for example, seventeenth-century English radicals evoking the memory of what they took to be a golden age of Anglo-Saxon liberty disrupted by the 'Norman yoke'.[7] But there are multiple gradations between such extremes: where, for example, should one place the transmitted 'memory' of slavery that may carry meaning for twentieth-century black Americans (in which elements of oral tradition may well be interwoven with knowledge derived from other sources, including films and novels and historical accounts),[8] or the 'memory' of the ancestors whose portraits may have hung continuously on the walls of aristocratic homes for two or three centuries, ingraining themselves in the memories of successive generations through visual familiarity and anecdotal commentary?

Complex relationships exist, in short, between the ways in which individuals remember their own experience, the ways in which they remember and transmit information more generally, the ways in which a sense of a more collective kind of past is cultivated within society, and the ways in which social life is organized. It is these connections that we have to explore further in the remaining chapters of this book, and we can begin to do this by picking up again the issue of the sense in which individual memory may be said to be social. Two rather different ways of 'socializing' the concept of memory have been apparent in recent literature. The first, which has been dominant in most historical studies of social memory, has generally identified the social with the collective: its interest has lain, if not always in the grander notions of 'collective memory', then at least in the analysis of group-specific mnemonic cultures and of group participation as a salient influence on individual recollection. The second – more common among social or anthropological or psychological theorists and among oral historians – has been interested less in groups than in social interactions. The first approach, insofar as it is interested in individual memory at all, inquires into the larger processes through which collectively developed cultures and conceptions of identity influence or determine the forms of personal recollection; the second is concerned more with establishing the ways in which remembering is occasioned by the dynamics of particular social relationships and exchanges – an approach which tends (though not invariably) to leave actual remembering individuals somewhat closer to the centre of consideration than is usually the case in studies which prioritize the influence of collective structures. The present chapter will seek to combine the two approaches, but its strategy will be to work towards an eventual engagement with the collectivist approach, along lines that are initially shaped more by interactionist concerns. The aim here is to navigate between extremes, avoiding on the one hand the kind of individualism that can see in the memory of the individual nothing but a sacred refuge of independent selfhood, fashioned from the mind's uniquely private and introspective connection to the earlier moments of its own being, and on the other the kind of facile language of common remembering that too readily ignores the hidden contestations, sullen resistances and silent oppressions of memory that can lurk beneath the surface of an apparent acceptance of common structures (as work on, for example, the histories of memory under Soviet regimes reminds us).[9]

Memory and social interaction

We may start by focusing for a final moment on the inadequacies of the stricter versions of mnemonic individualism. The view of remembering as an action of purely individual minds arbitrarily reduces the complex business of remembering to those of its elements that seem least communicable. No doubt something important in the experience of personal recollection – that vivid if transitory sensation of intimate recognition – is lost in translation from one mind to another. But something equally important to the experience of remembering – the possibility of connecting such impressions to a perception of the personal past that is sufficiently durable to animate a sense of identity and to confer a sense of direction – may depend precisely on our ability to articulate what we remember within the linguistic and cultural structures that we share with others, and to negotiate its meanings through social exchanges.

The exploratory potential of the strictly individualistic view of memory is also limited by what it takes for granted – the immutable mental self-sufficiency of the remembering individual. Concentrating on the incommunicability of the innermost sensations of personal memory, it fails to ask how memories are occasioned, or how the individual has come to be constituted as a subject capable of forming them, and therefore neglects the possibility that either or both of these processes may be, in significant respects, a social one. The over-rigid conceptual separation of the (supposedly internally directed) activity of remembering from the (externally directed) business of communicating what has been remembered prohibits any exploration of the idea that the individual's actual or anticipated involvement in communicative activity may itself be part of what brings memories into existence and may influence the shape they take. It is this idea that recent 'social constructionist' theories of remembering, as developed by psychologists such as Kenneth Gergen and John Shotter, seek to make central. From the standpoint of such theories, understanding of the world, including the understanding that we experience as memory, is not something that has its roots in some internal mechanism of the individual psyche, but is 'the result of an active, cooperative enterprise of persons in relationship'; what is basic is 'not the inner subjectivity of the individual, but the practical social processes going on "between" people'.[10] One of the more radical suggestions that such a line of argument can produce holds, indeed, that our very perception of memory as something deeply personal is itself ingrained through a kind of social conditioning: 'what we talk of *as* our experience of our reality is constituted for us very largely by the *already established* ways in which we *must* talk in our attempts to *account* for ourselves – and for it – to the others around us', Shotter writes.[11] In its harder forms, social constructionism tends to subvert the very notion of psychic individuality, but the ideas exist also in softer versions, which allow a greater place to individual subjectivity. Susan Engel has recently argued, for example, that 'most of the kinds of memory that we encounter in daily life go far beyond the intimate personal re-experiencing of something from the past', to involve 'public transactions of one kind or another', and that in some cases a memory must be regarded 'not only [as] a psychological entity within a person but [as] a social transaction between people'.[12]

One way of focusing our attention further on the issue of memory's relationship to social interaction is to linger briefly on the thought of the early twentieth-century psychologist Pierre Janet. For Janet, memory was not an innate and immutable capacity, present in the human species from the moment of its origin, and in human individuals from the beginning of childhood. Rather, both in the individual and in the species, it was a capacity – or more accurately, a set of practices – adaptively developed over time, as behaviour was pragmatically adjusted to meet the practical challenges posed at different stages in its development. Nor should memory be seen (as contemporary Bergsonian philosophy suggested) as a faculty embodying a kind of primal human intuition of temporality – a consciousness of the passage of time – for temporality was itself not a basic pre-conceptual reality; rather it was something that was mentally constructed, in ways that were intricately entangled with memory's own development. In short, memory was to be understood, not as a simple, 'consciousness' of a past whose status, as something separate from but meaningfully connected to the present, could be taken for granted but as a set of gradually evolving technical practices, the development of which had been instrumental in the cultural construction of temporal conceptions. The development of these practices had been rooted, Janet maintained, in pragmatic need – specifically, during the earliest and most basic phases of mnemonic development, in the need to retain information relating to particular circumstances (for example the approach of an enemy) so as to communicate that information to others and thus to make possible a joint response. In later stages of development, refinements in strategies and practices of mnemonic retention were always closely connected to refinements in the techniques of social communication. As the techniques of communication increased in subtlety and flexibility (for example through the development of new forms of narrativity), so memory became adapted to increasingly varied and complex social uses, in the performance of some of which it acquired the appearance of being an essentially introspective and self-affirming kind of mental activity. To dwell on this face of remembering was, however, to mistake some of its superficial effects for its basic functions: considered in its essentials, memory was always 'a social action', geared to the production of social effects through communicative exchanges.[13]

Though few of those who study memory nowadays engage in Janet's kind of species-historical theorizing, his basic emphases – on the fundamentally pragmatic and socially instrumental character of remembering, and on the intimate links between memory, culture and communication – remain suggestive. One strand of thought that can be drawn out of them leads to investigations of the ways in which the uses of memory, and therefore perhaps the actual characteristics of mnemonic activity, may be affected by major developments in the regimes of communication, like the transition from orality to literacy or the development of computer technology. (Aspects of this question will be explored further in the following chapter.) Another may lead us towards a further exploration of the idea that memory may be best regarded as a form of social practice. Recent psychological studies of cognitive development in early childhood – and specifically of the development of autobiographical memory – have an obvious bearing on this question.[14] Such studies reinforce the suggestion that remembering is an acquired skill, and that its acquisition is motivated by social need and realized through social experience. Young children, such research suggests, undergo a kind of apprenticeship in autobiographical remembering at the hands of older members of society, most obviously parents. The acquisition of recollective skills, like the acquisition of linguistic skills, forms part of the process of socialization through which the child is brought into contact with the norms and expectations of an adult-dominated society, and learns the means of exerting influence or securing benefits within that society. Indeed memory development and linguistic development are closely linked, since it is chiefly through the child's assisted participation in conversations and in the collaborative working out of narratives under the guidance of more experienced narrators that practices of autobiographical remembering are first developed. In its earliest phases, the child's reconstruction of his or her past experience is 'scaffolded' by adults: through questioning and suggestion, parents and others provide most of the structure and indeed of the initial content of the narrative that the child is encouraged to form and to regard as his or her own. Only gradually does the child take on the responsibility for structuring his or her own narrations and for extending them to include fresh events and experiences. Even then, the influence of the earlier scaffolding continues to be felt: different styles or patterns of remembering in later life may reflect the influence of different styles of parental prompting in the early stages – prioritizing, for example, factual information about the time and place of remembered events over evaluative information about emotional responses to those events, or vice versa. Gender and cultural differences in styles of remembering may also be explicable, at least partly, in terms of different patterns of adult encouragement at this early stage.[15]

The implications of such studies, based on work with late twentieth-century European and American children, for an understanding of memory acquisition in other societies and other historical periods need of course to be cautiously considered.

Parent-child relationships may be very differently organized in different societies, and may not always be the decisive ones for a child's development, and autobiographical remembering may not always carry the same significance as the primary indicator of mnemonic competence that it does in our own 'self'-obsessed culture. In other cultural settings, learning to tell stories about one's social community, or learning to repeat what adults tell one, or learning to reproduce certain kinds of rote-learnt material may carry greater weight than learning to tell stories of one's personal experience. But the more general implications of such research – that remembering is in many respects a learned capacity, that we learn it through social interactions, and that learning it is part of the more general process and experience of learning how to conduct ourselves in social settings – seem likely to be generally valid. Learning how to remember may be seen as a form of 'situated learning'– learning understood not as the simple cognitive acquisition of new chunks of knowledge, but as a facet of increasingly experienced participation in specific kinds of social practice.

The connections between memory-formation, social interaction and cultural initiation may be especially obvious in the context of early childhood development. There is no reason, however, to suppose that the adaptation of mnemonic behaviour to social setting ceases once the individual acquires the ability to remember 'independently'. 'Once we recall with and for others', Susan Engel remarks, 'the process of remembering depends as much on motivation and social contexts as it does on any neural network.' Indeed, she argues, once a memory is 'made public' (in the sense of being articulated in a social setting), 'the possibilities for disagreement, persuasion, and consensus become a dynamic part of the psychological process of remembering'.[16] In daily adult life, as well as in childhood learning, much of our remembering is performed either with or for others: it is closely linked to communication, and may be influenced by our perceptions of other people's expectations. A person may recount episodes from past experience differently, depending on whether he or she is reminiscing with friends, giving evidence to the police, being interviewed by an oral historian, or writing his or her memoirs, and while the differences may on one level be presentational, it seems likely that different interactive settings may actually promote different patterns of recollection in the individuals who are involved in them. As oral historians have long begun to notice in reflecting on the social dynamics of their own research, whether the setting is supportive or confrontational, controlled or freely evolving, strictly geared to a particular purpose or randomly directed, whether it involves strangers or close acquaintances, and whether those involved are of the same or of different classes or genders, are all aspects of a situation that can shape the way remembering in that situation is conducted.[17] Social psychologists, meanwhile, have begun, through conversational analysis, to focus attention on the strategies which come into play when remembering is conducted as a collaborative or group activity. David Middleton and Derek Edwards have shown, for example, how a collaborative group may collectively develop a way of structuring their recollective conversation. Such a structure serves, they suggest, not simply to assist group members in pooling and comparing their separate reminiscences, but also in establishing 'a mutuality of understanding' within the group – a mutuality which, in their view, frequently has as much or more to do with the sharing and communicating of affective or evaluative responses to the matter being recalled as it does with the production of an accurate and orderly narrative description.[18] Once we start to view remembering as something that is often socially structured and possibly collaborative, it becomes clear that it may be influenced by a wide variety of social considerations: people may find it more important to develop an account of things that is coherent, or that commands general assent within the group, or that minimizes friction, or that enhances self-esteem, or that legitimizes certain claims or structures of authority than to build a detailed and accurate picture of past reality. Remembering in social settings is not to be analysed as if it were a form of computational data-processing, but as an activity at least partially geared to the production of social effects.

Like other kinds of interactive activity, remembering is often subject to a kind of division of labour. Individuals accustomed to remembering in a collective setting may develop areas of specialization: one member of a family, for example, may be the one who remembers family birthdays and anniversaries; another, the one who holds the detail of financial transactions; another, the one who contributes information about earlier generations, or who initiates the stories that are retold at family gatherings. Such divisions of labour relieve individuals of the overpowering need personally to keep track of all the remembered information they wish to have access to: the reproduction of this information comes to depend less on the kind of generalized recollective brainstorming in which everyone tries to remember the same things than on effective communication between specialists in different recollective areas. Remembering becomes a 'socially distributed' activity – an affair of collaboration and mutual reliance. We should be wary, however, of assuming that when an activity is distributed, it is necessarily systemically harmonious: this may be more or less true of computers, but is seldom true in human societies. In remembering, as in industrial production, divisions of labour are seldom frictionless: if they promote efficiency in certain respects, they also embody relationships of power and dependence, and generate differences of experience or of perspective that can breed resentment and contestation. Nor, of course, can we divorce a consideration of the ways in which mnemonic functions are socially distributed from a broader awareness of the structures of power and dependence that govern social existence more generally: different recollective specialisms are often generated less by mutual convenience or by a genuinely shared perception of the need for mnemonic efficiency than by differences – and possibly inequalities – in people's social position. Collaboration between those who are differently positioned may be necessary, but may not always be an exercise in harmonious social combination. Isabelle Bertaux-Wiame's interviews with elderly men and women who had migrated to Paris between the World Wars illustrate this point. Bertaux-Wiame draws attention to differences in the way her male and female informants narrate their past experience. These differences relate not only to the types of things recalled – men focusing on memories of work, women more on memories of family – but also, and more particularly, to ways of telling the story. Male informants, for example, make heavy use of the pronoun 'I', framing their life stories as sequences of deliberate actions embodying the 'rational pursuit of well-defined goals' by individuals who are, so to speak, the essential actors in their own stories; women, by contrast, tend to use 'we' or the French 'on', thus articulating a more collective mode of identity, structured more by relationships than by personal action. In Bertaux-Wiame's account, these differences of perspective work, in the case of married couples interviewed together, to produce a complex blending of tension and dependence:

In an interview with a couple, one can see these deep differences brought out in the clashes which sometimes arise between the husband and wife in their accounts of the past. The man may tell the story of his life with a concern for chronological accuracy; but he will be constantly turning to his wife for help. For it is she, rather than him, who holds the family memory for dates – a memory nourished by innumerable stimulants in familiar objects and sur- roundings, faces, photographs and so on. And with the backing of this knowledge, she will keep on trying to intervene to correct her husband's account. Her corrections will always be in the same direction – to subdue the 'I'. The husband recounts an incident with himself as actor. She will retrieve a web of contradictory influences from the surrounding environment within which to place it, and her interventions will quite obviously frustrate her husband in his attempt to reconstruct his life story as the biography of a self-willed individual.

Here, the husband relies on the wife for remembered information that he needs to give anchorage to his own egocentric (and patri- archalist) account of life's experience, yet this information is provided with strings attached, subtly but persistently threatening to embroil him in a quite different, and less flattering, conceptual- ization of that experience. Remembering is interactive, but the relationships that the interaction brings to the surface are not ones of easy complementarity.[19]

Memory, groups and social belonging

In exploring the interactive aspects of individual memory, we have inevitably already begun to encounter the influence that structures of collective organization and experiences of group membership can exert on the activity of remembering. Any durable pattern of social interactions tends, after all, both to generate and to require a certain organization and a certain conception of group belonging – and to be a member of a group or community is, on one level, simply to be embroiled in a certain set of structured social interactions and to have a sense of this embroilment as constituting an element in one's social identity. Unlike the experimental groups that are sometimes conjured into existence for the purposes of psychoanalytical research, 'real life' groups and communities – families, clubs, religious or educational communities, political parties, businesses, military units, workplace teams, groups of friends, voluntary associations, and so on – are seldom organized purely for mnemonic performance. In some cases, admittedly, a recollective or commemorative function may be an important element in a group's *raison d'être*: associations of military veterans may, for example, exist partly to honour the memory of fallen comrades, and partly to give the veterans themselves facilities for mutual reminiscence. More usually, however, groups are organized primarily for the performance of other functions: the production, exchange or sharing of material goods; warfare or security; religious worship or political campaigning; culture, debate or leisured sociability. In practice, however, even groups whose principal functions are not ostensibly primarily mnemonic provide occasions for recollective exchanges, and generate needs for remembered information. Almost any group that exists for any length of time comes, therefore, to develop at least an informal mnemonic organization. In some cases, this organization is scarcely distinguishable from the general structuring of the group's activities: remembered knowledge is exchanged and circulated through the relationships and on the occasions that are routinely generated by the group's other business. In other cases, groups develop a more distinguishable kind of mnemonic apparatus, concentrating mnemonic activities on particular kinds of special occasion (anniversaries, family or old boys' reunions, etc.), instituting special mnemonic practices (commemorative rituals, portraiture, compilation of photograph albums, etc.), and perhaps establishing specialized practitioners (priests or tribal griots, remembrancers or archivists) whose contribution to the life of the group lies in the maintenance of remembered knowledge or in managing and orchestrating its production. In either case, groups may be considered both as forums for the production and reproduction of shared knowledge pertaining to the past of the collectivity, and as environments that condition the ways in which individuals remember. Analysing the relationship between these two functions – identifying the points of connection between individual recollection and collectively developed structures of consciousness – is a central challenge for the study of memory's social dimensions.

To speak of 'groups' is, of course, to employ an extremely general social category. Groups vary widely, and in multiple respects. Some exist for very immediate and short-term purposes, and dissolve once these purposes are accomplished or forgotten; others exist as standing structures whose durability and adaptability assures a transgenerational existence. Some are informal and possibly fluid (a group of friends, a social circle); others are formally organized and structured institutionally, with rules and definite conditions of membership. Some are founded on face-to-face relationships between individuals who live and work together; others are structured by the remoter connections which media of communication and sharing of knowledge or belief can set in place. Some are impermeable and exclusive, one is born in them and dies in them; others have a membership that is always in flux, with individuals joining or leaving. Some make total claims upon their members, requiring them to forgo or to sever other social connections; others permit or even assume their members' simultaneous possession of other group identities. Some are internally differentiated, with sub-communities that differ in function or in status (officers and other ranks within a military unit, clergy and laity within a church, different departments within a business); others have a more egalitarian or communal type of structure. Some are organizationally embedded in larger communities (as a class is embedded in a school, or a company in a regiment); others have a greater organizational autonomy. Any of these differences may have implications for the kind of mnemonic culture that a group develops, for the types of retrospective knowledge that it produces, and for the kinds of remembering that it facilitates.

In the broadest of terms, groups need retrospective knowledge for three kinds of reason. Firstly, even when their core activities are not in themselves mnemonic, they need such knowledge to ensure the satisfactory performance of these activities. Businesses need to maintain their records of past transactions; associations that offer benefits in exchange for contributions need to keep track of membership; political parties need to interpret their previous successes and failures; modern families planning a holiday or a birthday party consult their experiences of earlier and similar occasions. Like individuals, groups or communities can scarcely get on with anything without grounding their performance in knowledge derived from past experiences.

Secondly, groups need retrospective knowledge in order to maintain and to communicate the sense of corporate or collective identity on which their continuing coherence ultimately depends.

In practice, any durably existing group develops over time a certain body of retrospective information – couched sometimes as a developed narrative, but often as a looser collection of legend and anecdote, folklore and topographical reference – whose significance lies not so much in what it can contribute to the pragmatic performance of the group's core activities, as in what it says to the group's members about the social entity of which they are a part – about the group's origins and aspirations, the experiences that have shaped it, and what it means to be a member of it. While the build-up of such information over time may be partly accidental, a certain effort is made, in most groups, to organize it and to ensure its internal transmission. Being familiar with it is part of what holds the members of a group together; becoming familiar with it is part of what is involved in becoming, in the fullest sense, a member of the group in question. Information of this kind is not, of course, always clearly distinct from the kind of information that directly services the group's practical activities: knowledge of traditional techniques of production may, for example, contribute simultaneously to present production and to the producers' sense of being part of a traditional community; tales of a military regiment's past deeds of collective valour may, precisely by nourishing the soldiers' sense of a glorious tradition, also enhance the regiment's effectiveness as a fighting unit.

Thirdly, groups may need retrospective knowledge in order to maintain and to advance their position in relation to other groups or to broader institutional structures. Groups do not, after all, exist in a vacuum: their need is not just for legitimacy and status in the eyes of their own members, but for external recognition. The ways in which they present and organize their own retrospective knowledge may well reflect this, as much as it reflects any more internally-motivated need for unity and coherence. In some cases, indeed, shifts in a group's relationship to wider social or institutional structures can significantly revise the ways in which its members' sense of the collective past is framed. Rosalind Thomas has shown how this was the case with family traditions in ancient Athens. Prior to the development of the institutions of Athenian democracy in the fifth and fourth centuries BC, aristocratic Athenian families were conscious of their remote legendary origins, but paid little attention to more recent ancestry. It was only when confronted with the working of democratic institutions (and in particular of the democratic jury courts) that they acquired both the motive and the institutional opportunity to rehearse a more recent family tradition. Vital importance was now attached, in the context of legal proceedings, to an individual's ability to demonstrate his family's record of service to the Athenian state. Families were driven to cultivate a kind of familial memory, focused on relatively recent generations, for which they had previously had little practical need. But if the democratic system 'encouraged a new kind of family tradition', it also, in Thomas's view, produced an increasing standardization of its forms: the more families geared their self-images to the working requirements of the democratic system, the less place they could find in their traditions for specific pieces of orally transmitted information that might complicate or undermine the spotless record of service that was being constructed. In public at least, family histories became increasingly interchangeable.[20] In another study, Marcus Funck and Stephan Malinowski have analysed the 'masterful creation, selection and deployment of memory' by the German aristocracy, showing how the families of an aristocratic order threatened by the industrializing and democratizing tendencies of the modern era responded not just by reinforcing their traditional stock of mnemonic techniques (focused on family trees, hereditary seats, court ceremonies etc.), but also through an aggressive deployment of autobiographical writing that served – again in strikingly uniform fashion – to establish the image of aristocrats as natural leaders of society and vigorous opponents of the democratic rabble.[21] Other forms of contestation call forth other adaptive cultivations of past-related knowledge, designed to foster new claims to power, property or status, or to bolster old ones against new challenges.[22] For groups as for individuals, remembering can be as much about claiming as about identity.

How does individual remembering by group members relate to all of this? Variously, of course, depending again on the nature of the group and of its embeddedness in the broader social environment. On one level, obviously, acts of individual recollection, communicated to others, are always contributing potential elements to the fund of materials from which a sense of the collective past can be composed. The process of social negotiation by which some of these elements are invested with a lasting kind of significance for a broader circle of group members than entertains them originally is a continual one. The sociologist Gary Alan Fine has coined the term 'idioculture' to refer to the 'system of knowledge, beliefs, behaviors and customs' – and more particularly, the corpus of group-specific 'folklore (stories, myths, anecdotes, etc.) – that groups develop through the interactions of their members, and that those members refer to in organizing their collective activities. The internalization of such an idioculture is, for Fine, a vital criterion of group membership, but his attention is focused also on how the idiocultures are themselves developed. For him, there are five criteria that have to be met if a given item of potential folklore is to lodge itself in the idioculture of a particular group: the item has to relate to experiences that at least a significant proportion of a group's members have in common; it has to be usable in the context of interactions between members of the group; it has to be functional in relation to the group's perceived collective needs and those of its members as individuals; it has to be 'appropriate' (in the sense of working to maintain rather than to undermine the hierarchies of power and status that pertain within the group as at present constituted); and it has to have been brought to prominence through its connection to some 'triggering event' in the development of the group as a social unit whose members are conscious of possessing a common identity. Individuals, one might suggest, are both contributors to such an 'idioculture' and investors in it; the processes of idiocultural formation are ones through which they connect their own experiences of group membership to a broader sense of what is essential or significant in the group's evolving collective identity.[23]

Story-telling of one kind or another seems central to this process. In one of his more curious case studies (in a range of them that runs from the Manson family to Little League baseball teams), Fine explores the processes of idiocultural development among American mycologists (mushroom enthusiasts). Becoming a member of the mycological community requires, it seems, a narrative investment of self:

> . . . mushroom stories provide public recognition of a shared world of discourse. By permitting the elaboration of a social world through the mechanism of talk and narrative, mushroomers announce to each other that they 'belong' together. By placing themselves at the center of these stories, these individuals announce that they are willing to claim public membership within the group and serve

symbolically as the focus of entertainment – not only as entertainer but as topic. Narrator and audience build community together, and as the position of narrator changes into that of listener, the communal role of stories is made evident to all by their lived experience as actor and audience.[24]

Fine designed his studies of 'idioculture' for analysing the mental dynamics of relatively small-scale groups, in which the sense of the past is of a past that is more or less in living memory. No doubt, the processes he describes continue to operate in groups that achieve a more durable existence, and whose funds of retrospective knowledge come to include references to a past that nobody living can personally remember. Here, however, the symbolic ingredients that individuals make use of in establishing their connection to a larger social entity are no longer so clearly rooted in the continuing daily experience of interaction with other group members, for what at least some of these ingredients must now evoke is the larger existence of the group as (in the term that Benedict Anderson coined for nations) an 'imagined community'.[25] Such communities are constituted less through immediate personal connections than through assumptions of shared identity and imagined kinship. These assumptions are applied, furthermore, in ways which cut imaginatively across the experiential separation of people who are not each other's contemporaries: the communities that are imagined are communities not just of the living, but of the living with the dead and (by projection) the yet-to-be-born. To say this is not to say that imagined communities are pure abstractions, assembled in a world of ideology that has no points of contact with mundane social interactions; rather, the imagining of such communities is generally framed in ways which allow such interactions to acquire new levels of significance, by being viewed from what is supposedly a more durable perspective. Thus, for example, the family to which we feel we belong may be *both* the family unit of which we have practical experience in the present (with its personal relationships and interactions, and its 'idioculture' of the kind that Fine has studied) and the more enduring – but from a present standpoint less tangible – entity of whose hereditary continuities we feel this unit to be somehow the projection. Managing the connection between such longer and shorter perspectives on our social being is part of what being a member of an imagined community is about.

One of the ways in which such connections are established is through the embedding of data or stories relating to earlier phases in a group's existence in the memories that individuals may have of socially meaningful experiences – for example, of formative encounters with older or more senior group members (grandparents, mentors, older colleagues, etc.), or of processes of social or cultural initiation. Scholars have drawn attention, for example, to the ways in which messages about group identity, or about the legacy of past collective experiences, can be conveyed through the repetition of 'family stories' or 'family myths', focusing on the actions or experiences of earlier family members. For Anne Karpf, stories of this kind are 'a kind of DNA, encoded messages about how things are and should be, passed from generation to generation'.[26] The psychiatrist John Byng-Hall has given an example from his own family history. The story of the unfortunate eighteenth-century Admiral Byng, executed on his own quarterdeck for supposed cowardice in the face of the enemy, has passed as a family legend among Byng relatives, imbuing successive generations with a sense of the need to face dangers and avoid retreats. It has also, in its passage, influenced the family's larger narrative culture, giving prominence to further anecdotes that articulate similar themes in relation to episodes from the lives of later family members. What matters in such a case, Byng-Hall suggests, is less the detail of the original story (some of which is anyway inaccurate) than 'the context of listening and the context of recalling' – the ways in which the story becomes part of each generation's remembered practical experience of growing up as a family member.[27]

Formal commemorative occasions can also play a part in soldering the connections that individuals may feel to a larger past. When the members of a group assemble to celebrate an anniversary or to commemorate a founder or benefactor, or even to celebrate the career of a retiring colleague or to honour the memory of a recently deceased member, the life of the group in the present is structured, momentarily at least, around the evocation of past events or experiences. Such events may even, in some cases, be designed explicitly to connect the past that is in living memory to the past that lies beyond it. Polybius describes how the conventions of Roman funeral oratory served, in honouring the recently departed, also to remind participants in the ceremony of the longer tradition to which the deceased citizen was being connected:

the speaker who pronounces the oration over the man who is about
to be buried, when he has delivered his tribute, goes on to relate
the successes and achievements of all the others whose images are
displayed there, beginning with the oldest. By this constant renewal
of the good report of brave men, the fame of those who have
performed any noble deed is made immortal, and the renown of
those who have served their country well becomes a matter of common
knowledge and a heritage for posterity.[28]

Much of the efficacity of commemorative practices lies in repetition:
by becoming a familiar element in people's social experience, such
formally structured evocations of the past, and the more loosely
structured patterns of reminiscence that may take shape around
them, become part of the remembered texture of individual lives.

Awareness of objects and places can also be instrumental in
developing and reinforcing such connections. Family heirlooms
come accompanied with reminders of the ancestors with which
they are associated, or at least of the latest phases of their
transmission ('I had this from my grandmother', 'this has been in
your father's family for generations').

Attachment to places – either to ones that are presently occupied
or to ones that are remembered – can have a similar function in
allowing people to maintain their emotional connections to a
longer collective past. Amanda Lillie has shown the fervour with
which the exiled fifteenth-century Florentine aristocrat Palla Strozzi
held on to his ancestral properties on Florentine territory, and to
the sense of family that was attached to them. Making provision
in his will for one dilapidated property, Strozzi noted:

> And I do this because it was built from its foundations by our ancestors
> and forefathers, messer Jacopo and Palla his son, father of Nofri my
> father, and therefore my grandfather. And I want as far as it is possible
> for me to ensure that the site and place and farm should remain
> with our family and our descendants, in memory of he who built it
> and raised it from its foundations, and because of the place where
> it is: that is Carmignano, where there have always been men the same
> as us and of our lineage.[29]

For an aristocrat of another country and later era, Joachim von
Winterfeld, it was trees that did the trick: 'As I walk through woods
of birch and oak, past tall elders and across cuttings, my ancestors
accompany me every step of the way. I live immersed in the past,
and not simply my own. I feel myself to be a link in a long chain.'[30]

Memory and the devices of culture

We can gain a further perspective on the ways in which the activity of remembering in social settings connects individuals mentally to broader social frameworks and larger group identities if we delve more deeply into the cultural dimension of this activity. To say that remembering is, in important ways, a social activity is to say, of necessity, that it is a culturally mediated activity – that our ability to remember things in a stable manner, and to communicate what we remember, depends on the availability of cultural devices.

Culture, for the purposes of this discussion, is understood to be composed of the systems of signs, and of the practices involving the deployment of such signs, that have been evolved in human societies, and that are used by individuals within those societies, for the conversion of subjective mental data into meanings that are externally communicable, and for the communication and circulation of these meanings within society. Culture is, by definition, a social phenomenon: its forms and uses are shaped by, and themselves contribute to shaping, social relationships and social exchanges.

Culture is also a multi-layered affair. It consists, most basically, of whatever forms of symbolic expression have achieved sufficient systemic stability to be of use in the generation and transmission of meaning in social settings – of language in its oral and written forms, but also of systems employing gesture or non-verbal sound or pictorial representation. On the basis of these general systemic resources, however, societies have developed a wide range of more focused and specialized conventional practices, each adapted to different social and cultural uses, and each imparting different structuring features to a particular type of cultural activity: generic forms of written or oral or musical composition, gestural or rhetorical styles, particular modes of artistic representation, forms of ritual performance, and so on. Understanding the meanings that can be articulated through the use of a particular cultural device (a text, an oral utterance, a performance, a visual image or material artefact) at a particular moment involves relating that device not simply to its immediate context and to the general expressive possibilities of whatever linguistic or symbolic systems it manipulates, but to a complex background of conventional use.

Culture works by casting our inner subjective impressions into forms that have a stabler – and therefore more communicable

– objective existence. Once it is thus understood, its affinities with memory become obvious. Like memory, culture is both an individual and a social resource. Again like memory, it is a medium of retention, and thus a facilitator of deferred action: registered within the formal structures and vehicular devices of culture, the thoughts and mental impressions of a particular moment acquire sufficient stability and persistence to become objects of reference and generators of effects at later moments and in different settings. In short, like memory, culture equips human beings with means of transcending the limitations that would otherwise be imposed on consciousness by a relentless preoccupation with the needs and impressions of the immediate moment. But to speak only of affinities between culture and memory is to understate the case: culture is our basic mnemonic support system, without which memory as we understand it would scarcely be conceivable. It seems at least highly questionable whether the resources of individual minds, cut off from all cultural support, would be adequate, given the constant flood of fresh impressions assailing them at every moment, to give any kind of stable organization to their retentive capacities. In practice, our ability to draw distinctions among our impressions, to give some of them priority status, to establish thematic linkages between impressions relating to different phases in our existence, to delve back in memory for information from the past that is relevant to our present position, relies heavily on the cultural apparatus we have available.

In exploring memory's relationship to culture further, it is helpful to highlight three kinds of duality in the way that culture is put to use: between *internal* and *external* uses; between *private* and *public* uses, and between uses for *storage* and uses for *memorialization*.

The first of these distinctions involves different forms (or meanings) of 'objectification'. To objectify an impression is to capture it in a form that has sufficient fixity to be memorable and in principle communicable. Doing this does not necessarily mean projecting the impression into or onto an external object. In some cases, the cultural apparatus that assists us mnemonically consists of mental 'software' – narrative templates, cultural stereotypes, mnemonic formulae, systems of classification, rhyming patterns, etc. that individual minds can internalize, and the use of which may not always therefore have to be externally articulated. 'Software' of this kind is by no means necessarily ephemeral: certain rhyming

patterns or mnemonic formulae ('Thirty days hath September
...') have persisted in culture for centuries. Perhaps the most
extensively studied forms of mnemonic cultural software are the
techniques and devices of the ancient and medieval and Renaissance
'art of memory'.[31] Specialists in the 'art of memory' advocated a
range of ways of disciplining the mind in the business of retention
and retrieval. The best-known of these – the so-called method of
loci, or places – was based on spatial visualization: mental images
standing for the things to be remembered would be arranged in
an imagined space – placed, for example, within the separate rooms
of an imagined mansion – and then recaptured when needed by
mentally visiting those rooms in sequence. Such a method was suited
especially to the needs of those – lawyers or politicians, for example
– who needed to recover not just an assortment of facts, but the
sequence of ideas in a projected argument.

The most obviously observable mnemonic uses of culture
are, however, inevitably those in which objectification involves a
physical externalisation – in texts or objects or standardized ritual
performances. The crucial links between memory and this kind of
objectification were affirmed by the Russian social psychologist
L. S. Vygotsky:

> The very essence of human memory is that human beings actively
> remember with the help of signs. It is a general truth that the special
> character of human behaviour is that human beings actively manip-
> ulate their relation to the environment, and through the environment
> they change their own behaviour, subjugating it to their control. As
> one psychologist [Dewey] has said, the very essence of civilization
> consists in the fact that we deliberately build monuments so as not
> to forget. In the knotted handkerchief and the monument we see
> the most profound, most characteristic and most important feature
> which distinguishes human from animal behaviour.[32]

A lot is packed into this short passage: an emphasis on the
purposeful (or 'active') character of remembering; an insistence
on the fundamentally mnemonic character of cultural constructs;
an explicit connecting of what is essential in the collective human
achievement ('the very essence of civilization') to the distinctiveness
of human (as opposed to animal) memory. Equally interesting is
Vygotsky's choice of examples, which illustrates the second duality
in culture's mnemonic uses – between the public and the private.
Conventionally at least, the knotted handkerchief is a device used

by individuals to send mnemonic messages to themselves at a future moment. Its general meaning (the indication of an intention to remember something) is culturally shared, but the specific meanings with which it is charged on particular occasions are private and personal. A monument, by contrast, is conventionally a way of going public: it uses a form drawn from shared culture to develop a message that is itself intended to be shared or communicated or passed on to future generations.

The distinction between public and private mnemonic uses of cultural devices is not, of course, a rigid one: it is possible for a cultural object or device to bear both kinds of use simultaneously, or indeed (whether intentionally or otherwise) to assist in weaving public and private uses together, or in negotiating the relationship between them. The Vietnam War Memorial in Washington, for example – a long, low granite wall incised with the names of individual Americans killed in the war – is at once a public (though not an official governmental) commemorative statement and a facility adaptable to private remembrance, expressed through silent contemplation or touching of a particular name or deposition of objects privately associated with one of the deceased.[33] (When the Smithsonian Institution held a public exhibition of these ostensibly private mementos, it complicated the weave still further.)

Whether their uses are public or private, cultural devices can have two quite different kinds of mnemonic function: they can assist either in mnemonic operations of storage or in ones of memorialization. Operations of these two kinds have in common the fact of being designed to forestall forgetting, but they embody different strategies for doing this, and are usually informed by different motives. In storage, the purpose is pragmatic: data are, so to speak, put into reserve (whether in some mental territory of knowledge that is not currently in conscious use, or in an external storage system such as written text), with a view to being available for practical use at future moments. The aim is for the data to be retained, without cluttering up the foreground of anyone's consciousness in the intervals before they are required. Thus, for example, an individual stores the record of his financial transactions in an account book, or a government bureaucracy organizes its archives in ways designed to assist its later operations. In 'memorialization', by contrast, the forestalling of forgetting is envisaged less as a pragmatic precaution than as a moral imperative or pious duty: thus individuals hang portraits of their deceased ancestors, nations and municipalities erect statues of their honoured citizens, war memorials publicly list the fallen, whose 'name liveth for evermore'. Storage works by suspension; its operations are archival; its objective is availability. The point of 'memorialization', by contrast, lies in reminding: it seeks to ensure that the things to be remembered are constantly close to the surface of consciousness, and to the core of moral perceptions. Storage aims to permit deferral, while memorialization aims to ensure persistence, of a conscious engagement with the data that culture helps memory to retain.

Like the distinction between public and private, this one is, of course, fluid and contingent: how it works is culturally variable. Books are obvious devices for storing information, but this does not mean that they cannot function also as monuments or memorials, especially in societies where printed literature is a scarce commodity, laborious to produce, and where a book may be regularly and solemnly displayed and read, perhaps aloud in a communal setting.[34] Nor should we overlook the sheer difficulty of the task that memorialization purports to set itself. The kind of remembering it requires is demanding and exhausting: it requires a strong commitment of the rememberers to the moral duty that it embodies and to the more general social benefits (secure identity, social cohesion, moral elevation) that are supposed to stem from performance of that duty. The structure of some memorializing practices reflects the difficulty of sustaining this commitment continuously: remembrance is concentrated on particular occasions, such as saints' days or anniversaries, whose regular occurrence is considered a sufficient guarantee of commitment to the memory in question. In other cases, memorialization may be only briefly successful: the world abounds in rituals that have gone flat and monuments to the enduring memory of people who have nevertheless been forgotten.

Sometimes, on the other hand, the sheer comprehensiveness of a memorializing intention – the determination actively to remember everything – can blur the distinctions between archival storage and memorial preservation. The 'memory books' (*yisker biher*) compiled after the Second World War, by committees of survivors in exile, to commemorate specific Jewish communities obliterated during the Nazi ascendancy offer examples of this. Combining various kinds of written material (histories, autobiographical reminiscences, newspaper articles) and illustration (including photographs), and combining fresh material with material drawn from earlier sources, such books bear significance both as physical monuments (objects intended to stand for the vanished thing they commemorate) and as textual compilations (transmitting their memorializing and mnemonic intention through layout and language, and through the ways in which different texts are brought together). A passage from one such book testifies both to the memorializing purpose and to the comprehensiveness of the retrieval that the texts are supposed collectively to facilitate:

> The Kalish Book describes the daily life of the Jewish Community, its struggle for economic, cultural and social existence from the early days until the end. In these pages the survivors of the Community have done their best to set up a Memorial to their brethren. May it serve as a landmark for the coming generations of our offspring.[35]

Nathan Wachtel has written of the 'all-encompassing, nearly encyclopedic restitution of the Jewish world of Poland' that the *yisker biher* embody: 'Many a page is comprised of enumerations, quotations, lists, – of persons, places – inventories so that nothing will be lost of that which once was.'[36] No doubt the books were not intended as works of reference in the conventional sense, yet the very fullness of their memorializing intention – the effort to preserve in memory not just specific episodes or individuals, but the whole life of a vanished community – forces a recourse to techniques of storage: the book as monument can commemorate a totality, but the details of that totality cannot all be simultaneously held in the minds of those for whom the memorial is important.

Culture's assistance to individual memory does not lie only in the facilities it provides for storing or communicating remembered information. It lies also in the wide range of socially meaningful emotional or affective inflections, imparted to the activity of remembering, that it allows human beings, both individually and collectively to articulate and to communicate. 'Remembrance', 'mourning', 'reminiscence', 'nostalgia', 'celebration', 'commemoration', 'grievance', 'regret' – these are only some of the terms that are used to distinguish particular mnemonic or recollective comportments, within which memory can be, variously, affectionate or resentful, sorrowful or joyful, bonding or contemplative, solemn or convivial. Culture helps give form to these comportments, by providing appropriately structured occasions for their adoption (funerals, reunions, fireside get-togethers, commemorative ceremonies), by supplying material prompters and signifiers (widow's weeds, sacred relics, souvenir ashtrays, family photo albums), and by giving us gestures and languages that are tailored for their expression. Thus, an Australian soldier writes, in 1917, to the father of a fallen comrade:

> I am trying to express the sympathy we his mates feel towards you and your family in losing him. We lost a cheery good pal and staunch comrade and understand your deepest feelings. Struck down by a shell – George died as he lived – a man – a soldier striking for Honour and Freedom and I am glad to know I was counted among his friends.[37]

Conventional formulae – of sympathetic understanding, of loss, of comradeship, of soldierly valour – are used here to give a particular affective structure to the memories that are evoked, and to communicate those memories in ways that are geared to a purpose of consolation.

Individuals do not, of course, adopt such comportments only in private; they may also be participants in public activities that are similarly structured. Tensions can arise, in such cases, over what are actually to be considered the culturally appropriate means of conveying a particular mnemonic attitude. Can one, for example, commemorate the dead of a civil war by erecting a dining hall? The lawyer John Codman Ropes thought not, when Harvard's Memorial Hall was proposed in the 1860s:

> Is it a Memorial Hall after all? It is a Dining Hall called a Memorial Hall. But does calling it a Memorial Hall make it a Memorial Hall? . . . The solemnity which always surrounds death is an essential element in producing the moral impression, which our Memorial is designed to make. Let us not weaken it.[38]

The fact that such a hall could still be bedecked with commemorative paintings and stained glass did not persuade Ropes of the propriety of thus combining the messages of 'honor and hospitality' in a building destined (as Henry James later put it) to dispense 'laurels to the dead and dinners to the living'.[39]

The cultural devices that individuals use in articulating mnemonic and recollective comportments are themselves indicative of broader cultural – and therefore sometimes social – identities. In selecting the narrative stereotypes that helped them to formulate their memories, Luisa Passerini's informants implicitly identified themselves as members of a range of communities (family, work-group, political club, etc.), each of which possessed its own familiar repertoire of cultural forms.[40] In everyday life, no doubt, such gestures of cultural identification often pass unnoticed: we use many cultural devices so habitually that we do not think of ourselves as making statements about social or cultural identity when we do so. Sometimes, however, the gesture is more plainly significant. This may be because the cultural device in question in some way alludes directly to the conditions of membership of a particular community, as when the framing of life memories in the form of a conversion narrative establishes a religious believer's credentials as a member of the community of the elect. Or it may be because conditions of cultural contestation or persecution have given political significance to the choice of cultural resources. Thus the use which the Latvians studied by Skultans made of motifs drawn from earlier Latvian folk or national culture in structuring their autobiographical recollections marked a rejection of, or at least an inability to make intelligible personal use of, the ways of narrating experience that were authorized and promoted by the Soviet regime.[41]

If the use of particular cultural forms to express or to assist memory may be a marker of identity and of community, the forms that bind can also, in obvious or subtle ways, differentiate. The practice of the Catholic confessional, in which the priest receives and judges the penitent's articulation of guilty memory, maintains and marks the penitent's participation in the community of the Church; it also, however, maintains the functional separation of priesthood and laity, and the relationships of authority and dependence between them. The generic conventions of certain kinds of autobiographical writing can have a similar double effect. Ann Fabian has shown the impressive array of autobiographical story-types (beggars' tales, soldiers' tales, convict narratives, slave narratives, tales of imprisonment, tales of captivity by Indians), each possessing its own generic features and offering a template for the narrative encapsulation of a different kind of social experience, that were a feature of nineteenth-century American literary culture. Such narrative genres fed off each other (escaped slave narratives, for example, reworking elements of language and metaphor familiar from earlier narratives of imprisonment or religious conversion), weaving multiple variations around the recurrent motifs of 'confession, conversion, and captivity'. Each of them offered a particular set of 'poor sufferers' the means of structuring memory and experience for public consumption – and thereby, perhaps, making money or advancing a particular cause. Their function was also social: telling the right kind of story in the right kind of way could bring a socially disadvantaged author a degree of acceptance in society. Fabian's emphasis is on the accrediting function of generic conventions – the ways in which autobiographical materials cast in a familiar narrative mould secure the status of truthfulness in the eyes of an audience sensitized by previous exposure to such forms of sentimental literature. The same templates that allowed unfortunate authors to win a degree of sympathetic recognition from the reading public also, however, by committing them to a 'poor and humble' narrative stance, implied their acceptance of a deferentially subordinate position within society.[42]

Like remembering in conversational settings, remembering enabled by cultural devices may be marked by divisions of labour, and shaped by relationships of power and dependence. The ability to make use of such devices is seldom evenly distributed, whether because their operation requires resources (of time, raw materials, monetary wealth, manpower, intelligence or education) that are unequally possessed, or because efforts have been made artificially to restrict or control their use. Mastery over particular devices – the ability to read or write, the ability of the oral poet or tribal griot to deliver the contents of oral tradition through mnemonic and story-telling techniques, the authority of the priest to perform the central commemorative ceremonies of the cult, the master craftsman's special knowledge of the traditional skills of the craft – confers social power, whether directly through the dependence in which it places those who wish to have the benefit of the device in question but are excluded from its direct use, or through the prestige that is publicly accorded to the specially qualified practitioner. Such mastery may be jealously guarded and hedged with restrictions, and may become, as a result, at once a badge of identity and a vehicle of authority for a particular social group – either one actually constituted by its members' monopoly over the mnemonic capacities in question, or an otherwise existing group (a clergy, an aristocracy) that simply adds this monopoly to its other means of social influence.

Differential access to the cultural resources that are useful for remembering produces inequalities in mnemonic capacity, sets limits to identity, and breeds – potentially at least – sentiments of exclusion. In fairly obvious ways, exclusion from the best available technologies for storing information over time, or from the means of accessing information that has been stored by means of such technologies, can be a source of social disadvantage, as the plight of illiterates in a society dominated by literacy makes clear. But the point can apply also to exclusion from the culturally recognized means of adopting socially or psychologically significant mnemonic comportments. Ruth Kluger, whose father perished during the Holocaust, has written of the difficulty that she has in preserving his memory:

> I keep wanting to celebrate him in some way, to find or invent an appropriate way of mourning, some ceremony for him. And yet celebrations and ceremonies are not my thing. I suspect them of mendacity, and often they strike me as ridiculous. Nor would I know where to start. In the Jewish tradition only men say the kaddish, the prayer for the dead. (Who is keeping you from saying any prayer you please? my friends ask. But it wouldn't count, couldn't be part of a prescribed communal ritual, so what would be the point?)[43]

Kluger's problem, as she perceives it, lies not in an absence of memories of her father to draw on, but in her exclusion from the cultural means of remembering him 'in the right way'. Her affective needs are moulded by a religious culture that prescribes particular practices of remembrance, but are frustrated by the gendering of religious functions which prevents her, as an isolated Jewish woman, from personally making use of the appropriate cultural device. Her sensitivity to this particular cultural exclusion shapes her critical attitude to the religious tradition:

> If it were different, if I could mourn my ghosts in some accepted public way, like saying kaddish for my father, I'd have a friendlier attitude towards this religion, which reduces its daughters to helpmeets of men and circumscribes their spiritual life within the confines of domestic functions. Recipes for gefilte fish are no recipe for coping with the Holocaust.[44]

Cultural devices, as this example reminds us, are not merely pieces of expressive technology; they are also forms of social practice. The use of them activates or generates social relationships. In some cases, as with the kaddish, that use is so much part of a traditional pattern of activity that the cultural device seems operable only within an already established – and possibly highly restrictive – set of social relationships, which it serves merely to reinforce; in other cases, there may be greater room for improvisation in the way a device is employed, and thus in the social relationships that its employment is instrumental in establishing or developing. In either case, however, cultural devices assist us in forging relationships, both real and imagined, that can contribute to our sense of somehow belonging to durable transgenerational communities or networks of affinity. They do so not simply by allowing us to be communicators and recipients of information about the past of these communities or networks, but by embedding the transmission of this information in the patterns of life that constitute our regular social existence. Two examples may help us to explore this idea a little more fully.

The food historian and cookery writer Claudia Roden has written of the role which cooking plays in sustaining her own sense of connection to a past from which she might otherwise be distanced. 'Jewish food', she writes, 'tells the story of an uprooted, migrating people and their vanished worlds. It lives in people's minds and has been kept alive because of what it evokes and represents.' Her own experience, as the daughter of a Cairo Jewish family, transported to England following the Israeli-Egyptian war of 1956, illustrates this. Referring to her childhood, she writes of how the smells and tastes of traditionally prepared food, blending with her parent's constant reminiscences, kept the memory of life in Cairo alive in exile. But the connection is textual as well as sensory:

> When I look through the old notes and recipes given by relatives and friends soon after they [her parents] left Egypt, it rekindles memories of our old life in a vivid way. They are written in French and interspersed with remarks about who gave the recipe long ago in Egypt, how much the dishes were appreciated by a certain person, and the occasion on which they were served. Each recipe has a name. There is 'kobeba Latifa', 'fromage blanc Adèle', 'hamud Sophie', 'pasteles Iris', 'blehat Rahel', and so on. Most of the people are dead now. They were my parents' generation. But their recipes keep their memory very much alive, at least for me.[45]

Several strands of memory are woven together here: memory of a
lengthy culinary tradition, memory of particular people, memory
of a social circle more generally, memory of parents, memory of
place, memory of smells and tastes, memory of the author's
childhood as both a social and a sensual experience. Roden's
awareness of the past is mediated, simultaneously, through traditional culinary practice, through the mnemonically triggering
effects of sensory experience, and through engagement with the
writing that one generation has passed on to another. The written
recipes serve as textual reminders at once of people and of practices,
and the collection of them, compiled at the time of exile, is a
reminder not just of the social world that produced it, but of the
moment at which that world was disrupted, and the continuity of
the tradition possibly endangered: while facilitating a mental
connection, it also marks a separation.

In Roden's account, we see the effects of a transmission –
of textual materials and of associated practices – from the standpoint of the recipient. But social bonds can also be formed at the
moment of a cultural resource's production. In her diary, Elizabeth
Grant of Rothiemurchus, whose memoirs supplied an example for
an earlier chapter, described how these memoirs were written:

> After breakfast and my little walk I write the recollections of my life,
> which I began to do on my birthday to please the girls, who eagerly
> listen to the story of their mothers' youth, now as a pleasing tale, by
> and by it will be out of a wish to feel acquainted with people and
> places I shall not be at hand to introduce them to. This effort at
> memory amuses me extremely. I live again my early years, among
> those who made the first impressions on my mind, many of them
> gone where I am perhaps slowly but very surely following, and I recall
> places very dear to my imagination, which were I now to see I should
> probably, from the changes made in them, know no more. I am glad
> I thought of this way of occupying my quiet day, a part of it at least,
> the hour or two thus employed steals easily away. The pleasure of
> talking over these bygone times with my children attaches us the
> more to one another. As we become more confidential in our
> intercourse, we make the tale profitable too by the comments we
> engraft upon it, and best of all it encreases my content with the
> present, the contrast between my maiden days and married life being
> to all rational feelings so much in favour of the latter.[46]

The significance of Grant's memoirs, for the building of a sense
of family, lay, then, not just in their content, but in the process of

their production. On one level, this production established the business of remembering as part of the daily and weekly routine of her own existence as a middle-aged married woman. On another, it was part of a strategy of recollection which supplied her with a necessary – and seemingly a comforting – perspective on her present existence. On a third, it was a means of establishing bonds within the family, both between herself and her daughters and, prospectively at least, between the daughters (and perhaps also members of future generations) and the people and places of an earlier family history – bonds which, in the first of these cases at least, were established as much through the business of narrating and listening and commenting as through the information actually conveyed. But the content of the memoirs can perhaps also be re-examined in the light of these relationships. What was the significance, for daughters, of maternal recollections that found their essential point of focus not in the Ireland where they themselves were being brought up, but in the Highland Scottish environs of the mother's own youth? Consider how the very recognition of the inevitability of displacement is used by Grant, in the following passage, to reinforce the status of Rothiemurchus (her childhood home) as the point of reference for her own generation's sense of family belonging:

> Once 'over the water' we were at home in Rothiemurchus, our beloved Duchus, which, through all the changes of our lives, has remained the spot on earth dearest to the heart of every one of us. We have been scattered far and wide, never now *all* to meet again. We children have grown up and married and have had new interests engrafted on our old feelings, and have changed our homes and all our surroundings, and most of us have lived long, busy years far away from the Highlands, yet have we never any one of us ceased to feel that there was the magnet to which all our purest, warmest, earliest, and latest affections were steadily drawn. No other place ever replaced it, no other scenery ever surpassed it, no other young happiness ever seemed to approach within a comprehensible distance our childhood in Rothiemurchus.[47]

The powerful statement that this passage makes, not just of Grant's own nostalgic attachment to the places of the happier phases of her childhood, but of the capacity of the memory of place to sustain the emotional bonds of family across time and distance, seems peculiarly relevant to females in a landed society dominated by male primogeniture. For daughters, destined to pass from one family to another through marriage, the cultivation of memories of place might be tinged with a certain nostalgic sense of separation, but might also mitigate the effects of social rupture, by attaching the sense of belonging less to the harsh and exclusive dictates of a male-dominated system of property and dependence than to the idea of an affective community, in which male and female might participate more equally. By thinking about the textual emphases of a memoir such as Grant's together with the social relationships that were involved in and developed through its production, we can achieve insights not just into the ways in which memory is harnessed to the production of collective senses of identity, but also into the gendering of such a process.

Theorizing memory in social settings: Bartlett, Halbwachs and others

Since individuals live their lives as members of social groups of one kind or another, their personal remembering, and their communication of that remembering to other members of the groups they belong to, contributes to the processes by which groups develop a sense of a collective identity extending over time. In remembering their own experience (its formative moments, significant encounters, locations and human relationships), and in discussing these memories with other people, they deepen their own and other people's sense of attachment to larger social entities, and participate also in the passing on and interpretation of stories and references to a more distant or extended past that possess a resonance in the collective setting. In short, individual remembering both reflects and contributes to the sense of a collective past that members of a group collectively relate to. It is in deepening an understanding of these processes that it is helpful to turn now to explore the thinking of the two early twentieth-century scholars most commonly cited as founding fathers of social memory studies: the British psychologist Frederic Bartlett and the French sociologist Maurice Halbwachs.

In the first part of his *Remembering: a Study in Experimental and Social Psychology* (1932), Bartlett used controlled experimental methods to develop his basic contention of the schema-dependent and reconstructive character of individual remembering. In the much shorter second part, drawing evidence not from psychological experiments but from folklore studies and from the observations of anthropologists and colonial administrators among the indigenous peoples of Southern Africa, he extended his argument that this reconstructive activity is one in which 'both the manner and the matter of recall are often predominantly determined by social influences'.[48] By this he meant, more specifically, that individual recollection is shaped, in vital ways, by the individual's relationship to group-specific social and cultural structures. In thus separating himself from purely individualistic conceptions of remembering, Bartlett was also, however, careful to distance himself both from Jungian notions of a 'collective unconscious' and from ways of talking about memory in groups that seemed to attribute to the groups themselves an actual power of recollection. The hypothesis of such a 'memory of the group' could never, in his view, be more than 'an interesting but uncertain speculation'; the role of group-based cultures in 'determining and directing the mental lives' of individuals (and especially their remembering) could be regarded, by contrast, as 'a matter of certainty and of fact'.[49]

Bartlett's account of what he called the 'social mechanisms of recall' in individuals rested on a general conception of how social groups are formed and sustained. He summarizes this as follows:

> Every social group is organised and held together by some specific psychological tendency or group of tendencies, which give the group a bias in its dealings with external circumstances. The bias constructs the special persistent features of group culture, its technical and religious practices, its material art, its traditions and institutions; and these again, once they are established, become themselves direct stimuli to individual response within the group.[50]

Bartlett nuances this basic picture in various ways: he recognizes, for example, that the 'psychological basis' of group organization may evolve as the group itself becomes more complex and multifunctional, and that customs, traditions and institutions may constrain people not just directly, but also through the social 'sentiments' (presumably of identity and loyalty and common purpose) that develop around them. The essential theory remains simple: the active mental impulses that underpin a group's existence (which can be anything from a desire to secure food and shelter or a shared set of pugnacious instincts to a desire to propagate particular religious ideals) shape its forms of organized culture, and these in turn condition the ways in which individuals within the group respond to external stimuli – including the ways in which they mentally connect freshly encountered data to previous experience. Through the mediating influence of group-specific culture, the 'social bias' of the group is translated, in the case of each individual, into 'an active tendency to notice, retain and construct specifically along certain directions' – in effect, to remember particular kinds of things, and to organize the memory of them in particular ways. Cultural and social organization conditions individual remembering in two ways: 'First, by providing that setting of interest, excitement and emotion which favours the development of specific images, and secondly, by providing a persistent framework of institutions and customs which acts as a schematic basis for constructive memory.'[51] Memory is guided and supported, in short, both by the individual's active emotional involvement in the group to which he or she belongs and by the group's own forms of collective organization.

In Bartlett's view, the influence of group-based cultural dispositions on acts of remembering was evident in the 'manner' as well as the 'matter' of recall: the 'temperament' of each group (Bartlett's shorthand for 'that group of preferred organised reactions which have crystallized into its institutions, customs and beliefs')[52] was reflected not just in what its individual members typically remembered, but in the modes of narrative and verbal presentation (including such aspects as tone of voice and degree of animation) through which the remembered data were articulated. He argued, for example, that the detailed linear narratives provided by Swazi trial-witnesses, which so infuriated colonial magistrates impatient to get to the heart of the case, reflected the cultural priorities of a social group which was heavily dependent on rote recital for the transmission of news and information, which possessed a relative abundance of time for the performance of tasks, and which was relatively unfocused and unorganized in its social interests.[53]

While Bartlett's central focus was on the social shaping of individual remembering, he also drew attention to the adaptive processes that were involved in the formation of a group's culture. In particular, he focused on the ways in which groups assimilated freshly-imported cultural elements (stories, images, rituals, institutions) into their existing repertoire of cultural practice. The mechanisms involved here were, according to Bartlett, ones of 'social conventionalization': the incorporation of a new element into a group's working culture, and thus its survival as part of the cultural legacy transmitted within the group from one generation to another, depended on its being gradually adjusted in ways which reduced its discordance with the cultural setting to which it was being introduced. If these adjustments did not result in the element in question losing its existence as a separate cultural feature, it would eventually achieve stability in a form more attuned to the norms of the culture as a whole, and to the social impulses of which that culture was the articulation. Bartlett likened these processes of 'social conventionalization' to the processes by which individuals participating in 'repeated recall' experiments progressively modified the materials (stories or images) that they were asked to recall at regular intervals, bringing those materials into line with their existing mental schema. For him, in other words, there were close similarities between the processes of cultural adjustment by which social groups responded to fresh experiences and shifts in historical circumstances and the processes of reconstructive recollection by which individuals made sense of their own experience.[54] In Bartlett's immediate argument, the point of this comparison is to prime his measured response to putative analogies between individual and collective mental operations: he wishes to argue that while the hypothesis of a 'memory of the group' functionally analogous to that of the individual is inherently speculative, the notion of group cultures as embodiments of some kind of guiding collective 'temperament' is conceptually helpful. From a more general perspective, however, the significance of the comparison lies in the way that the juxtaposing of individual and collective processes deepens Bartlett's presentation of mental relationships to the past as essentially rooted in the cultural development of human societies: not only are the memories entertained by individuals conditioned by the group-specific cultures in which those individuals are embedded; those cultures are themselves composed of elements that are adjusted over time to fit the evolving needs of the communities that generate them.

This is as far as Bartlett's thoughts run in this direction, however. His principle focus is on the ways in which individual remembering is affected by group culture, not on the ways in which that culture is related to the larger workings of society. His lack of interest in a more sociological mode of inquiry is marked both by his tendency to assume that the only path to an investigation of collective aspects of remembering lies through the empirically unanswerable question of whether groups themselves have a capacity to remember, and by his apparent reluctance to envisage social situations of any complexity. Bartlett's social world is a simple and stable one: the individual is always positioned unproblematically within a particular group, and groups themselves are clear-cut and self-contained, each founded on identifiable social impulses, each possessed of a culture that coherently and functionally reflects those impulses, each essentially separate from other groups. There is no apparent need, within such a model, to consider how remembering may be affected by passage from one group to another or by membership of several groups at once, or how group cultures may be moulded by intersections or interactions or conflicts between different groups, by the location of one group within another, by amalgamations of groups, or by the splintering of larger groups into smaller ones.

For all of this, we must turn instead to the ideas developed by Bartlett's contemporary, the French sociologist Maurice Halbwachs, first in his *Les cadres sociaux de la mémoire* (1925) and then in the draft materials published posthumously as *La mémoire collective* (1950). Halbwachs's thinking resembles Bartlett's in its emphasis on the reconstructive character of remembering and on the role of group-specific cultural frameworks in shaping individual recollection, but he makes a far more ambitious attempt to integrate his account of how individuals remember into a larger theoretical analysis of the workings of society. For him, the interest of the 'social frameworks of memory' lies not only in their influence on individuals, but in their status as social products. Where Bartlett repeatedly shies away from the idea of a 'memory of the group', Halbwachs gives the impression of eagerly embracing it, through his formulation of the notion of 'collective memory'. The actual significance of this difference is a little elusive, since Halbwachs's statements about 'collective memory' and about its relationships to individual remembering are sometimes obscure and inconsistent, but it betokens a deeper difference in intellectual mentality. For Bartlett, the psychologist, it is the mental processes of individuals that have an empirically observable kind of solidity: social structures, for all their importance, seem hazy by comparison. For Halbwachs, the Durkheimian sociologist, it is the dense texturing of social existence that seems real, and the workings of the individual mind that seem, by contrast, fragile and unstable. Bartlett's basic conception is of stability: each individual remembers in ways which have certain regular features, and these are taken to be manifestations of a stable and unitary kind of cultural formation. Halbwachs's conception is of fluidity: individuals remember in ways which are fluctuating and discontinuous, and this reflects the fact that the social environment they inhabit is a complex and shifting one.

These points will become clearer if we probe Halbwachs's thought in greater detail. Much of his argument, in *Les cadres sociaux* particularly, was framed as a sustained critique of the view of memory he associated particularly with the philosopher Henri Bergson. In the Bergsonian view, memory was an actual survival of past experience, lodged in the individual mind as a sequence of impressions that could be reactivated: when individuals remembered, they simply drew on this inner fund of impressions, in effect reliving their past experiences. Against this, Halbwachs argued that past experiences did not survive in any integral form, that remembering was not a reliving but a reconstructive representation of those experiences, and that this reconstruction was based not on the individual's inner mental resources, but on the deployment of inherently social – indeed collective – frames of reference. The argument was pressed home initially through a comparison of remembering and dreaming. In dream, Halbwachs claimed, we are indeed removed from social influence, but what happens then is quite different from what happens when we remember. The impressions that come into our minds in dream are derived from our previous experiences, but they do not in any stable or intelligible way refer us back to those experiences: all we have in dream are jumbled fragments of past perception, and our sensation is therefore not of retrospection (or even of reliving), but of a continuous flow of immediate present experience. Remembering, by contrast, depends on the recognition that particular impressions relate to past rather than to present experience, and remembering things in any sustained or coherent way involves a more detailed 'localization' of these impressions – the mental assignation of them to particular moments or periods in our past existence (and perhaps also to places that were significant for us during certain phases of that existence). To be able to localize our impressions in this way, and to begin to build them into coherent structures of memory, we must have basic ways of mapping our remembered existence. The mapping devices that we possess, Halbwachs insists, come to us not from inward contemplation, but through our involvement in society. We remember not as isolated individuals, but as beings whose whole life is absorbed in social interactions of one kind or another, and whose individual identity is not separate from those interactions, but effectively constituted by them.[55]

It was to express this view of remembering as a facet of social existence that Halbwachs coined his conception of the 'social frameworks of memory' ('cadres sociaux de la mémoire') – or, in the stronger formulation he sometimes preferred, the 'frameworks of collective memory' ('cadres de la mémoire collective'). The basic thrust of his argument was summarized as follows:

> One can remember only on condition of finding again, within the frameworks of collective memory, the place of the past events which interest us. A recollection [souvenir] is so much the richer for reappearing at the meeting-point of a greater number of these frameworks, which in effect intersect with each other and partially overlap each other. Forgetting is explained by the disappearance of these frameworks or of a part of them, whether because our attention is no longer capable of focusing on them, or because it is focused elsewhere (distraction is often only a consequence of an effort at attention, and forgetting results almost always from distraction). But forgetting, or the deformation of certain of our recollections, is explained also by the fact that these frameworks change from one period to another. Society, depending on circumstances and on its point in time, represents the past to itself in different ways: it modifies its conventions. As each of its members bends himself to these conventions, he inflects his recollections in the direction in which the collective memory is evolving.[56]

To grasp the significance of this passage, we must unravel Halbwachs's central concepts a little further. The first points to be made concern the actual nature of the 'cadres sociaux de la mémoire'. Halbwachs's own attempts to give conceptual content to this term were convoluted and at times opaque, but certain basic elements emerge from his thinking. The first is that the term's reference is not to social structure in itself (though there are obviously connections to this), but to social mentality: the 'cadres sociaux de la mémoire' are structures of thought or of mental representation that are generated within society, and that guide the efforts of members of society to relate their impressions of their own past existence to broader patterns of social existence. At their most basic level, the 'cadres' assist individual remembering by foregrounding those features that are shared by given sets of events – their possession of a common location, a common cast of participants, a common relationship to particular themes or issues in a group's development – which make it possible to view those events as part of a more general social experience. In their more developed forms, they articulate more general conceptions of the character and history and general outlook of the social groupings whose experience gives rise to them. The 'cadres sociaux de la mémoire' possess a stability and a character of conceptual generality that distinguishes them from the 'memory-images' ('images-souvenirs') of the individual, but they are not, according to Halbwachs, fundamentally different in their raw material: 'the framework [cadre] also is made of recollections [souvenirs]'.[57] In arguing this point, Halbwachs set out to reject the distinction conventionally drawn between memory (an evocative experience based on private mental 'images') and conceptual thinking (a rational activity based on the deployment of abstract 'ideas'). For him, remembering and conceptual thinking were intimately entwined and mutually reinforcing: mental representations of past events and people always contained an element of conceptual arrangement, while 'there is scarcely a general notion that is not for society an occasion to refer back to such and such a period of its history'. [58] The 'cadres sociaux de la mémoire' promoted, and were themselves the product of, this mutual penetration of ideas and images, within individuals and within society.

Groups were at the core of remembering, for Halbwachs. As he argued at some length in *La mémoire collective*, 'in reality we are never alone':[59] our experience is always an experience inflected by group membership, and it is this aspect of it that allows us to remember it. The experiences we recall are ones we shared with others, or in which we were somehow aware of our relationship to a larger collectivity. But Halbwachs's claim is not simply that our memories are of group-related experiences, but that our ability to reconstruct those experiences depends on our present ability to view them from the mental standpoint of the groups to which they relate. By this he means not that we must mentally return to the precise attitudes that we had as a group member at the time of the events or experiences to which our memories refer, but that our perspective on those events or experiences must continue to be moulded by a participation in or an identification with the group (or groups) in question. If the group itself has ceased to exist, or if our own connection with it has come to an end, our ability to recall things that we experienced as members of the group will be curtailed.[60] Halbwachs allows some flexibility: individuals may go on feeling a mental and emotional attachment to a group after the group has been dissolved or they themselves have lost touch with its other members, and this may enable them for a while to retain the memories that are attached to it. But memories that are not reinforced by regular interaction with other group members are bound to be insecure, always liable to be obliterated by the new memories that arise once individuals enter into new social connections. The 'cadres sociaux de la mémoire' are a reflection, in other words, of our patterns of group involvement: individual memory is shaped by those patterns, and evolves as the patterns themselves are transformed.

Halbwachs recognized that individuals have complex social existences and social histories: his theory is not premised, as Bartlett's tends to be, on a unitary relationship between individual and group. His handling of the apparent distinctiveness of individual memories reflects this. Halbwachs insists that individuals never occupy a social vacuum: both their experience and their remembering of that experience are always moulded by their group connections. He accepts, however, that the different members of a group will not remember things in an identical manner, and that some at least of our memories have the superficial appearance of being purely private evocations of personal experience. His explanation of this, however, is not that there is some quality of individuality in memory which lies outside the influence of the 'cadres sociaux', but that individuals are differently positioned in relation to those 'cadres sociaux'. Each individual is at a point of intersection between several different social circles, and therefore between different group-specific currents of thought, whose relationship to each other also shifts over time. The different members of a group share certain experiences, but their memories of those experiences (and indeed the extent to which they are able to remember them) will be affected not just by their common membership of the group in question, but by the ways in which their involvement in that group is inflected by their simultaneous relationship to other group identities, both at the time of the original experience and at the moment of recollection. (A group of men who have cowered together in a trench under enemy fire have common elements of experience to look back on and may feel a powerful sense of common identity, but those of them who were also members of a group of regimental officers – and perhaps also of a broader 'officer class' – may construct this experience differently from those who were rank-and-file soldiers. The common experience of being one of a group of students may carry different meanings for students who are connected to different kinds of family background; and the memory of it will not be the same for students who have followed a variety of subsequent career paths but stayed in touch with each other as a group of friends as it is for a student who has lost touch with his student contemporaries but gone on to become a lecturer in the same department.) Individual remembering is shaped as much by the intersection and combination of different collective influences, as by the stability of particular collective identities. The memories which appear most personal are, for Halbwachs, simply those that are sustained by the most complex patterns of multiple social connection:

> Here again, as the recollection reappears through the combined effect of several overlapping series of collective thoughts and since we cannot attribute it exclusively to any one of them, we imagine that it is independent, and contrast its unity with their multiplicity. One might as plausibly suppose that a heavy object, suspended in the air by a host of stretched and interconnecting threads, remains hanging in a void, supported only by itself.

For Halbwachs, the individuality of the remembering subject is an illusion generated by the complexity of social existence:

> The succession of recollections [souvenirs], even of those which are the most personal, is always explicable by the changes that are produced in our relationships to the various collective milieux, that is to say, definitively, by the transformations of those milieux, taken separately, and of their ensemble.[61]

Developing these arguments in *La mémoire collective*, Halbwachs let slip the suggestion that each individual's memory might be regarded as 'a viewpoint [point de vue] on collective memory'.[62] In fact, *La mémoire collective* replaces talk about the 'cadres sociaux de la mémoire' with talk about the relationships between individual and collective memory. Even in his earlier work, however, Halbwachs had already made it clear that he regarded the 'cadres sociaux' not just as socially generated templates for individual recollective activity, but as manifestations of a mnemonic capacity that was actually collective. For him, indeed, saying that 'the individual remembers by adopting the viewpoint of the group' was tantamount to saying that 'the memory of the group realises and manifests itself in individual memories'. The 'cadres sociaux' were not frameworks brought into being through the combining of memories that were individual; rather, they were 'the instruments that collective memory makes use of to recompose an image of the past which is in accord, in each epoch, with the dominant thoughts of society'.[63]

The idea that groups – families, for example – were themselves the possessors of memory was not, Halbwachs claimed, a simply metaphorical one. For while recollections of family life would take different forms in the consciousness of different family members, these differences should not prevent the recognition of a deeper connectedness:

> from the fact that they have mixed with each other in the same daily life [mêler], and that perpetual exchanges of impressions and opinions amongst them have tightened the bonds whose strength is sometimes felt the more acutely the more they try to break them, the members of a family perceive well enough that in each of them the thoughts of the others have developed ramifications that can only be followed, and whose overall design can only be understood, by bringing all these thoughts back together and somehow rejoining them.[64]

What Halbwachs seems to have meant by this strikingly obscure passage is that the practical experience of being a member of a family, and of interacting continuously with other family members, imbues the individual with a general conception of the family as a social formation that is not dependent on his or her own limited reactions to other family members in specific settings. This general conception (embodied in notions of kinship, inheritance, familial roles, family tradition, family history, etc.) frames the individual's sense of his or her own position within the family, and constitutes a kind of common matrix for remembering by different family members. At once a conceptual framework and a collective representation of the group past, this view of the family is generated and sustained within the group through the experiences and interactions of family life. Internalized by individuals as part of the process of becoming a family member, it is reinforced in those individuals through their repeated exchanges with each other. Viewed from one angle, this continuously sustained collective self-image is the content of the family's 'collective memory'; viewed from another, it forms the 'cadre social' for the individualized recollections of family members.

While the contents of a group's 'collective memory' possess a certain stability relative to the ebb-and-flow of individual impressions, they are also, in Halbwachs's view, continually evolving. Within any group, two elements in 'social thought' are apparent – 'on the one hand a memory, that is to say a framework composed of notions that serve us as landmarks [points de repère], and that refer exclusively to the past; on the other, a rational activity that has its starting-point in the current conditions of society, that is to say in the present'.[65] This rational activity (itself ultimately grounded, according to Halbwachs, in a more broadly grounded kind of social memory) regulates the operations of the group's social memory and modifies it as circumstances evolve.

Despite his efforts to give it substantial content, Halbwach's 'collective memory' remains an elusive concept. Individuals, he affirms, remember in ways that are moulded by the collective memories they have internalized, but while he discusses some general features of such memories – most notably their mental organization of the time and space dimensions of the group's experience[66] – he offers surprisingly little insight into how their contents are generated and reproduced. His emphasis falls, in fact, much more on the individual's mental dependence on group-specific structures of consciousness than on the social dynamics of the process by which such structures are maintained – by which, in other words, groups themselves organize the business of remembering the collective past.

It is here that the work of a later French sociologist, Roger Bastide, has seemed helpful in remedying the deficiencies of Halbwachs's conception. Bastide's concern in his own detailed research was to understand the conditions which either facilitated or disrupted the maintenance of a traditional knowledge of African religious traditions among the descendants of Africans transported as slaves to the Americas. For him, the key to the understanding of remembering and forgetting lay not in the general perception that memory was always attached to groups, but in a more specific attention to the way groups were organized. A group, for Bastide, was not a conglomerate entity to which a coherent memory could simply be attributed, but rather 'a system of interindividual relationships'. If it might be important to understand (with Halbwachs) that the remembering individual was a point of intersection between groups, it was equally vital to understand that any group was 'a place of exchange' and of interaction between individuals who might have different functions in the social process of remembering. Like the different elements in a nervous system, Bastide argued, each individual in a group is 'endowed with activity, receiving stimuli from others and rendering them in return, with the result that these activities form a network of complementarity'. What allowed the elements of a collective past to be maintained and reproduced, possibly even in a radically new social setting, was not so much (as in Halbwachs's model) some basic continuity of the group as an entity whose 'standpoint' could be mentally adopted by individuals, but rather the maintenance or reproduction of a particular structured pattern of social interactions:

> memories [of African religious traditions] are so caught up in the weft [trame] of the African village, of its human gatherings, that they are resuscitated only where this village is remade in another land, where the human gathering can establish itself on its old basis.

In religious ritual, for example, different groups of individuals have different roles in a performance whose mnemonic value emerges only when all these roles are activated together. For Bastide, then, the contents of collective memory – the knowledge of the group's past that it mobilizes and reproduces – are not held in some kind of central group intelligence; nor are they inherent as a coherent whole in the mind of every individual. Rather, contact is maintained with the collective past through interactive exchanges within the group, between people whose different positioning in the group's structures gives them different perspectives. The individual encounters collective memory as one who participates in its productive processes, and who has a sense of the larger pattern to which his or her own activity contributes. At a basic level, indeed, collective memory as Bastide defines it is to be conceptualized not as a shared memory for particular kinds of historical information, but as the operational memory that allows the group to structure its collective mnemonic operations: 'collective memory is a group memory, but it is the memory of a scenario – that is to say, of the connections between roles – or indeed the memory of an organization, of an articulation, of a system of relations between individuals'.[67]

Occasions on which groups evoke aspects of their collective past are not always structured as ritual occasions; nor do all groups develop the kind of formal divisions of mnemonic labour that tend to be a feature of such occasions. But Bastide's insights can help us, nevertheless, in giving a depth and precision to the analysis of social memory processes. By emphasizing the need to attend to the specific social dynamics of the occasions on which the past is remembered, and to the ways in which the dynamics of these occasions are related to the structuring of social life more generally, Bastide helps us to overcome the rather nebulous collectivism that can sometimes be a feature of Halbwachsian approaches. He helps us again to connect the analysis of knowledge to the analysis of social process, reminding us, for example, of how much of our awareness of being connected to a past may be composed less of cognitive attachment to particular pieces of information than of experience of participation in the social occasions on which that past is evoked, celebrated or re-enacted.

It may be helpful to focus thinking on some of the issues that have been touched on in this section through a final couple of examples. The first deals with a relatively static kind of scenario – that of the mnemonic life of medieval monastic communities, especially those subject to the Benedictine rule. Janet Coleman has shown how the life of such communities was regulated by a strict discipline of communal religious observance whose intended purpose was precisely to sever whatever mnemonic connections monks might have to the secular world beyond the monastery itself. The minds of monks were to be focused relentlessly on the matter of salvation: what they were to remember was not 'the past or events in the extramural world', but the commandments of God, the dangers of hell, and the images of eternal life. The crucial feature of the monastic discipline, in this respect, was the meticulous and monotonous cycle of daily religious offices around which the whole existence of the community was structured. Taking a lead from Halbwachs, Coleman views the structural organization of time as a key dimension of the social organization of memory. In society beyond the monastery doors, she argues, individuals would gain experience of different time schemes, applying to different areas of social activity, and thus develop varied kinds of memory. In the monastery, one time-scheme prevailed utterly, cutting the community's mental structures off from the world outside and holding memory within its rigid cyclical rhythms – allowing the monastic memory to become, in effect, 'a storehouse of divine texts' rather than of personal recollections.[68] In Coleman's Halbwachsian reading, the structures of monastic life deprive the monk of all possibility of sustaining a mental connection to the social frameworks of his earlier existence: amnesia with regard to earlier experience becomes the very basis of social and therefore of personal identity. (In Bartlettian language, one might say that the psychological basis of the group – the impulse towards salvation – imparts a bias to its culture, manifested especially in its liturgical arrangements, which in turn imposes a set of schema on individual remembering that effectively blocks the mental registration of anything other than holy or sacred messages.)

This, at any rate, was the Benedictine ideal. In an article focused on early Anglo-Saxon monastic experience, Catherine Cubitt paints an altogether more varied picture of monastic remembering. Strictly regulated incubators of holiness though they were designed to be, monasteries were living communities that could not in practice separate themselves entirely from the world around them. Individuals entered them at different stages of life (some as child oblates, some after active lives in the world outside) and attained different kinds of status within them, as well as exercising different functions (to do with the provision of food, for example) whose perform-ance gave them different working rhythms and may possibly have produced informal groupings which might have at least some rudiments of a separate mnemonic culture. The rhythms of litur-gical life dominated and co-ordinated the life of the community, but not to the complete exclusion of other experiences of tempo-rality. Relationships developed in the course of monastic training – between masters and pupils and among pupils themselves – that might again be important in shaping the way life in the community was remembered. Models of holiness were derived not just from sacred texts, but from the personal example of teachers and memories of earlier monastic leaders, so that the remembered pasts of monastic communities might themselves be a source of edification. Not all of monastic remembering, in short, was channelled through the regular liturgical disciplines of the community, or had sacred text as its immediate object, and even sacred texts themselves could be experienced in different social settings – through reading in the refectory as well as through liturgical performances. Text did not replace personal experience, Cubitt argues: rather, memories of the two were fused together.[69]

Where this example highlights the complex ways in which formal structures and informal relationships could interact in modelling the operations of social memory within relatively enclosed communities, the second – drawn from work on memory and redundancy in the modern computer industry by the sociologist Richard Sennett – explores some of the ways in which the social organization of memory may be affected by dramatic changes in the structuring of economic and social activity at a societal level. According to Sennett, the impact of new technologies of communication in the late twentieth century generated corporate structures that were geared, organizationally, less to monolithic durability than to adaptability in the face of shifting market forces. Rapid turnover of staff and of projects, organizational structures designed to facilitate rapid bouts of expansion or downsizing, flexible and geographically extended networks of contracting and employment based on the potential of the Internet, became the prevailing realities. One effect of this was to undermine traditional notions of the stable 'career' – the working life-time spent gradually acquiring seniority in the service of a single company, or at least in one profession or specialized branch of activity. Increasingly, the normal experience became one of frequent shifts in employment, periodic re-skilling or adaptation to new working structures, focus on short-term projects rather than long-term development, and endemic risk of redundancy or unemployment. Sennett argues that these changes in corporate structure and in working experience have had important (and, in his view, damaging) implications for the way memory functions in society. On the one hand, memory has become less and less an element in the organizational structures or value-systems of industrial corporations themselves: new-style companies simply are not organized in such a way as to cultivate traditions, to value loyalty and length of service, or to sustain a sense of company history. On the other hand, memory becomes more and more the means by which individuals struggle to achieve a stable sense of selfhood in a working world whose institutional frameworks no longer reliably support such a sense. Memory is privatized and individualized: it becomes 'like a form of private property, to be protected from challenge and conflict' – a kind of refuge from the competitive world of modern capitalism, rather than a means of confronting its realities.[70]

Whether or not one shares Sennett's conviction of the perniciousness of this turning-inwards of memory upon the subjective life of the individual, his account of the ways in which modern forms of capitalism structure remembering and forgetting offers insights whose relevance extends beyond the analysis of late capitalist society. It draws our attention to three things in particular. The first is that human institutions (or organized communities) possess widely varying kinds of mnemonic economy. The strength of memory within a particular group or institution – and the extent to which that group or institution actively cultivates and encourages a sense of its own past – are by no means a straightforward function of how long it has existed, or of how powerful or vigorous it is in its hold on the lives of its members. Some institutions channel power into promoting and focusing acts of remembering; others are relatively indifferent to them, or may even actively discourage them, or promote them very selectively.

Secondly, Sennett's analysis reminds us, institutions and their mnemonic cultures do not exist and evolve as isolated entities, but as part of the more general structuring of society, responsive to larger economic, social, political or cultural evolutions. Save in the rarest of circumstances, the significance of the ways in which memory is structured and managed within particular institutional or group frameworks is only likely fully to emerge when these are related to a larger picture. The strength and coherence of retrospective awareness within one group or institution may be connected to its weakness or lack of focus within another. Changes in a society's economic or political arrangements, or in its governing ideologies, may erode the mnemonic cultures previously operative in certain parts of its social and institutional structure, but may establish new concentrations of mnemonic activity in others.

Finally, Sennett's analysis reminds us of the complex relationship that exists between memory as a vehicle for conceptions of individual selfhood on the one hand, and the social and institutional framing of mnemonic activity on the other. Even memories strongly focused on self must be socially contextualized, for selfhood is not an immutable given: it has different meanings and different levels of importance under different conditions. The association of memory with an individual rather than a corporate kind of identity is itself a cultural variable, influenced by general social conditions; in some cases (as in Sennett's example), selfhood may seem to provide a focus for mnemonic activity developing outside the prevailing institutional structures of society; in others, where these structures provide clearer and stabler channels for mnemonic activity, memories that are personal in character may either seem less important, or be more closely interwoven with senses of collective identity.

Notes

1 Schrager, 'What is social in oral history?', p. 287.
2 Eakin, *How Our Lives Become Stories*, p. 75.
3 The formula is borrowed from Prager, *Presenting the Past*, pp. 70–89.
4 M. Bloch, *The Historian's Craft* (Manchester, 1992), p. 33.
5 M. Hirsch, *Family Frames: Photography, Narrative and Postmemory* (Cambridge, Mass., 1997), p. 22. For further discussion of 'second-generation' Holocaust memory, see A. Hass, *In the Shadow of the Holocaust: the Second Generation* (Cambridge, 1990); A. Karpf, *The War After: Living With the Holocaust* (London, 1996); T. Fox, *Inherited Memories: Israeli Children of Holocaust Survivors* (London and New York, 1999).
6 E. Zerubavel, *Social Mindscapes: an Invitation to Cognitive Psychology* (Cambridge, Mass., 1997), pp. 91–2.
7 C. Hill, 'The Norman Yoke', in C. Hill, *Puritanism and Revolution: Studies in the Interpretation of the English Revolution of the Seventeenth Century* (new edn., London, 1997), pp. 46–111.
8 For discussions of African-American memory, see, for example, G. Fabre and R. O'Meally (eds), *History and Memory in African-American Culture* (Oxford, 1994).
9 See, for example, Watson (ed.), *Memory, History and Opposition Under State Socialism*; S. Nuttall and C. Coetzee (eds), *Negotiating the Past: the Making of Memory in South Africa* (Cape Town, 1998).
10 K. Gergen, 'The social constructionist movement in modern psychology', in his *Refiguring Self and Psychology* (Dartmouth, 1993), p. 136; J. Shotter, 'Social accountability and the social construction of "you"', in J. Shotter and K. Gergen (eds), *Texts of Identity* (London, 1989), p. 137. See also J. Shotter, 'The social construction of

remembering and forgetting', in D. Middleton and D. Edwards (eds), *Collective Remembering* (London, 1990), pp. 120–38.

11 Shotter, 'Social accountability', p. 141.

12 S. Engel, *Context is Everything: the Nature of Memory* (New York, 1999, pp. 9, 19. See also, for example, J. Wertsch, *Voices of Collective Remembering* (Cambridge, 2002). For discussion of differing degrees of constructionist radicalism, see K. Gergen, 'The place of the psyche in a constructed world', in his *Social Construction in Context* (London, 2001), and for a useful survey and critical analysis of recent psychological approaches to the social and cultural aspects of remembering more generally, S. M. Weldon, 'Remembering as a social process', in D. Medin (ed.), *The Psychology of Learning and Motivation*, vol. 40 (San Diego, 2001), pp. 68–116.

13 P. Janet, *L'évolution de la mémoire et de la notion du temps* (Paris, 1928), pp. 181–390.

14 The account given here is indebted to the useful summary of this research (by two of the leading scholars in the field) in K. Nelson and R. Fivush, 'Socialization of memory', in Tulving and Craik (eds), *The Oxford Handbook of Memory*, pp. 283–96.

15 See, for example, R. Ely and A. McCabe, 'Gender differences in memories for speech', in S. Leydesdorff, L. Passerini and P. Thompson (eds), *Gender and Memory* (Oxford, 1996), pp. 17–29, a volume whose essays are valuable in exploring the gendered aspects of remembering from a variety of angles.

16 Engel, *Context is Everything*, pp. 9, 18.

17 On such issues see esp. A. Portelli, 'Research as an experiment in equality', in Portelli, *The Death of Luigi Trastulli*, pp. 29–44, and the essays in Part I of Portelli, *The Battle of Valle Giulia*.

18 D. Edwards and D. Middleton (eds), 'Joint remembering: constructing an experience through conversational discourse', *Discourse Processes* 9 (1986), pp. 423–59.

19 I. Bertaux-Wiame, 'The life history approach to the study of internal migration: how women and men came to Paris between the wars', in P. Thompson (ed.), *Our Common History: the Transformation of Europe* (London, 1982), pp. 192–3. The interactive setting of these interviews also, of course, includes Bertaux-Wiame herself as interviewer: had husband and wife been remembering things together without a third party, or had the interviewer been male rather than female, the tension of perspectives would no doubt still have been there, but might have worked itself out differently.

20 R. Thomas, 'Ancient Greek family tradition and democracy: from oral history to myth', in Samuel and Thompson (eds), *The Myths We Live By*, pp. 203–16.

21 M. Funck and S. Malinowski, 'Masters of memory: the strategic use of autobiographical memory by the German nobility', in Confino and Fritzshe (eds), *The Work of Memory*, pp. 86–103.

22 See, for example, P. Geary, *Phantoms of remembrance; Memory and Oblivion at the End of the First Millennium* (Princeton, 1994), pp. 115–33, on medieval monastic memory.

23 G. A. Fine, 'The Manson Family: the folklore traditions of a small group', *Journal of the Folklore Institute* 19:1 (1982), pp. 47–60.

24 G. A. Fine, 'Community and boundary: personal experience stories of mushroom collectors', *Journal of Folklore Research* 24:3 (1987), pp. 231–2.

25 B. Anderson, *Imagined Nations: Reflections on the Origins and Spread of Nationalism* (revised edn. London, 1991).

26 Karpf, *The War After*, p. 17.

27 J. Byng-Hall (interviewed by P. Thompson), 'The power of family myths', in Samuel and Thompson (eds), *The Myths We Live By*, pp. 216–24.

28 Polybius, *The Rise of the Roman Empire* (Harmondsworth, 1979), p. 347.

29 Quoted in A. Lillie, 'Memory of place: *luogo* and lineage in the fifteenth-century Florentine countryside', in G. Ciapelli and P. Rubin (eds), *Art, Memory, and Family in Renaissance Florence* (Cambridge, 2000), pp. 209–10.

30 Quoted in Funck and Malinowski, 'Masters of memory', p. 87.

31 See the classic study by F. Yates, *The Art of Memory* (Chicago, 1966).

32 Quoted in D. Bakhurst, 'Social memory in Soviet thought', in Middleton and Edwards (eds), *Collective Remembering*, p. 210.

33 See K. A. Hass, *Carried to the Wall: American Memory and the Vietnam Veterans Memorial* (Berkeley and Los Angeles, 1998).

34 See, for example, Le Goff, *History and Memory*, pp. 72–3.

35 Quoted in N. Wachtel, 'Remember and never forget', *History and Anthropology* 2 (1986), p. 312.

36 Ibid., pp. 308–18 (quotation p. 310). For more on these books, see J. Kugelmass and J. Boyarin (eds), *From a Ruined Garden* (New York, 1983).

37 Quoted in J. Damousi, *The Labour of Loss: Mourning, Memory and Wartime Bereavement in Australia* (Cambridge, 1999), p. 12.

38 T. Brown, *The Public Art of Civil War Commemoration: A Brief History With Documents* (Boston, Mass., 2004), p. 27.

39 H. James, *The American Scene* (London, 1907), p. 61.

40 Passerini, *Fascism in Popular Memory*, pp. 17–63.

41 Skultans, *The Testimony of Lives*, esp. ch. 10.

42 A. Fabian, *The Unvarnished Truth: Personal Narratives in Nineteenth-Century America* (Berkeley and Los Angeles, 2000).

43 R. Kluger, *Landscapes of Memory: a Holocaust Girlhood Remembered* (London, 2003), p. 23.

44 Ibid., p. 24.

45 C. Roden, *The Book of Jewish Food; an Odyssey from Samarkand and Vilna to the Present Day* (Harmondsworth, 1997), pp. 3–4.

46 Passage from Grant's journals (8 June 1845), quoted as preface to Grant, *Memoirs of a Highland Lady*.

47 Grant, *Memoirs of a Highland Lady*, pp. 24–5.

48 Bartlett, *Remembering*, p. 244.

49 Ibid., pp. 299–300, and 280–300 generally.

50 Ibid., p. 255.

51 Ibid., pp. 253–5.

52 Ibid., p. 257.

53 Ibid., pp. 264–6.

54 Ibid., pp. 268–80.

55 M. Halbwachs, *Les cadres sociaux de la mémoire* (Paris, 1994), chs. 1 (on dream) and 4 (on localization). Translations from Halbwachs here are my own, but references will be given to the abbreviated translation published as M. Halbwachs, *On Collective Memory*, L. Coser (ed.) (Chicago, 1992) (hereafter Coser).

56 Ibid., pp. 278–9 (Coser, p. 172–3).

57 Ibid., p. 98 (Passage not reproduced in Coser).

58 Ibid., p. 282 (Coser, p. 176).

59 M. Halbwachs, *La mémoire collective* (Paris, 1997). Again translations are my own, but references will also be given to the English-language translation: M. Halbwachs, *The Collective Memory*, with introduction by M. Douglas (New York, 1980) (hereafter Douglas), in which this passage is on p. 23.

60 See especially ibid., pp. 50–61 (Douglas, pp. 22–30).

61 Ibid., pp. 95–6 (Douglas, p. 49).

62 Ibid.

63 Halbwachs, *Les cadres sociaux*, p. viii (Coser, p. 40).

64 Ibid., p. 146 (Coser, p. 54).

65 Ibid., p. 290 (Coser, p. 183).

66 See chs. 4–5 of Halbwachs, *La mémoire collective*.

67 R. Bastide, 'Mémoire collective et sociologie du bricolage', *Année sociologique* (1970), pp. 65–108, esp. pp. 84–97 (quotations pp. 84–5, 91–2).

68 J. Coleman, *Ancient and Medieval Memories: Studies in the Reconstruction of the Past* (Cambridge, 1992), pp. 129–36.

69 C. Cubitt, 'Monastic memory and identity in early Anglo-Saxon England', in W. Frazer and A. Tyrell (eds), *Social Identity in Early Modern Britain* (London, 2000), pp. 253–76.

70 R. Sennett, 'Disturbing memories', in P. Fara and K. Patterson (eds), *Memory* (Cambridge, 1998), pp. 15–19, 23–5.

❦ 4 ❦

MEMORY AND
TRANSMISSION

The previous chapter explored the social and cultural dynamics of memory at a relatively localized level. Its concern was with how the mnemonic life of individuals is shaped by its immediate social contexts, and with how this shaping is related to the development and maintenance of mnemonic cultures in relatively small-scale social groups – families or monastic communities, rather than nations or the universal church. The next two chapters will broaden the perspective. How does knowledge of a larger social past take shape within society? How does some of this knowledge, shared and disseminated, come to be regarded as knowledge pertaining to specific kinds of corporate identity – the identity of nations, for example? How is the sense of such a large-scale corporate past publicly articulated, focused and organized, and how does its development intersect with the ways in which individuals and smaller groups within society remember and comprehend their own existences? Such questions may be posed in relation to any society whose forms of political and cultural organization are not confined to the kind of limits that allow its members to be constantly in direct social interaction with each other – but they take on a particular edge when we consider modern societies. The members of such societies are required, in active and continuous ways, to view themselves as participants in the larger community of the nation, which makes demands upon them both morally and institutionally, and which implicitly requires the subordination of other collective interests. What it means to be a member of such a national community – and how happy one feels about it – depends at least partly on how the nation's past as a continuous entity is imaginatively configured, for it is in the representation of a nation's past that people find the markers of its present identity and future prospects – of the heritages it transmits, the interests it embodies, the destiny that lies before it. For this reason among others, the nation as an 'imagined community' (in Benedict Anderson's sense) has been the primary focus of much of the recent literature that has focused on the 'production of the past' within human societies, – and it is with the modern nationalist forms of a sense of the past that my discussion in Chapter 5 will be largely concerned. The issues raised in the present chapter will, however, be ones that are relevant to the discussion not just of national, but of other forms of collective identity. These issues relate less to the politics of any particular past than to the broader cultural processes by which a sense of the past, of whatever kind, is made possible in human societies.

At a crude level, it may be asserted that events and experiences can find a lasting place in social memory to the extent that (i) human societies have developed communicative techniques that allow information to be transmitted over lengthy periods, and (ii) conceptions of collective identity have taken shape whose sustenance requires the support of organized accounts of collective past experience – especially, in the modern period, of a community's experience as a nation. Scholarly contributions to the study of social memory have tended, accordingly, to have two different kinds of focus. Some have focused essentially on issues of *transmission*, exploring the impact of different media of communication on the retention and formulation of past-related knowledge. Others have been concerned with issues of public *representation* – with analysing the cultural productions (texts, images, commemorations, etc.) through which specific understandings of a collective past have been articulated at particular historical moments, and with exploring the politics of this representational activity. The separation of my two chapters broadly replicates this division.

It is important, however, to stress the artificiality of such a separation. Any suggestion that the 'production of the past' has two neatly distinguishable phases – a phase of politically disinterested transmission, in which data enter circulation, followed by a phase of politically contentious representation in which they are arranged into ideologically resonant accounts of a collective past – can only be misleading. Contests of power and interest are woven into every phase and level of the social memory process. Access to the media through which transmission of information is effected, and motivation to use those media to influence the way the past can be viewed, are not evenly distributed within society. Peasant families, illiterate and preoccupied with the daily struggle for survival, have less opportunity to transmit information to posterity, and less reason to wish to do so, than do aristocratic families or monastic establishments that command the services of scribes and that are concerned to ensure the perpetuity of claims to property or social status. Without education and financial or material resources, archives cannot be organized, and Kirk Savage correctly observes that 'public monuments do not arise as if by natural law to celebrate the deserving: they are built by people with sufficient power to marshal (or impose) public consent to their erection'.[1] In any given situation, the messages that are transmitted across generations will disproportionately reflect and promote the interests of certain groups in society.

The channelling and framing of information about the past is also often closely connected to processes of institutional development. J. G. A. Pocock has argued that the development of a human knowledge of the past is rooted in the processes by which people become aware of structural continuities in the way certain kinds of social activity are organized. A person engaged in such activities develops, according to Pocock, 'a particular image of the past, in the form of a projection into it of the continuity with which he is associated, and a particular conception of the way in which its continuity in the past authorizes or otherwise ensures its continuity in the present and future'. Thus, for example, the lawyer becomes aware of a structured history of legal decision making; a member of a powerful family becomes aware of the ancestry that is the guarantee of present and future status.[2] For Pocock, in other words, a socially rooted interest in the past is shaped, at least initially, around the need to sustain the viability and the legitimacy of specific institutionally structured projects. Institutional development is usually a development in the way power is organized and exercised in some area of a society's activities, or possibly in society generally. Bureaucracies arise, one of whose functions is to develop and transmit and articulate the historical knowledge which both advances and legitimates their own activities. The development of such institutional and bureaucratic structures – be they secular or ecclesiastical, governmental or legal – can indeed be instrumental in producing shifts in the way information passes within society more generally, and in the credit that is attached to information coming from different sources. Michael Clanchy has shown, for example, how the transition from [orally transmitted] 'memory to written record' in medieval England was driven by the evolving needs of the royal judicial and administrative system. One of the effects of the transition was to loosen the connections between the legal process and ordinary people's sense of community. 'The remembered past is unobjective', Clanchy writes, 'but it is meaningful and valid to more people because they participate in its transmission'. By shifting credit from a past that was retained in the minds of ordinary people to one that had to be anchored in written documentation, the agents of royal authority enhanced the power and prestige of their own bureaucratic operations, and began to separate the accredited public perception of a collective past from the mnemonic processes of individuals and local communities.[3] The operations of power leave their mark not just on the representations of the past that are produced within society, but on the social relationships that govern transmission.

Even at a purely conceptual level, anyway, it is scarcely possible to keep the notions of 'transmission' and 'representation' neatly separate. Representations of the past, in text, image or performance, are integrally part of processes of transmission, for any such representation is simultaneously the expression of a current understanding of the past (which must be understood in relation to present political and cultural needs), and a link in the chain of communications by which information which will be available for incorporation into future representations is passed on to further recipients. The same is not, perhaps, so clearly true the other way round, for while there is no doubt a sense in which every communication of data involves an act of representation, much of this representational activity, as it occurs in the course of everyday life, is geared to purposes that do not specifically require the formulation of an understanding of the past as such. The information transmitted in such cases is presented not as information 'about the past' but as information relating to present concerns and transactions. The preservation and transmission of this information is presumably motivated by the assumption that it will be useful in the future, but this need not be an assumption that it will be useful essentially in helping people to formulate a view of what will by then be the past. Only retrospectively, and through a crucial shift of perspective, does anybody come to think of this information as 'belonging to the past', and hence as useful in constructing representations of which the past of a given community or social formation is the essential object. Alongside the transmission of this information, however, there may well be a transmission of information that is already structured as knowledge 'about the past' (or which, although still structured ostensibly as information about what is going on in the present, is clearly presented with a view to influencing the ways in which present events will be incorporated into the accounts of the past that are formulated at a later moment). In most cases, it is information packaged in this way that provides the initial working templates within which larger assemblages of data come to be organized into the broader understandings of the collective past that are current at any given moment.

Under the general heading of transmission, it is helpful to distinguish *tradition* from *communication*, the former involving a transmission of habits through repetitive practice, the latter a transmission of ideas or information through the use of spoken or written language, of visual imagery, or of other systems of communicative signs (music, gesture, morse code, etc.). Like many of the distinctions drawn in this book, this one is not absolute: any tradition requires there to be some communication, and any system of communication requires a certain level of traditional practice in order to be effective. Yet, while the two terms should not be taken as standing for mutually exclusive patterns of behaviour, the distinction between them can helpfully draw attention to variations in the way transmission is effected, between individuals and between generations.

Tradition

In tradition, the connections that are established between generations, or between earlier and later moments in a society's existence, are supplied by continuities of practice – by people, whether unconsciously or deliberately, taking the way things have been done before as the effective model for their own activity. What constitutes tradition is not so much the total absence of change – societies are never completely static and even the most traditional patterns of behaviour evolve slowly over time – as the close relationship between knowledge and repetitive practice. The knowledge which is present in tradition is not knowledge of a past that is felt to be conceptually and cognitively separated from the present, but the knowledge of established and inherited ways of doing things – a working knowledge grounded in practical experience, rather than in feats of intellectual representation.

Practice is often physical as well as mental. Traditional knowledge is therefore often, in a literal sense, embodied knowledge – knowledge rooted in the body's habituation to particular postures or patterns of movement. A former brickworker in an Ulster village, describing the working practices of his trade to a visiting ethnographer, resorts (even though bedridden) to a kind of physical re-enactment:

> 'And there was a way of turnin it. You shoved it in like that, do ye see, and just turned it over nicely.'
>   Mr. Boyle rams the short shovel into the pudding of clay and gracefully, slowly turns his wrists, revolving a shaft of air above the bedclothes. His memory is banked in specific gestures and words. Repeating the motions of work, his body releases its remembrance into his mind, and as he repeats the industry's technical terms, associations form within and a full, textured memory spreads outward from points of detail.[4]

Physical movements, here, are not merely illustrative of what is being remembered and described for the ethnographer's benefit; they are integral to the very process of recollection.

Habit, whether physical or mental, lies at the core of tradition. Paul Connerton helpfully outlines the difference between habit and simple disposition:

> The term disposition suggests something latent or potential, something which requires a positive stimulus outside ourselves for it to become actively engaged. The term habit conveys the sense of operativeness, of a continuously practised activity. It conveys the fact of exercise, the reinforcing effect of repeated acts.[5]

Once a way of doing things becomes habitual, the performance of the requisite actions no longer depends on a recollection of the occasions on which these actions were first performed: knowledge and memory become procedural rather than episodic. Habit in the strict sense, however, is limited to the lives of individuals. The apparent transfer of habit from one generation to another which constitutes tradition occurs when social conditions and mechanisms exist which allow successive generations somehow to ground the patterns of activity that become habitual for them in the modes of practice that are already habitual for the generations that precede them. Tradition always involves an element of learning: traditional skills and techniques cannot simply be inherited in their fully developed form, but have to be acquired afresh by each new practitioner. In traditional learning, however, the communication of knowledge remains closely connected to a context of existing practice: one absorbs what one needs to be a carpenter by watching other carpenters and by practising under their initial guidance, not by reading manuals of instruction or attending theoretical lectures.

Tradition works through normativity, through routine, through the conforming of individual behaviour to socially prescribed patterns. The sense of the past that it generates is less a perception of historical change, than a feeling of temporal depth rooted in continuities of practical experience. But tradition is not to be understood as mindless persistence. Generally, it involves at least a measure of social reverence – a disposition to value, rather than simply to repeat, the ways of one's ancestors or the established usages of one's community. Even in prehistoric communities, the archaeologist Richard Bradley has suggested, people 'did not make artefacts or build structures according to a traditional format because they were unable to think of anything else', but rather as a purposeful 'way of adhering to tradition and maintaining links with what they knew of their past'.[6] To say that the social mechanisms of tradition minimize discontinuities between past and present is not to say that they leave no room for any kind of supposedly retrospective knowledge: myths of origin, genealogies, and bodies of ancestral legend, transmitted from generation to generation, may play an important part in legitimizing, and therefore in sustaining, traditional arrangements and behaviours. The communication of such bodies of knowledge may, however, itself often be enacted through ritualized social practices that are themselves notably traditional in character: religious ceremonies, ritual dance, recitations of epic poetry. In such cases, tradition and communication are fused together: a single performance serves both to articulate and to transmit significant knowledge of symbolic figures and moments in a group's collective past, and to sustain the members of that group in their sense of being members of a community that is constituted and held together by patterns of traditional practice.

Media of communication

If tradition transmits knowledge along the connecting lines of a continuous context of social practice, the media of communication make it possible for mental data to pass from one such context to another. Through the processes of externalization, data acquire the potential to outlive the practical and experiential settings that have produced them; their distribution comes to depend at least as much on the practical robustness of the media of communication themselves as on any general continuity in social habits and social relationships. They become, in a sense, detachable commodities, available to be combined with materials of different origin in fresh packages of knowledge appropriate to different situations.

Here, we must add a further duality in culture's mnemonic operations to the three (internal/external, public/private, storage/memorialization) that were referred to in the previous chapter: by externalizing remembered data, culture makes that data available both for *dissemination* and for *concentration*. On the one hand, that is to say, they allow particular items of data to be circulated or separately communicated to a potential multitude of different recipients, and to be lodged in different locations; on the other, they allow data originating in different places or at different moments or in different remembering minds to be brought together in a single location. Often, of course, movements of these two different kinds are closely and systemically connected: modern print culture, for example, pulls data from different sources together into books, which it then disseminates in mass-produced form to different locations, in at least some of which these books are then concentrated in libraries or collections. Indeed, if one treats individual minds (as well as things such as libraries, archives, museums, collections, books, newspapers) as places where data drawn from different sources are brought together, it makes sense to say that any dissemination of data (or of objects encapsulating data) that is not completely abortive involves the distribution of that data to different points of concentration.

Thinking about the different implications of dissemination and concentration for the survival and transmission of data (or of objects encapsulating data) is nevertheless a useful way of starting to think about the contributions which different media of communication may make to the processes by which a knowledge and

sense of the past are developed within human societies. Dissemination increases the chances that data have of surviving by multiplying the social locations in which they will have to be eliminated (whether through coercion or through natural wastage) if they are to disappear entirely. How effectively this protects them in practice depends on other factors: societies that have a highly developed capacity for dissemination may also, after all, have developed a culture of discardability – of junk mail, of deleted e-mails, of disposable nappies and cardboard coffee cups. In practice, survival may depend at least as much on concentration. In practice, the long-term survival of data tends to depend on some combination of dissemination and concentration, and can in some cases be assured for a time by concentration alone – as when a piece of information is preserved only in a given document within a given archive. By assembling data or materials in a given location, concentration allows them in many cases to be more effectively protected from decay or random destruction (though disasters such as that of the library of Alexandria remind us that it may also, in some cases, expose a host of materials to a single destructive blow). Equally importantly, however, concentration allows the data (or objects) that are concentrated to be given durable structural interconnections, of a kind that may facilitate their survival, not as random elements, but as a coherent complex (an archive, an ordered collection, an organized body of knowledge), designed perhaps to answer specific social or institutional needs.

Most of human communication is not, of course, geared to the intended production of long-term effects. The practicalities of day-to-day social and economic exchanges require modes of communication that are fluid and improvisational: conversation works best when we do not always seek to make our utterances sententiously memorable. Most conversational exchanges (and most quickly-scribbled notes and e-mails) are swiftly forgotten, and few people see any social tragedy in so much forgetting. Sometimes, of course, the materials of conversational exchange do achieve a wider dissemination: rumours of a dramatic, threatening or scandalous event can travel rapidly along multiple lines of social exchange, mobilizing or terrorizing substantial numbers of individuals in a short period, as happened for example with the rumours of brigandage and aristocratic plotting that swept parts of the French countryside in the *grande peur* of 1789.[7] The mechanisms of conversational exchange are, however, seldom very effective at ensuring the build-up of data from one generation to another: for this, a more definite structural patterning, either of the social relationships that give direction to communication, or of the way the data are themselves organized, appears necessary.

In some cases, for example, aspects of the way a society is socially organized may provide specific occasions or structured settings that regularly promote or facilitate the transgenerational communication of ideas, information and attitudes. Marc Bloch drew attention, for example, to the conservative inflection which he claimed was imparted to the mental training of children by the standard patterns of work in peasant societies:

> Because working conditions keep the mother and father away almost all day, the young children are brought up chiefly by their grand-parents. Consequently, with the molding of each new mind, there is a backward step, joining the most malleable to the most inflexible mentality, while skipping that generation which is the sponsor of change. There is small room for doubt that this is the source of that traditionalism inherent in so many peasant societies.[8]

While Bloch's emphasis here is on the transmission of traditionalist attitudes rather than of specific bodies of information, the structuring of intergenerational relations that he refers to might also shape and facilitate the latter form of transmission. Similar opportunities for the conversational mentoring of younger by older members may be found in many other patterns of social existence.

Despite such opportunities, societies or communities that are pre-eminently dependent on oral exchange for the passage of information from generation to generation tend to experience a fairly continuous turnover of transmitted information. Those who have studied such societies have generally drawn a significant distinction between the relatively detailed knowledge that may be possessed of things falling within 'living memory' (commonly defined as the combined memory spans of the generations with which those living at a given moment have themselves come into contact) and the much sparser awareness that is generally possessed of things or people belonging to earlier periods. The practical extent of 'living memory' obviously depends on a variety of demographic and social factors, including life expectancy, parental age at childbirth, and geographical mobility. Within the limits set by these factors, information about the past can be transmitted with the authority of personal experience; the receipt of it can be strengthened by the kinds of affective engagement that come from personal acquaintance with the person imparting it; the information can be linked by both giver and receiver to issues of genuine common interest; and those who impart the information can be interrogated, encouraged, pressed for further detail by those to whom it is communicated: information is therefore more likely to be retained, and more likely to be evoked in the context of current activities and concerns, than is the case with information relating to earlier periods. In many social situations, therefore, and not only in societies that are predominantly illiterate, the edge of living memory has been, for most practical purposes, the horizon of any detailed awareness of a collective past. Emmanuel Le Roy Ladurie found that the inhabitants of the village of Montaillou around 1320 whose conversations were reported in Inquisition records had information on nothing before the lifetime of their previous feudal lord,[9] while Françoise Zonabend found in the third quarter of the twentieth century that the inhabitants of Minot in Burgundy gave no sign of having any knowledge of particular events in the life of the village between its alleged foundation by the ancient Gauls and the time of their own grandfathers. Their awareness of the intervening period was apparently reducible to the perception of a seemingly undifferentiated traditional continuity:

> 'People in the old days did it by tradition. . . . Our grandfathers knew the custom' . . . Tradition, custom, two terms which have the same value as reference and describe ways of speech and action which can as easily belong to a distant past as to a living person's life span. In this way all evocation of the past gives the impression of having actually been witnessed. It is immersed in the same time-flow and refers to one time, that of the community.[10]

The inhabitants of Minot contrasted this seamless continuity of the past with the dramatic changes that had overtaken village society in their own lifetimes. Indeed, the unspecific character of their awareness of even relatively recent periods of collective history may well be attributable partly to the way in which the post-war transformation of village society destroyed some of the more obvious channels for transgenerational communication: it was around 1950, for example, that the grandparent-centred patterns of child-rearing to which Marc Bloch drew attention gave way to ones in which parents were the central figures, and that the practice of holding *veillées* (evening gatherings that were an occasion for older inhabitants to hold forth on old times in the presence of the young) was abandoned in Minot itself. Without such facilitating structures, the limitations of ordinary verbal exchange as a means of passing information across generations were all the more starkly revealed.

To draw attention to these limitations is not, however, to deny that oral communication can be effective in conveying bodies of mental data across a succession of generations: examples abound of myths, legends, fairy-stories, folktales and other bodies of material that have been sustained over centuries largely through oral transmission. For this to happen, however, the data in question have to be structurally organized for memorability, in a way that removes them from the ordinary ebb-and-flow of conversational communication. Perhaps the most universal way of making mental data durably memorable is through narrative organization. As Fentress and Wickham put it, 'a story is a sort of natural container for memory; a way of sequencing a set of images, through logical and semantic connections, into a shape which is, itself, easy to retain in memory' – in effect, 'a large-scale *aide-mémoire*'.[11] The presentation of ideas or information in narrative form confers memorability partly through the dramatic sequences and relationships that are established within the story itself, and partly through the story's relationship to conventions of genre that are culturally familiar. But narrativization is also an inherently selective process: data that cannot readily be assimilated to the narrative structures that are adopted get 'filtered out in transmission'.[12]

Casting mental materials as a story enhances their chances of being passed from generation to generation. Where reliance is on orality alone, however, the maintenance and reproduction of a story is itself a complex mnemonic exercise, requiring the active participation of each of the minds through which the story passes. Patterns of rhyme and metre, formulaic phraseology, assonance and alliteration, arrangement of stanzas, cadence and intonation, have all been important elements in the mnemonic techniques that specialists in story-telling (be they bards or epic poets or ballad singers) have made use of in composing and reproducing complex and extended oral narratives.[13] Where the art of memory of the rhetoricians trained its practitioners to tag the materials they wished to remember internally, in the techniques of oral epic poetry, the tagging is itself externalized: the mnemonic devices that permit a narrative to be orally reproduced and communicated are built into the narrative itself as compositional features. As Fentress and Wickham put it, 'from the smallest poetic units to the largest, from the basic auditory structure to the syntax and the structure of meaning, the form of poetry in oral societies is ordered so as continually to provide the reciting poet with signposts showing him the way to proceed'.[14] By grasping and working within the set patterns and operating constraints of a particular genre of composition, oral practitioners such as those who transmitted the Homeric epics or the medieval 'Song of Roland' were able to reproduce and communicate impressively substantial bodies of narrative in relatively stable form. As Parry and Lord showed long ago in their work on South Slav epic poetry, the reproduction in question was not a verbatim recollection based on rote memorization; rather, each successive oral performance would have involved a complex combination of remembering and composition, with recollected details finding their appropriate narrative places through a kind of structured improvisation.[15] Each recitation of an epic would no doubt have differed from earlier ones in points of verbal detail, but the reproduction of basic compositional features would have allowed stories to retain a certain continuity of shape and meaning across numerous recitations.

Not all orally transmitted stories necessarily require such elaborate feats of mnemonic organization. Family myths and other items of group-specific folklore can sometimes possess a kind of anecdotal brevity that allow them to be retained and transmitted with relatively little technical effort. Here again, however, oral transmission has, over time, a tendency to modify what it communicates. Stories that survive from generation to generation tend to be refined and simplified: details which seemed important in the early stages of a story's transmission – the precise locations and timings of particular events, for example – get omitted, while elements that seem more continuously meaningful become more salient. Specificity yields to mythic resonance, and often to a kind of generic recognizability. While family stories, for example, will still have details that are specific to particular families, their tendency to deal with concerns that are common to many families – issues of origin and inheritance, conflict and community, fortune and misfortune, shame and honour – makes it unsurprising that they seem at times to draw on a common stock of narrative motifs. Folklorists studying American culture have, for example, noted the common occurrence of certain types of 'family misfortune story' (relating to loss of inheritance or squandering of opportunity) or courtship narrative, while a study of memory in families descended from slaves in Brazil refers to the similar appearance, in different family traditions, of stories of enforced marriages between young female slaves and elderly enslaved men.[16]

The importance of oral transmission is by no means confined to societies in which the techniques of literacy are undeveloped, or are confined to a small sector of the population. Even in societies that are heavily dependent on reading and writing, much of day-to-day communication is oral, and orality has a vital role in commenting on, interpreting, debating and adapting the messages that are proffered in written text. Scholars have become increasingly disinclined to draw rigid distinctions between 'oral' and 'literate' realms of culture, and inclined rather to explore the ways in which orality and literacy are interconnected.[17] Yet, while we must avoid too crude a model of the transition from a culture of orality to one of literacy, there is no doubt that the availability of written text as a medium of communication has transformative effects on the ways in which knowledge relating to the past is formulated and transmitted within human societies, and that the effects of this transformation are carried further as skills and habits of literacy are carried beyond a specialized elite, and as societies develop increasingly sophisticated networks and technologies of textual production and dissemination. The present discussion is not the place to review the enormous literatures in disciplines such as history and anthropology that have explored the social and cultural impact of literacy and of print culture: a few points only will be highlighted.

By fixing messages or information in textual form, writing gives these mental data an objective existence outside the minds that formulate them. This has four kinds of effect. The first is simply to make possible the formulation and transmission of more complex, more fluid and ramified bodies of ideas or information. The ability to write things down frees people from the need to concentrate, at every moment in the formulation of ideas which are to be transmitted, on the primary practicality of shaping those ideas in a readily memorable form. Since not everything must be constantly held in memory, individuals can more easily assemble ideas and information from a range of sources, can arrange them in new and experimental combinations, and can formulate them with a degree of abstraction or structural uncertainty that would be impossible in a purely oral culture. Instead of having to be continuously encapsulated in memorable formulae, understandings of the world or of the past of one's community can be articulated diffusely, with a wealth of detail that is not always firmly held in place by mnemonic structures. Since it is possible to hold on to more information, there is also not the same necessity as there is under conditions of orality to strip what is to be remembered down to what is obviously functionally relevant to present concerns. Oral societies, remarks Ong, 'live very much in a present which keeps itself in equilibrium [. . .] by sloughing off memories which no longer have present relevance': thus, in a well-known example, the genealogies that are transmitted among the Tiv of Nigeria are continually adjusted to fit the present social relationships that they serve to support.[18] In more literate societies, information that is redundant in terms of immediate need may have a greater chance of survival.

Secondly, literacy establishes new possibilities of reference. Most obviously, it introduces the concept of a record, as something distinct from a memory. Under conditions of orality, episodes in the past are knowable only by interrogating the memories of living individuals, who either remember the episodes or remember hearing about them from others. Information held in memory is the only form of evidence, and the only way of testing or questioning evidence is to compare one person's memory with that of others. Since there is no idea of an external record to which present recollections can be compared, there is no way of checking the reworking of the past that goes on as memories evolve and pass from one generation to another. 'In this environment', writes Michael Clanchy, 'historical facts are hard to grasp, and harder to transmit in their original form from one generation to the next. The memory, whether individual or collective, tends continually to transform the information it receives.' Furthermore, as Clanchy points out, once episodes have passed out of memory, there is, in an illiterate society, no way of recapturing them and reincorporating them into society's historical vision.[19] Nor, finally, do societies without written records have obvious means of developing a linear and graduated chronological understanding of the past: once events have passed beyond the edge of living memory, the connections that are established between them are likely to be based less on a sense of precise chronology than on relationships of meaning perceived from a present standpoint. The introduction of written text modifies this situation in several important ways. By giving stable definition and material longevity to the view of an event that is formulated at a particular moment, written texts constitute a record of that event that can be 'referred back to', thus allowing the representations of the past that are contained in memory to be tested against an apparently stable external standard. It also becomes possible, at least in principle, for events that have passed out of memory to be recovered through the rediscovery of written records. In short, the durability of written text tends to encourage a conceptual separation of historical knowledge from memory's continuous workings. One effect of this is to replace the constantly updated past of oral tradition with a past that (in Ong's words), is 'felt as an itemized terrain, peppered with verifiable and disputed "facts" or bits of information'.[20] The durability of text, and the increasing facility with which the new technologies of printing allow it to be copied and therefore consulted simultaneously by different people, introduce new concepts of accuracy in the transmission of mental data from generation to generation: the structured improvisations of the oral poet yield to the meticulous copyism of the scribe (and in due course to the mechanical reproductive accuracy of the printing press, of the photocopier, of the fax machine). Mere memory comes to seem vague and unstable: notions of evidence, authority, truthfulness, authenticity are re-focused on the seemingly tangible stability and objectivity of written text.

Thirdly, by freeing the storage and the concentration of information from their heavy dependence on the mnemonic and organizational capacity of individual minds, writing dramatically increases the possibilities of storage that societies and individuals may have available. It becomes possible to archivize material systematically for future use. Archivization embodies not simply a basic possibility of accumulation that is not present in purely oral cultures, but also new possibilities of organization – material can be catalogued, arranged in sequences and thematic patterns that are geared to a range of institutional projects, rather than simply to the immediate need for mnemonic retention. Information that is stored can also be brought together at later stages in combinations that were not originally envisaged: it becomes a flexible resource, through which the past can be continually re-investigated and re-interpreted.

Fourthly, by allowing data to be communicated by means other than face-to-face exchange, writing enhances and streamlines the possibilities of dissemination. Written messages can be transmitted over substantial distances and across significant periods of time without having to pass through numerous intermediaries, each of whom may modify the message in transit. To the extent that text can be copied, furthermore, the same data can be communicated simultaneously to different audiences and placed in concentrated storage in different physical locations. Here, of course, the effects of a shift towards literacy were massively reinforced by the development and spread of printing. Literacy and printing together have the effect not only of spreading information more widely, but also of dramatically transforming the social experiences of transmission and reception. The immediate interpersonal communications in particular social contexts that govern oral transmission are replaced by a state of affairs in which information is decontextualized, and framed for communication to an abstract audience whose individual members may have direct contact neither with the author nor with each other.[21] Texts become points of focus for 'textual communities'[22] defined by their absorption and interpretation of particularly bodies of textual material. The formation of such textual communities may also, in the long run, contribute to the development of new kinds of cultural and even political identity, which in turn supply a focus for particular formations of past-related knowledge.[23]

In the last couple of centuries, further waves of new technology – photography, telegraphy, telephony, recording, radio, film, television, computers and the internet – have further transformed the ways in which information circulates and the potential it has for passing from one generation to another. The impact of these technologies has been various. Some have worked primarily to enhance the possibilities of storage, and to accelerate or make more flexible the ways in which stored data can be organized, processed and analysed. Others have worked primarily to improve the speed and to multiply the directions of communications, allowing messages to be circulated and exchanged – in some cases with almost instantaneous effect – within ever-expanding networks of social connection. Like the onset of literacy and of print, such technologies have, in transforming the modalities of communication, also had the effect of grouping people in new virtual communities, either of consumers (viewers, listeners) or of active participants, defined by their relationship to particular channels or flows of information. Through the continuing development of technology, and of the social relationships that are developed through its use, the production of potential ingredients for long-term patterns of social memory formation continues to evolve.

Material and environmental aspects

It is important also to attend to the material and environmental aspects of social memory processes. Oral and written communications take place in physical settings, and an interaction with those settings, and with the objects that are part of them, is frequently part of the way in which messages about the past are received. Indeed written texts are themselves generally presented as material objects – books, letters, inscriptions, etc. – whose materiality as well as whose textual content may be significant in the process of transmission. A family bible, for example, bears the messages of religion and sacred history that are inscribed in it as writing, but may also, as a physical object, serve as a reminder of past family members or occasions.

A wide variety of different kinds of objects assist remembering, and thus contribute, directly or indirectly, to the processes by which data and ideas are passed from generation to generation. Some are specifically designed to fulfil such a mnemonic or information-bearing function; others, designed for other purposes, acquire such functions more inadvertently, coming into the category of 'objects around which remembrance accrues through contextual association'.[24] Some function as mnemonic prompters which assist individuals in recalling and reproducing specific kinds of information: thus the Maori use knotched staves to assist their genealogical recitations,[25] while the court spokesman of the Asante uses the ceremonial stools of earlier rulers, with their associated objects, as the focus for narrations of dynastic history.[26] Such objects may be significant, however, not simply for the mechanical assistance they provide in recitation, but for the symbolic link that they establish to the past that is being recalled.

In other cases, objects offer an assistance in processes of individual remembering that is less formally structured, and that derives rather from the mental associations that have been formed between particular objects and particular moments, people or places in the individual's past experience. A souvenir from a childhood holiday may evoke memories both of place and of occasion, and of childhood more generally; a photograph album may help in ordering memories of people or phases in remembered existence. In these cases, the mnemonic effect is at least partially pre-intended, but memories can also be triggered by objects – items of clothing, utensils, trinkets, pieces of jewellery – that have no formally inbuilt memorializing or commemorative function, but that are simply capable, when encountered in certain circumstances, of activating certain recollections. In 'memory involving things', as Alan Radley remarks, there is usually a certain mixture of intentional and fortuitous connections.[27]

The mnemonic effects of objects may be confined to the life and consciousness of an individual but they may also – as in the case of public monuments – be intended to be more general, and may come – as in the case of monuments, but also possibly of other less formally commemorative artefacts – to have an influence that is transgenerational. Portraits and heirlooms and saintly relics are obvious examples of objects that may pass from one generation to another within a group or community, offering regular 'reminders' of people or moments in that group's past, and hence also of the group's own continuous existence. The ability of objects to 'carry memory' from one generation to another depends, of course, on their being commented on and interpreted, for the mnemonic meaning of objects is not intrinsic to the objects, but is a social construction. In some cases, objects like monuments or heirlooms carry their own commentary with them, in the form of written inscriptions which identify the things to which the object refers, or which comment on its production and transmission. Thus, a funerary monument may bear an inscription which names the deceased and comments on his estimable qualities, and perhaps on the mnemonic mood that has caused the monument to be erected by his widow or colleagues or descendants. In other cases, the mnemonic significance of an object is established only by oral communications which occur as it is passed from generation to generation. But though their status as mnemonic markers may have to be periodically reasserted, physical objects can help to keep an awareness of the past – or of certain points of reference in the past – alive without the need for endless portentous announcements: their very presence as familiar elements in people's day-to-day material surroundings serves to prevent the elements of the past with which they are associated from 'falling out of mind'.

Objects are themselves environmental features: their significance is tied up not just with their materiality, but with their spatial arrangement, and with the ways in which this arrangement is connected to structured experiences of living in particular physical and social settings. The mnemonic functions of a portrait, for example, depend not simply on its ability to remind the viewer of the particular past individual who is represented, but on the ways in which it is hung – its relationships to other similar images (for example in a chronological series indicative of patrilineal descent within a particular family, or in a collection commemorating the successive holders of a particular office), and the ways these images are encountered as people move through or occupy space (their concentration in certain rooms of the house, their sequential arrangement, etc.).

Like textual messages, indeed, material objects are subject to rhythms of concentration and dissemination that can enhance and modify their mnemonic potential. The very act of collecting and arranging certain objects together – as in a museum, for example – can be the thing that is decisive in making those objects the vehicle of a historical message. In her study of nineteenth-century German collecting, Susan Crane quotes an address to the Oberlausitz Academy of Science in 1829 about one such project of collection:

> so long as these Denkmäler remain disparate and dispersed as mere curiosities, they will be threatened by neglect and even destruction. United in a collection, they receive a greater value and will become instructive, inasmuch as they place the olden times and conditions of our nation before our eyes and under our attentive observation, actively report on them, and bring new light to those earlier cultural conditions, morals and habits.[28]

Mnemonic significance may become attached, in such cases, not just to the objects that are gathered together, but to the physical or architectural space in which they are grouped and arranged – the museum, the archive, the library, the public square in which statues are displayed.

But the dissemination of objects can also generate new kinds of mnemonic significance. When stones from the dismantled Bastille were carried, at the instigation of the revolutionary entrepreneur Palloy, as a gift to each French *département* (and smaller ones crafted as tablets engraved with the Declaration of the Rights of Man and of the Citizen to each administrative district), the aim was to give each corner of provincial France its physical reminder, both of the royal despotism of which the Bastille had become the symbol, and of the symbolic moment of liberation that its destruction represented.[29] The global distribution of bits of the Berlin Wall after its destruction, though more haphazard and commercialistic, achieved arguably similar mnemonic effects.[30] Distributions of objects carrying associations with places of religious pilgrimage, or of mass-produced commemorative objects such as medallions or commemorative mugs, can also be instrumental in giving particular references to the past a widespread currency, and in developing social networks around them.

Translocations of objects through concentration and dissemination are part, but only part, of the creation of what we may call a mnemonic environment.[31] A mnemonic environment is not necessarily – or usually – an environment constructed purely and intentionally for the purposes of remembering; what is meant is rather the general environment in which people live in a particular time and place, envisaged in terms of its mnemonic functions. As in the case of objects, the mnemonic functions of a lived environment are usually a mixture of ones that have been deliberately contrived, and ones which have arisen without formal planning. Mnemonic significance may be concentrated in formal symbolic features – like monumental complexes – that have been artificially inscribed on the landscape with a specific memorializing intention. But it may also be laid on the landscape diffusely and informally. Any landscape, whether 'natural' or 'artificial', within which social activity is conducted over a period of time, will tend to develop mnemonic connotations of an associative kind for those who live in it: contemplation of particular places brings back memories of things that happened there or people who lived there. At their most informal, these associations exist only in individual minds.

Sometimes, however, they are shared and externalized, preserved in oral story-telling or the names that are given to particular locations (Dye's Meadow, Brick Kiln Wood, Harper's Ferry) – and thus acquire a measure of transgenerational durability.

The investing and perceiving of mnemonic significance in environmental or topographic features is a fluid and complex business – a matter at least as much of use as of original intention. Distinctions between what is 'natural' and what is artificially constructed are not necessarily decisive here. Richard Bradley has drawn attention, for example, not just to the artificial monumental constructions of which prehistoric societies were capable, but also to the ways in which natural landscape features (rocks, caves, springs, rivers etc.) could be constituted through social practice as loci of mnemonic significance.[32] History happens, furthermore, in ordinary places, and by happening there can sometimes transform mundane topographic features into shrines laden with mnemonic significance. The execution of the last resisting fighters of the Paris Commune of 1871 in the corner of the cemetery of Père Lachaise transforms an unremarkable wall into the Mur des Fédérés, a focal point of commemorative piety for the French Left. In other cases, archaeological sites may be invested with a similar kind of 'monumental' significance.[33]

Mnemonically significant sites can also, however, possess a range of non-mnemonic uses: churches or civic monuments stuffed with commemorative sculpture serve as meeting places and centres for commercial activity. Sometimes, indeed, a coupling of mnemonic and non-mnemonic functions is part of an original commemorative intention, as when, for example, a war memorial takes the form of a public garden, or streets of terraced housing bear the names of military victories. The mnemonic crafting of the environment intersects constantly with its other aspects.

Mnemonic environments are things people inhabit, things with which they enter into habitual relations. They are things people move through or around in, sometimes ceremonially, sometimes with mundane purposefulness, sometimes casually, sometimes speculatively or questingly. Sometimes mnemonic experience is the point of the movement, sometimes merely a side-effect; sometimes it is carefully organized, sometimes merely random; sometimes it is focused on collective activities in a deliberately public setting, sometimes it is idiosyncratically personal. But the experience of living in such environments and of engaging with their stimuli remains, along with the experiences of oral and of textual communication and reception, a vital part of social memory's continuously unfolding processes.

Notes

1 K. Savage, 'The politics of memory: black emancipation and the Civil War monument', in J. Gillis (ed.), *Commemorations: the Politics of National Identity* (Princeton, 1994), p. 135.

2 J. G. A. Pocock, 'The origins of study of the past: a comparative approach', *Comparative Studies in Society and History* 4:2 (1962), pp. 211–13.

3 M. Clanchy, 'Remembering the past and the good old law', *History* 55 (1970), pp. 165–76 (quotation, p. 176); and more generally M. Clanchy, *From Memory to Written Record, England 1066–1307* (Oxford, 1979).

4 H. Glassie, *Passing the Time in Ballymenone: Culture and History of an Ulster Community* (Bloomington, 1982), p. 555.

5 P. Connerton, *How Societies Remember* (Cambridge, 1989), p. 94.

6 R. Bradley, *The Past in Prehistoric Societies* (London, 2002), p. 11.

7 G. Lefebvre, *The Great Fear of 1789: Rural Panic in Revolutionary France* (New York, 1973).

8 Bloch, *The Historian's Craft*, pp. 33–4.

9 E. Le Roy Ladurie, *Montaillou: Cathars and Catholics in a French Village, 1294–1324* (London, 1978), pp. 281–2.

10 F. Zonabend, *The Enduring Memory: Time and History in a French Village* (Manchester, 1984), pp. 2–4 (quotation, p. 2).

11 Fentress and Wickham, *Social Memory*, p. 50.

12 Ibid., p. 74.

13 See, for example, Fentress and Wickham, *Social Memory*, pp. 41–86; W. Ong, *Orality and Literacy: the Technologizing of the Word* (London, 1982), pp. 33–45; D. Rubin, *Memory in Oral Traditions: the Cognitive Psychology of Epic, Ballads, and Counting-Out Rhymes* (Oxford, 1995), esp. pp. 194–226.

14 Fentress and Wickham, *Social Memory*, p. 43.

15 A. Lord, *The Singer of Tales* (new. edn, Cambridge, Mass., 2000). For further discussion, see Ong, *Orality and Literacy*, pp. 57–67.

16 S. Brandes, 'Family misfortune stories in American folklore', *Journal of the Folklore Institute* 12:1 (1975); S. Zeitlin, ' "An alchemy of mind": the family courtship story', *Western Folklore* 39:1 (1980); M. de L. M. Janotti and Z. de P. Rosa, 'Memory of slavery in black families of São Paulo, Brazil', in D. Bertaux and P. Thompson (eds), *Between Generations: Family Models, Myths and Memories* (Oxford, 1992), pp. 164–5.

17 See, for example, B. Stock, *The Implications of Literacy: Written Language and Models of Interpretation in the Eleventh and Twelfth Centuries* (Princeton, 1983); A. Fox, *Oral and Literate Culture in England 1500–1700* (Oxford, 2000).

18 Ong, *Orality and Literacy*, pp. 46–8;

19 Clanchy, 'Remembering the past', pp. 165–8.

20 Ong, *Orality and Literacy*, p. 97.

21 Ibid., pp. 100–1.

22 For the notion of textual community, see Stock, *The Implications of Literacy*, passim, esp. pp. 90–2; B. Stock, 'Textual communities: Judaism, Christianity, and the definitional problem', in his *Listening For the Text: On the Uses of the Past* (Baltimore, 1990), pp. 140–59.

23 See, for example, Anderson, *Imagined Communities*, pp. 46–9; Wertsch, *Voices of Collective Remembering*, pp. 62–5.

24 E. Edwards, 'Photographs as objects of memory', in M. Kwint, C. Breward, J. Aynsley (eds), *Material Memories: Design and Evocation* (Oxford, 1999), p. 222. For more discussion of material aspects of memory, see this volume and, for example, E. van Houts, *Memory and Gender in Medieval Europe, 900–1200* (Basingstoke, 1999), ch. 5; N. Saunders (ed.), *Matters of Conflict: Material Culture, Memory and the First World War* (London, 2004).

25 J. Mack, *The Museum of the Mind: Art and Memory in World Cultures* (London, 2003), pp. 41–2. Mack's book gives a host of further examples of mnemonic objects and their uses in different cultures.

26 J. Goody, 'Memory in oral tradition', in Fara and Patterson (eds), *Memory*, pp. 77–8.

27 A. Radley, 'Artefacts, memory and a sense of the past', in Middleton and Edwards (eds), *Collective Remembering*, p. 55.

28 Quoted in S. Crane, *Collecting and Historical Consciousness in Early Nineteenth-Century Germany* (Ithaca, NY, 2000), p. 81. For more on memory and museums, see, for example, S. Crane (ed.), *Museums and Memory* (Stanford, 2000).

29 H.-J. Lüsebrink and R. Reichardt, *The Bastille: a History of a Symbol of Despotism* (Durham, NC, 1997), pp. 131–4.

30 See B. Ladd, *Ghosts of Berlin: Confronting German History in the Urban Landscape* (Chicago, 1997), pp. 7–12.

31 For an important study of 'mnemonic landscape', see R. Koshar, *From Monuments to Traces: Artifacts of German Memory, 1870–1990* (Berkeley, 2000).

32 R. Bradley, *An Archaeology of Natural Places* (London, 2000).

33 See, for example, M. Dietler, 'A tale of three sites: the monumentalization of Celtic oppida and the politics of collective memory and identity', *World Archaeology* 30:1 (1998), pp. 72–89.

❦ 5 ❦

SOCIAL MEMORY AND
THE COLLECTIVE PAST

From the materials and messages that are transmitted within society, specific representations and larger understandings of a collective past are continuously woven. Events, experiences and personalities that have left an impact in people's thinking get incorporated into narratives or organized accounts of the society's or the nation's past. Some of these accounts prove ephemeral, others durable; some acquire widespread currency, even perhaps a kind of official status, while others retain the status of challenging alternatives, or become the property of a particular section of society; some are publicly proclaimed, others remain private or clandestine. Through the encounters, actual and potential, between different versions, the politics of the past – the politics generated by processes of social memory in the larger society – emerges as a crucial, though often a deeply contested, aspect of the cultural life of human societies. Before exploring this aspect of culture further, we must pause to reflect more fully on what we mean by having a sense of the past, and on the relationship that such a sense may have to more specific acts of representation or evocation.

In social and historical discourse (if not in strict philosophical necessity), the past is always the past of something – a group, a community, a state, a nation, a race, a society, a civilization. It is in relation to such an entity that the significance of events is determined, that narrative coherence is established, that the possible lessons or legacies of the past are perceived. For there to be a past worth worrying about, there must always be the imaginative supposition of a continuity in social existence, and such a continuity is generally envisaged from the standpoint of identification: the past in question is *our* past, the past that gives meaning and value to our continuing existence as a collectivity, the past that belongs to us as a constitutive element in our common identity. Representations of the collective past hinge, in other words, on backward projections of current perceptions of identity: the past takes mental shape by being viewed as the breeding- and testing-ground of today's social collectivities, which are themselves interpreted, by the same token, as the possessors of an organic durability rooted in the deep continuities of an earlier history. Collective pasts of the kind that can confer this kind of dignity on the communities to which they are connected are seldom simply 'out there' waiting to be discovered or remembered. Their construction involves, at the very least, a selection from the available materials, and is frequently in practice accomplished by bolder acts of appropriation – for example, through the identification of earlier dynastic histories as 'national' ones, or of ancient tribal peoples such as the Goths or Gauls or Sarmatians or even the Trojans as the ancestors of modern nationalities. Composing a collective past – for example, a national one – means construing certain elements and materials (stories, episodes, texts, objects, places, personalities, beliefs, achievements, institutions) as 'belonging' to this past rather than to any other, or at least as having a place in this particular past that is sufficiently special to constitute a kind of privileged connection (as was implied, for example, when Frenchmen, without denying that other nations might be Christian, persisted in regarding their own nation as the 'eldest daughter of the Church'). Even where – as is not always the case with modern nationalities – institutional continuities in the past provide a core of materials already organized as the materials of a particular national history, the ways in which a vision of the national past is composed are always liable to be contentious, and to evolve over time, as political and social circumstances change: thus, national histories that were once focused on the growth of monarchical institutions or the doings of an aristocratic elite may be refocused as stories which cast the common people as the essential animators of the nation's identity and destiny, while histories formerly shaped to reveal the heroic genius of a racially homogeneous national folk may be revised to fit a new perception of the nation as a multi-ethnic community. Evolutions in a given national community's social politics and international positioning can produce situations in which several different historical conceptions, articulating the experience perhaps of different generations, coexist within that community. Thus, for example, the memories of elderly Australians may still link them to an era in which their defining emotional links were to the history and interests of the English mother-country, while slightly younger ones identify with a conception of the Commonwealth that prioritizes the histories of its white (and especially Anglophone) settler peoples, and younger ones still may look to a conception of the nation as a vibrantly forward-looking multi-ethnic entity whose supposed connections to a British colonial past are tenuously residual or tediously anachronistic.[1] Processes of political change often present those who seek to craft historically-rooted collective identities for national communities with the problem of how to deal with the symbolic debris of earlier conceptions: how should a republican and democratic polity engage with the emblems of a once dominant monarchical tradition; how should a post-colonial society view the cemeteries whose function was to commemorate the dead of the colonial power?[2] Whatever the perceived nature of the national community, and however strong the emphasis on its supposedly immutable character, representations of its past are always forged in tension with possible alternative conceptions, and are seldom simple replications of the way that past has been evoked previously.

The past is also, by definition, a relative concept. It makes sense only when conjoined to a present, and indeed a future. Having a sense of the past gives a meaning to, but also draws meaning from, present experiences and expectations. The nature of the relationships that are perceived to exist between past and present may vary from society and to society, and may evolve as societies develop. Eric Hobsbawm has linked evolutions in collective attitudes to the past to escalations in a society's experience of social innovation. In largely static societies, he argues, the past supplies a 'pattern' of practice that life in the present largely reproduces: there is no rupture, and therefore no need for formal mental distinction, between past and present. In societies experiencing a greater level of innovation, past practices remain significant as points of reference, but no longer exert such a limiting influence on present possibilities. At best, in this phase of development, the past supplies a selectively applicable 'model', the uses of which may be ideologically complex: the idea of a 'return' to past practice (whether to an ancient constitution, to an earlier set of values or to a traditional mode of production) may be either conservative

or radical in its practical implications, but can never in practice
produce the integral resuscitation of earlier modes of being. As
innovation becomes more and more an accepted and systemic
feature of social experience, Hobsbawm suggests, attitudes to the
past undergo a further change: the purpose of defining the past
is now less to 'return' to it (even selectively or figuratively) than
to reject it or transcend it. The past becomes the negative marker
against which the necessary progress of society is measured.[3] While
Hobsbawm's model is necessarily schematic, it reminds us helpfully
of the varied and complex orientations that people and groups in
society can have to the elements of a collective history, and to the
ways in which that history is mentally organized. Ruptures as well
as continuities leave their impressions on the way a collective (for
example, national) past is composed, and trigger different responses
in different quarters. For some, a return to Victorian values may
be the means to national regeneration; to others, those values may
be the symbolic markers of a past that must be left behind. For
some, in nineteenth-century France, the French Revolution was
the decisive moment in the foundation of the country's modern
nationhood; for others it was an unfortunate breach in national
history that had to be repaired. Tensions of this kind, between
different perceptions not just of the past, but of the modalities of
the past's connection to the present, are integral to the way that
social memory processes have unfolded in modern societies.

What each successive wave of social actors relates to, whether
positively or negatively, is of course not so much the reality of past
experiences, as the ways in which the past has been imagined,
evoked and represented by previous generations of social actors.
One important emphasis of recent scholarship has indeed been
on the need to appreciate the continuous nature of the debate on
the past that takes place in human societies: understandings
or representations of the past are not fashioned from scratch at
each particular moment to meet the overweening political needs
of that particular moment, but are always likely to have been
influenced by a previous history of debate and representation.
Jeffrey Olick puts the point cogently: in tracing the representational
histories of particular past events, 'we must not treat these histories
as successions of discrete moments, one present-to-past relation
after another; images of the past depend not only on the relationship between past and present but also on the accumulation of

previous such relationships and their ongoing constitution and reconstitution'.[4] The past is flexible, but its flexibility at any particular moment is significantly conditioned by its previous history of use.

A history of use is social as well as intellectual: to understand the ways in which previous understandings and representations of the past can influence later ones we need to consider not simply the narrative contents of those understandings and representations, but the social contexts in which they have been deployed. In some cases, as John Davis has argued, the social conditions under which views of the past are produced may establish patterns that are essentially reactive: each successive generation in a village community, for example, may establish its ascendancy by overturning the view of the past that the preceding generation had relied on. In other cases, for example where social identity depends more on concepts of lineage than on ones of generation, the social pressure may instead be to maintain the impression of continuity between previous and present understandings.[5] Structural differences of this kind may affect not simply the ways in which people in communities like villages or tribes understand the collective pasts of these localized communities, but also the ways in which they connect themselves and their communities to the continuously negotiated interpretative categories of a larger national history.

Collective pasts are fluid imaginative constructions. Only a small proportion of the texts, images or performances that we may speak of as offering representations of, for example, the past of a nation make any pretence of mapping that past as a coherent and detailed whole. For most people and for most purposes, having a sense of such a past is a vaguer and more impressionistic experience, at once elusive and allusive – less a matter of having the past precisely plotted than of possessing a few relatively central symbolic references – significant events or persons, story-lines, places, concepts, visual images, etc. – around which broader associations of meaning can be flexibly organized.

In speaking of the cultural productions that articulate this kind of sense of the past, it may often be more accurate to speak of a past being evoked than of it being represented. What is represented is often a detail (an episode, action, place, person, object), but the function of this detail is evocative: in depicting it, the creator of a text or image alludes to something larger, but not necessarily precisely defined, of which the detail is taken to be a part. (An image of a medieval castle evokes a larger concept of the Middle Ages, or of feudalism, or of the past of a particular nation; a description of Stanley's encounter with Livingstone evokes the epic achievements and sacrifices of white men in Africa.) The perceived connections between these symbolic points of focus are not necessarily always to be regarded as primarily 'narrative' in character: they may, for example, be generated as much by spatial relationships between historic sites or by the sequential arrangement of events in a commemorative calendar or by the clustering of anecdotes that express a particular thematic message, as by any mutual reference of elements to a clearly agreed and developed historical story-line. Nor should we necessarily assume – as one kind of emphasis on narrativity may lead us to – that the points of focus for a sense of the past are always specific historical events. For while events – discrete moments of significant action such as the Battle of Waterloo, the granting of Magna Carta or Columbus's arrival in the Americas – are undoubtedly the salient features of many historical accounts, and are the principal points of reference also of many commemorative practices, a sense of the past can also give prominence and significance to more extended experiences – the rough equivalents, perhaps, of the 'general events' and 'lifetime periods' that Conway refers to in his model of individual remembering.[6] Thus a historical awareness of the First World War may incorporate a specific awareness of particular events – the first day of the Somme, Armistice Day, etc. – but may give equal or even greater prominence to a more general imagery of trench warfare or of mutilation and bereavement. Specific episodes from the medieval past – the Battle of Agincourt, for example – may be prominent in the narrative construction of a nation's past; many people's sense of that past may, however, focus as much on more general conceptions of the Middle Ages, either as an age of ignorance and brutality (encapsulated in images of serfdom and feudal tyranny, of pestilence and poverty) or as an age of faith (embodied in the glories of cathedral architecture).

Evocations of the past are only effective, however, if there is an audience which has some idea of the kinds of things that representations of detail may allude to. Acts of evocation presuppose, in other words, the existence of at least a degree of common understanding about the way a particular past is – or might be – constituted. By an 'understanding', I mean a structure of organizing assumptions that frames the possibilities of representation. Understandings of the past are communicated from generation to generation not just through the transmission of particular texts and images and of the bodies of data they contain, but through the repetition and reproduction of particular ways of arranging data. Specific modes of narrative emplotment – the habit of telling the past as a story of progress or of decline, of liberation or of enslavement, of providential control or stubborn survival or downfall and redemption or revolutionary advance – are obviously important here,[7] but other kinds of structuring device may also be significant. The sociologist Eviatar Zerubavel has drawn attention, for example, through a musical metaphor, to the contrast between two different types of historical 'phrasing', the one emphasizing the *legato* rhythms of gradual progression, the other the *staccato* of periodic ruptures and sudden shifts from one historical phase to another. He also explores – inter alia – the ways in which the imagined territory of the past can be given structure through concepts of descent and genealogy, of cyclical or of linear progression, of structural analogy (between different episodes or between different histories), and through what he calls 'the social punctuation of the past' – in essence, through periodization, with its twin impulses of 'intraperiodic lumping' (stressing the unity of a period over its discontinuities) and 'interperiodic splitting' (stressing the divisions between periods over possible continuities).[8] Taken together, such techniques help to make the past an imaginatively navigable terrain, and to give it a referential structure to which particular details can be related.

In recent years, a massive literature, both in history and in other disciplines (notably sociology and literary studies), has explored the field of social or public memory in pursuit of insights into how a socially available sense of the past is constructed, how it evolves, and how references to the past are put to use, both culturally and politically, especially within modern national communities. This work has drawn on many different methodologies and had many different kinds of focus. While some scholars have sought to trace and analyse general features of social memory in societies such as modern America or Israel, nineteenth-century Germany or early modern England,[9] others have traced and analysed the afterlife of specific episodes or experiences, showing how the early

seventeenth-century revolt in the Cevennes, the Battle of the
Alamo, the American Civil War or the Great Famine in Ireland
has engraved itself on later memory and public discourse, and
how the uses and understandings of such episodes have evolved
over time.[10] In other cases, the emphasis has fallen on the still
frequently traumatic memory and problematic legacy of episodes
still in or close to living memory – the First and Second World
Wars and the Holocaust especially,[11] but also, for example, the
1956 Hungarian Revolution, the Vietnam War, the AIDS epidemic,
or the South African experience of apartheid.[12] Alongside such
(loosely speaking) event-focused studies, other scholars have
dramatically expanded the field of 'reputation studies', tracking
the posthumous reputations and evolving symbolic uses of figures
as diverse as George Washington and Robert Emmet, Joan of Arc
and Shaka Zulu, Isaac Newton and Robert E. Lee – to say nothing
of legendary or dubiously historical figures such as Saint George
or King Arthur.[13] Across these various fields of study, different
approaches have been developed. Some have focused on the study
of public memorials and commemorative practices; others have
explored the uses and depictions of the past in historiography,
in museums and other 'heritage' institutions, in school textbooks
and children's literature, in fiction, film and television, or in
other forms of popular culture. Some have focused on narrativity,
others on monumentality, material culture or on the sense of
place. The present chapter makes no attempt comprehensively
to summarize or synthesize this vigorously proliferating body of
scholarship, but seeks simply to draw on elements of it in focusing
attention on certain aspects of the dynamics and politics of social
memory in modern national settings.

Events and their afterlives

The memory of an event or of a historical experience begins with
the event or experience itself. Even such a commonsensical statement requires some qualification. In the first place, of course, not
all events that come to have a place in public or popular memory
need ever actually have happened. Deeds of legendary heroes
such as King Arthur, or questionable episodes in the lives of figures
whose historical existence is recognized – like the episode of King
Alfred and the cakes or that of Washington and the cherry tree –

can acquire a powerful significance in the workings of social memory, and a status of truth in the eyes of successive generations, without necessarily ever having been through a phase of being episodes that anyone actually personally remembered. In the second place, even when it is clear that the events in question are not fabrications or folkloric impositions, events are not always self-evident things, whose status as potential objects of memory is clear from the start. In some cases, it is true, the establishment of this status is more or less instantaneous: if one group of people drops an atom bomb on another, it is pretty immediately clear that something has happened, of which future memory will need to take account, even if the broader historical implications of the event may be expected only to emerge more gradually. In other cases, it is the very fact of something at all memorable having occurred that emerges only after a delay: the falling of an apple on the head of Isaac Newton becomes an event to be noted only once its alleged effects in prompting Newton's scientific thinking have been worked out. Even where the immediate circumstances of an event are such as to make it clear that something dramatic and potentially meaningful is going on, the nature of this something may take time to come into focus. As David Cressy has pointed out, it was only gradually that it became clear, in 1588, that a set of naval skirmishes in the English Channel formed part of a larger drama of which the outcome would be the disintegration of the menacing Spanish Armada and the rescuing of England from the threat of invasion: the suspense and anxiety generated in the interim may have helped to ensure that the memories of that year would be ones not of simple victory, but of Providential deliverance.[14] When troops of the First and Third Corps of Confederate infantry were repelled in their massed attack on Union positions on Cemetery Ridge near Gettysburg on July 3 1863, forces on both sides certainly knew that they had been involved in a shudderingly violent encounter, and that this was part of a larger battle and of a larger war. Only gradually, however, over days but also over weeks, months, years and decades, was this encounter – named and made memorable as 'Pickett's Charge' – brought into focus for memory as the decisive moment in a battle which came itself to be perceived as the crucial turning point in a war which in turn came to be regarded as the crucial formative episode in modern American history. This perception of Pickett's Charge, which was vital to its positioning in later American memory, was not in any obvious sense an emanation of the immediate memories that participants in the action had carried with them from the battlefield. Rather, the meanings that were found in the action, both by participants and by other contemporaries (journalists prominent among them), were adjusted as the battle's outcomes became clearer, and as interpretations of what had been at stake in the larger conflict of which it was a part, and of the longer-term consequences of that conflict, evolved.[15]

Events may also take on significance from patterns of expectation that are rooted in the memory of earlier episodes. Knowledge of earlier Hebrew prophecies shaped perceptions of the life of Jesus of Nazareth, both during that life and afterwards; awareness of what had happened in England after the seventeenth-century restoration of the Stuarts helped to mould perceptions of what was happening in France when the Bourbons were restored in 1814.[16] In a more general sense, indeed, most events derive at least part of the meaning that is attributed to them from pre-existing understandings of what is going on, to which the memory of earlier events must make a contribution. As the events unfold, these understandings may themselves be modified, in ways which may in turn affect the ways in which earlier events are remembered.

Sometimes, perhaps because they are easily assimilated into widespread pre-existing patterns of expectation, events that will later have a place in social memory 'come into focus' relatively painlessly, assuming a place in public consciousness that is seemingly uncontentious, and that will alter only gradually as time proceeds. In other cases, however, contests over the appropriate ways of framing the memory of particular events may persist over a longer period, or may indeed emerge only gradually, as later events modify the perception of earlier experience. American controversies over the appropriate ways of remembering the dropping of the atom bomb on Hiroshima in 1945, which came to a head in the 'Enola Gay' affair of 1994, when vociferous opposition from veterans' associations and their political and journalistic allies forced the abandonment of a projected exhibition centred on the aircraft which had carried the bomb at the Smithsonian Institution's National Air and Space Museum, afford a good example of this.[17] For most Americans in 1945, the dropping of the Hiroshima bomb was experienced as a culminating moment of deliverance, whose meaning was to be derived from its connection to the struggle against Japanese aggression which had cost the lives of so many Americans over the previous three years. Its mental and emotional links were to the unprovoked attack on Pearl Harbor, to the heroism of American servicemen, and to the atrocities inflicted by the Japanese on civilian populations and prisoners of war. The casualties inflicted by the bomb itself were understood, from this perspective, as the necessary price of averting the far greater loss of life on both sides which it was assumed would have been incurred in an invasion of mainland Japan. The experiences of the post-war era, however, lent increasing weight to a different understanding, in which the bombing of Hiroshima was not a merciful ending, but an ominous beginning – a crucial moment in the escalation of the nuclear arms race which would jeopardize the security of the post-war world. From this angle, the significance of the 'Enola Gay' mission lay not in what it had concluded or in what it had avoided, but in what it had inflicted and in what it menaced for the future: the horrors visited on the population of Hiroshima became the central emblem of the devastation with which humanity was threatened. Beneath the surface of the 'Enola Gay' dispute, then, lay a tension between two ways of framing the remembered experience of 1945 that seemed dangerously incompatible. To understand the ferocity with which the dispute erupted, four decades after the events to which it ostensibly referred, we need, however, to understand the ways in which perceptions of 1945 had been refracted through the historical experiences of the intervening period. The point here is not simply that Americans living in the 1990s had an awareness of the geo-political effects of the development of nuclear weapons that made some of them unwilling to accept the basic evaluation of what had happened in 1945 to which others remained stubbornly attached: it is not simply a point about critical distance. Nor is it only, though it is partially, a point about generational rivalry – the resentment of a generation formed by the wartime experiences of the 1940s at the perceived devaluation of their contribution and marginalization of their perspectives by historical 'experts' mainly recruited from a younger generation. Largely, it has to do with the fissures in American society that were opened up firstly by the internal ramifications of the Cold War (McCarthyism on the one hand, the anti-nuclear movement on the other), and secondly by the experience of Vietnam. Without the antipathies which these experiences had generated, of which the post-Vietnam resurgence of a polemically vigorous style of conservative American patriotism was the most obvious manifestation, the virulence of the 'Enola Gay' controversy would be hard to understand.

Contestations over the appropriate narrative framing of episodes are only one of the things that can make the remembering of recent events or experiences socially problematic. Much attention has been paid to the ways in which individuals and societies register the effects of divisive or traumatic passages of collective experience: civil wars, national defeats, foreign occupations (with their accompanying experiences of resistance and collaboration), genocidal atrocities, episodes of state-sponsored terror. Experiences of these kinds produce ruptures, conflicts and insecurities within society at large and within the lives of countless individuals. Their emergence into memory is shaped, on the one hand, by the strategies which public bodies (governments, political parties, churches, etc.) adopt in the aftermath: the ceremonies of remembrance they officially institute, the amnesties they grant, the lip-service they pay to reconciliation or to vengeance, the judicial enquiries they set up, the encouragement they give to denunciations on the one hand and to acts of forgiveness or contrition on the other, the descriptions they give either of the old order to which they wish society to return or of the new one they wish to establish. But it is influenced also by the ways in which individuals handle the legacy of loss and bereavement, of suspicion and humiliation, of shame and resentment – by the secrets they keep and the ones they confess to, by their attitudes of recrimination or of forgiveness, by their thirst for justice or for knowledge of what has previously been concealed. Sometimes, in the aftermath of such experiences, public and private impulses to remember and commemorate are brought into a relatively harmonious kind of interaction, generating forms of remembrance that are effective both as political statements and as foci for private emotions, and allowing different parties to reach a measure of agreement on how the traumatic episodes are to be fitted in to the prevailing conception of the collective past. Sometimes, however, traumatic episodes leave a more lasting legacy of national division, or of discrepancy between public and private remembering, which prohibits such an easy resolution. Examples of the tensions that can arise in such cases, and of their implications for the ways in which individuals relate to the representations or understandings of the collective past that are available within their society, will be explored further in a later section of this chapter. For the time being, it is enough to note the ways in which experiences of national trauma or division can impart uncertainty even to the official policy of those who subsequently make it their business politically to manage the way such episodes are publicly acknowledged or responded to. Sheryl Kroen has shown, for example, how the public policy of the Bourbon monarchy restored in France after 1814 was vitiated by its inability to master the tensions between an official policy of forgetting that sought to reconcile those whom the Revolution of the 1790s had divided, by effectively behaving as if the Revolution had never happened, and the insistent emphasis which many of its supporters, especially within the Catholic Church, placed on the need for the crimes of the Revolutionary period to be publicly recognized, remembered and atoned for.[18]

Shifting political alignments may combine with the flow of subsequent events and the movement of generations to produce periodic shifts in the ways that a difficult phase of collective experience is evoked in public discourse, and in the kinds of political uses to which such evocations are put. In an influential study, Henry Rousso has delineated the workings in post-war French society of what he calls the 'Vichy syndrome', a 'neurosis' which in his view testifies to the traumatic effects of France's wartime experience of occupation, and more particularly, of the civil war between supporters of the Vichy regime and its Resistance opponents. Far from being linear in its development, the Vichy syndrome, in Rousso's view, passed through four distinctive phases of development. In the first, running from the end of the war to around 1954, memories of wartime rivalries and hostilities were still irrepressibly close to the political surface: 'constant calls to forgive, to reconcile, even to forget the past clashed with an urgent need to deal with the spontaneous return of repressed material'. In the second phase, lasting from about 1954 to 1971, and linked pre-eminently to the political ascendancy of General De Gaulle, memories of civil war and collaboration were 'repressed' through the cultivation of a 'resistancialist' myth which effectively identified the achievements of the wartime resistance movement with the nation as a whole. In the third phase, the resignation of De Gaulle and the emergence of a new political generation no longer personally anchored in the wartime past gave rise to a brief but dramatic 'return of the oppressed' in the early 1970s – a sudden upsurge of interest in wartime conflicts, mediated through film and historical writing, which decisively shattered the mythical façade of the previous period. This led into a fourth phase, identified by Rousso as one of a public 'obsession' with the previously repressed memories of the Vichy era, manifested for example in frequent recriminations against prominent politicians for their wartime pasts, and in the opening up of painful issues through the trials of wartime criminals such as Klaus Barbie and Paul Touvier.[19] Rousso summarizes the entire evolution in a graphic 'temperature curve of the syndrome', showing a phase of remission (punctuated by occasional 'bouts of fever') in the later 1950s and 1960s, with phases of 'acute crises' before and after.[20] By metaphorically pathologizing the phenomena he is describing (with the language of neurosis, repression, crisis, fever, remission, etc.), Rousso powerfully conveys the impression of Vichy memory as something chronically 'unsettled' – both in the sense of being liable to sudden explosions of intensity after phases of apparent quiescence, and in the sense of being still somehow in need of resolution. His interest lies, ultimately, less in the political functions of Vichy memory at any particular moment than in its status as the object and vehicle of a quasi-neurotic fixation, that has yet to find the kind of stable space between the mythically-straightjacketed 'repression' of painful recollections on the one hand and their obsessive reproduction on the other, on which a calmer understanding of the Vichy past's significance might be negotiated. Though open to criticism for its failure critically to discuss the implications of its metaphorical extension of a conventionally individualistic language of psychic disturbance to the description of collective cultural and political comportments, and though limited in its field of vision to the most obviously public manifestations of such comportments (political speeches, commemorative ceremonies, historiography, film, etc.), Rousso's study offers an illuminating approach to the sometimes painful and difficult modalities of a traumatic or disruptive episode's assimilation as an object of public discourse.

The ways in which an event or collective experience is registered in public and private consciousness at the time of its occurrence and during the period when it is still in living memory exert a powerful, though not necessarily a determining, influence on the meanings it may later be invested with. In some cases, what is transmitted to later generations may be less a stable memory than a legacy of the difficulties that contemporaries have had in coping with the impact of devastating or traumatic experience. Such an effect is revealed, for example, in Lucette Valensi's analysis of the mental impact of the Portuguese monarchy's devastating defeat at Alcácer in 1578. The initial reaction of many Portuguese to a defeat which removed the country's king (Don Sebastian) and army, decimated its aristocracy, and effectively ended its career as a mighty imperial power (preparing the ground, indeed, for the loss of its independent sovereignty two years later) was, as Valensi shows, one of denial and mental resistance. Although a dramatic narrative of the events in Africa was assembled by Portuguese writers over the ensuing decades, this initial reaction of disbelief left its mark in a persistent weaving of mythology which called the shocking reality of events in question, most obviously by sowing the idea of Don Sebastian's survival and possible future return. The later history of Portuguese evocations of 1578 is marked, for Valensi, by tension and oscillation between perspectives from which the loss of imperial grandeur can be mourned (and therefore in some measure left behind) and ones in which the 'Sebastianist' fantasy of a returning glory is kept alive. Social memory has been, on one level, a transmission of ambivalence.[21]

Over time, and especially once events and personalities have passed out of living memory, the basis for their retention in social memory is gradually modified. The significance that is attached to them becomes increasingly symbolic in character, a function less of their precise location in the unfolding sequence of events than of the place that can be given to them in schematic narratives of a society or nation's history, or of their capacity to embody moral or existential messages that are found meaningful at later moments. This is often clearest in the case of personalities. (Indeed, personalities are sometimes the pegs that are used to fix events in memory's patterns: the meanings of the American Revolution are evoked through memories of Washington, those of the Civil War through figures such as Lee and Lincoln, those of the Falklands War through Margaret Thatcher.) Barry Schwartz has shown, for example, how the durable place of Abraham Lincoln as a vital iconic figure in American memory was established not in the period immediately following his death, but in the opening decades of the twentieth century. The crafting of Lincoln's image at this point reflected the need for American symbols that could give a historical anchorage to the public democratic aspirations of the Progressive Era. The Lincoln that emerged was a figure in whom the majesty appropriate to a figure of towering historical importance (reflected, for example, in the Lincoln Memorial) was finely balanced with the imagery of Lincoln as common man (the Lincoln of the log cabin). 'Elevating Lincoln', Schwartz writes, 'the Americans affirmed their commitment to both commonness and greatness', celebrating in him a symbolic figure 'whose contradictory qualities reproduced the contradictions of American society'.[22]

Once constructed as elements with symbolic significance, events and personalities may of course be put to varied and evolving uses, both political and cultural. The Chilean naval officer Arturo Prat, killed in heroic battle against the Peruvians in 1879, and recrafted as an incarnation of civic virtue enlistable in campaigns against public corruption and private immorality, served in subsequent decades sometimes as an emblem for conservative conceptions of national unity, sometimes as the figurehead for radical or reformist attacks on conservative backwardness.[23] Sometimes, of course, shifting public attitudes produce dramatic reversals in symbolic significance: one generation's symbols of imperial nobility become another's emblems of imperialist and racialist aggression. But while the past is malleable, it is not infinitely so: symbolic significance is adjusted (and heroes and celebrated events go in and out of fashion) in ways that are always influenced by earlier constructions, and by the restraining effect of possible challenges to any radically new interpretation.[24]

Connections and commemorations

Events and personalities do not establish themselves in social memory as isolated containers of symbolic meaning: much of their significance comes from the ways in which they get connected to other events and to larger narrative structures. Thus, as Schwartz shows, Lincoln has significance partly in relation to Washington: juxtaposing and comparing the two heroes of American nationhood allows statements to be made about the nation's evolution or about the varied components of national character that could not be made by focusing on the one without the other, and shifts in the balance of public sentiments on these issues can be charted by detecting shifts in the relative emphasis that is placed on the two heroes (as reflected in patterns of publication, opinion polls, etc.).[25] Something similar happens with events, sometimes even as they occur. Lincoln's own Gettysburg address explicitly presents the current Civil War as the testing ground of the ideals of the American Revolution,[26] while the Thatcherian rhetoric of the Falklands War deliberately echoed the Churchillian vision of the Second World War. And again, such connections provide frameworks within which shifts in relative weighting can occur: the Glorious Revolution of 1688, presented in Whig mythology as the triumphant accomplishment of the ideals fought for in the 1640s, has paled as the status of the Civil War itself as the real English Revolution has been enhanced.

Couplings such as these occur within, and help to focus larger narrative structures. The ways in which particular events, or groups of events, are framed and located within such structures are instrumental in establishing the symbolic meanings that attach to them. Yael Zerubavel has shown, for example, how the understanding of symbolic episodes in Jewish and Israeli history (Masada, the Bar Kokhba revolt, the battle of Tel Hai) can be modulated as the boundaries of the 'commemorative narrative' in which they are incorporated are adjusted – either through curtailment (stopping the story at a moment of triumph or heroic resolution) or through extension (allowing momentary setbacks to become mere incidents on the road to eventual triumph).[27] As well as conferring meaning on particular events, such devices also help to give the collective past a kind of dramatic structure, in which the perception of longer themes (of long-term struggle, eventual success, downfall and recovery, corruption and redemption) is punctuated by moments of peculiar symbolic intensity. Here again, however, strictly narrative arrangements are not the only ones that can determine the associations that are formed between different elements in a society's repertoire of historical references. The gathering and arrangement of objects in a museum, the gathering of heroes into a national pantheon (whether a metaphorical one or an actual building containing their bodies or images), the arrangement of statues in a public space, the publication of compendia of past glories (*One Hundred Great Lives, A Book of Golden*

Deeds) or of series of children's stories (promising, as if in a tourist brochure, trips *With Clive to India, With Kitchener to Khartoum*), the erection of a Temple of British Worthies (in which Shakespeare, Locke, the Black Prince and Sir Francis Drake rub shoulders as Whiggish dignitaries), the arrangement of saints' days or anniversaries in a commemorative calendar are all instances of less obviously or less purely narrative connective arrangements.

A wide variety of practices – literary, cultural, ceremonial, artistic, monumental – combine, then, to structure the past of a particular nation or community as a flexible and multitextured – but not entirely formless – fabric of associations. Different groups or individuals within society will engage with the fabric on different levels, and perhaps with different parts of it, drawing out of it their own more specific mental patterns. Different age cohorts, for example, may hold different sets of events in memory, either as a result of specific generational experiences (such as participation in war or periods of economic hardship) or because of a more general tendency for people to be more responsive to events (or at least more capable of incorporating them lastingly into their general cognitive structures) during certain phases of their existence (for example adolescence or early adulthood) than during others.[28] Different religious or political groups may also be expected to synthesize their knowledge of the collective past somewhat differently. But broader regularities and deeper continuities in the repertoire of images and references relating to a collective past that members of a society hold in consciousness may also sometimes be apparent. Research by Michael Frisch, in which successive cohorts of his American college students were asked to list the first ten names they thought of in response to the prompt 'American History from its beginning though the end of the Civil War', and then to repeat the exercise leaving out presidents, generals and statesmen, revealed striking levels of consistency. In the case of the first list, heavily dominated by military and political figures, these may well have reflected the high school curriculum, but the equally remarkable patterns of consistency that emerged when these figures were left out (producing high scores for the likes of Paul Revere, John Smith, Daniel Boone, Harriet Tubman and especially Betsy Ross) suggest to Frisch the more deeply rooted persistence of historical symbols embedded in an inherited culture.[29]

The historical connections and emphases that are articulated in public culture are generally, of course, easier to uncover than those that may be at work in the minds of ordinary members of society. Yael Zerubavel has coined the useful term 'commemorative density' to describe the variable intensity with which different periods in a collective past are publicly celebrated or actively remembered. In any narrative presentation of a collective past, certain periods or moments are invested with stronger significance than others, and this is true also with the implicit 'master commemorative narrative' which in Zerubavel's view structures commemorative practice within a given society. (She defines commemorative practice fairly broadly, to include things such as songs, stories and school textbooks, as well as monuments, festivals and commemorative ceremonies.) Commemorative density, as Zerubavel defines it, seems to be both a qualitative and a quantitative concept: it refers both to the importance or significance that an event is deemed to possess within the implicit structures of the master commemorative narrative and to the amount of actual commemorative activity that is focused on it, in comparison to that focused on other events. (Zerubavel seems, indeed, to assume that these two things will go together.) In any case, the significance that the master commemorative narrative attributes to events that have a high commemorative density is not a purely historical significance (in the sense of being one that is attached to the event's perceived place in a sequence of causally linked historical occurrences): it is a symbolic or even mythical significance that allows such events to 'serve as paradigms for understanding other developments in the group's experience'. Zerubavel draws particular attention here to the way in which events that are assigned a symbolic status as 'turning points' in the collective past – and which are therefore positioned liminally between one perceived phase of experience and another – can take on a kind of mythic function which allows the commemoration of them to be a forum for mediation between potentially conflicting understandings of the past in question.[30]

Applied to the generality of a society's (loosely-speaking) commemorative productions, commemorative density is necessarily a somewhat abstract – though helpful – concept. Switching to the more limited context of analyses of specific types of commemorative activity allows such a notion to be explored further. Eviatar Zerubavel, for example, has analysed and compared the 'national commemograms' of different present-day countries, plotting the chronological distribution of the events commemorated by public holidays, and showing how these are typically grouped in distinctive historical clusters, usually relating either to the very distant or to the fairly recent past. For Zerubavel, national commemorative calendars come to embody tacit narratives that 'encapsulate nations' collective histories as strings of sacred peaks sporadically protruding from wide, commemoratively barren valleys of profane time'.[31] This may be a slightly misleading way of putting it, for (as is also clear in Zerubavel's account) such calendars are historical products which may in practice synthesize and juxtapose elements from different commemorative traditions. It is not always clear that the function of the calendar as a whole is one of evoking a unitary implicit narrative: indeed the way in which the arrangement of such a calendar is liable to plunge those who follow it backwards and forwards in time, rather than carrying them forward in an orderly chronological progression, tends to suggest otherwise. The effect of the calendar may sometimes be better understood as one of juxtaposition, allowing symbolic meanings that have roots in different narrative contexts to be blended and intermingled, not in a larger narrative structure, but in a looser framework of associations. The past may be constituted here less as a story, tacit or otherwise, than as a referential space. But if the basic narrativity of commemorative calendars may be variable, their tendency to assign official memorability overwhelmingly to episodes drawn either from a very distant or a fairly recent past – thus balancing a sense of the primordial with a sense of recent direction – remains important.[32]

A further dimension may be added to the study of commemorative density by exploring evolutions over time. Barry Schwartz has developed such an approach in a study of the historical imagery displayed in the United States Capitol Building. By plotting not just the distribution across time of the events and persons currently commemorated by images in the Capitol, but also the times at which different images were commissioned, Schwartz is able to map distinguishable phases in the development of the Capitol's iconographic presentation of national history, which he seeks to understand as reflecting the different priorities and constraints that operated at different stages in the development of national politics. His analysis is sensitive not only to fluctuations in the quantity of images relating to different periods in the nation's history, but also to variations in the type of image displayed. Prior to the American Civil War, the analysis suggests, the iconography of the Capitol concentrated overwhelmingly on images relating to the colonial period or the American Revolution. This was a reflection, Schwartz argues, less of any basic lack of interest in later events than of America's continuing political divisions: the imagery of national origins and founding heroes supplied the only agreed basis for a conception of national unity. After the Civil War, the focus shifted: less preoccupied with the fragility of national unity, America's representatives became more concerned to promote imagery which 'celebrated the weight of institutional structures and acknowledged social diversity'. Although a focus on the foundational era was not abandoned, images of it became anecdotal rather than epic, and episodes from the later antebellum as well as the postbellum period became more numerous, allowing a more continuous picture of the national past to emerge. There was also an increasing institutional emphasis on commemorating the holders of particular political or bureaucratic offices. In short, while the older iconography of founding heroes retained its place, new additions to that iconography began to affirm the stability and continuity of national institutions. What emerged, Schwartz suggests, was an iconographic pattern 'that attested to the fact that America, at last, had become an unrevolutionary culture'.[33]

Public commemorative activities are not, by any means, the only cultural vehicles that influence the formation of a sense of the collective past in human societies. (Any analysis of this process in our own society that dwelt on such activities but neglected school curricula and television would be radically flawed.) The emphasis that studies of social memory have frequently placed on the analysis of such activities is not, however, completely misplaced: commemorative occasions and ceremonies do indeed contribute distinctively, and in many social settings vitally, to making the past an active rather than a merely passive element in people's social awareness. Their contribution is on two levels: they are instrumental in constituting the past that is to be remembered, and the collectivity that is expected to do the remembering.

A commemorative occasion – be it a particular commemorative ceremony, or a larger event such as a centenary celebration that may have non-ceremonial as well as ceremonial components – is a social

occasion. It calls on the members of a community to participate in – or at the least, to witness – the articulation of whatever
element in the past is being evoked. Participation may be voluntary,
or it may be more or less insisted on as a condition of being
recognized as a member of the community; in either case, it may
be difficult in practice to avoid. In this sense, commemorative
activities help to elicit a sense of social connectedness, and to focus
this on the evocation of things in the past. Where a commemorative
occasion is a rare or one-off occurrence (as with the state funeral
of a recently deceased personage, or with the special festivities
that celebrate the centenaries or bicentenaries – rather than the
annual anniversaries – of particular events), the effect may be to
refocus – even if only temporarily – people's sense of the historical
underpinnings of contemporary identity. Often, however, the
effects of commemorative activity are deepened and extended by
repetition: participation in the collective evocation of certain past
episodes or experiences becomes part of the regular patterning of
social existence. As Jeffrey Olick has emphasized, the remembered
experience of past commemorative performances then becomes
an important contextual element in the shaping of each fresh commemorative occasion: participants in commemorative performances
will tend to structure their activity in the light of the messages that
have been articulated on previous occasions, the debates that have
arisen, and the expectations that this past history of commemoration has given rise to.[34]

Whatever their social effects, commemorative activities focus
attention on particular events. In doing so, they do not only reflect
the symbolic status that those events have acquired, but actively
enhance it – even if sometimes only momentarily. Symbolic significance is not a flame that burns steadily: it is retained by being
periodically revivified, and commemorative ceremonies help to
do this. The observance of a commemorative calendar allows
groups or societies to do the rounds of their symbolic references,
recharging them in regular order; more isolated commemorative
performances allow energy to be suddenly directed into a particular
corner of the symbolic system, in ways which may sometimes modify
the way the sense of the past is structured. In either case, the event
that is focused on receives a kind of special attention: those who
are involved in the commemoration, as witnesses or participants,
are required to attend to its meanings, to review the reasons for

remembering it, to remind themselves of its perceived significance for the community and for themselves – and may have the opportunity, in the process, to modify that significance.

But if commemoration replenishes the individual saliency of the events it specifically envisages, it does so by reaffirming (and perhaps adjusting or reworking) their connections to larger systems of meaning – to the totality of the communal past, to the broader moral life of the community. Commemorations of specific events seldom confine themselves to revisiting the detail of the events themselves: they are occasions for celebrating, evoking or reflecting on the potential of those events – the vistas they opened up, the destinies they advanced, the moral transformations they accomplished, the examples they bequeath. New York's 1892 festivities for the four hundredth anniversary of Columbus's 'discovery of America' celebrated the explorer not just as a successful navigator, but as the progenitor of an American civilization founded on freedom of religion, progress, enlightenment, education and honest toil; space was also left for celebrating him as a hero for Catholic Americans, and for bringing different ethnic communities together in honouring the first immigrant American, offered here as emblem of a multi-ethnic society.[35]

It is in this sense that commemorations are always as much about the present and the future as about the past. They offer occasions for communities to take stock of, to debate, and perhaps to adjust the meanings they find in their own history and the shapes they give to their collective identity – and for different constituencies within those communities to stake their claims to a share in the past, and in its present and future uses. This is especially clear in commemorations of foundational events. Heroic as they may possibly appear in themselves, founding moments are significant, by definition, mainly through what they are believed to have produced: they can only truly be celebrated by evoking and defining the communities they have given rise to. A rigorous comparative investigation of American and Australian centenary and bicentenary celebrations by Lyn Spillman shows how in both countries these anniversaries were the occasion for extensive explorations of the nature of national identity which went well beyond any narrative evocation of the foundational moments themselves, configuring nationhood not simply in terms of common history, but of such considerations as international recognition, political culture and a connection to land. Spillman's analysis allows us to see differences as well as similarities both between late nineteenth- and late twentieth-century articulations in either country, and between the two countries: over a hundred years, for example, Americans continued to emphasize the defining importance of their political culture, but became less inclined to connect national identity to land, while for Australians the land became symbolically crucial, and political culture less important. Equally important is a difference in the emphasis that is attached to the actual originating moments (the American Revolution on the one hand, the colonial foundation of 1788 on the other), and in the effect this has on larger historical conceptions. In the case of the United States, where the events commemorated are those which established America's independent nationhood, these events remain an important point of symbolic focus, and remain integral to an essential narrative of the nation's development as a political community. In the Australian case, where the original event is more 'disreputable' (the foundation of what was originally basically a penal colony), this event came to be more the pretext of commemoration than its real object, and visions of Australian history remained relatively vague and eclectic, focusing the sense of nationhood more on themes such as land than on a specific historical narrative.[36]

Tensions and contestations

By constituting certain events as symbolic markers of a particular vision of collective identity, and by enlisting members of society collectively in the articulation of that vision, commemorative practices can be a force for political and social cohesion. An emphasis on this aspect of commemorative performance is often expressive of a more general emphasis on social memory as a terrain in which coherent and homogeneous collective identities are grounded. 'A shared memory', writes JonathanVance, 'is one of the cornerstones of a society as we understand it. Individuals who constitute any social order share a common vision of history that locates the community in time and space, giving it an appreciation of its own past as well as a sense of its future'.[37] In a similar vein, Anthony Smith asserts:

> An essential element, perhaps the essential element, in any kind of
> human identity is memory. [. . .] In the case of collective cultural

identities, such as *ethnies* and nations, later generations carry shared memories of what they consider to be 'their' past, of the experiences of earlier generations of the same collectivity, and so of a distinctive ethno-history. Indeed, their ethnicity is defined, first of all, by a collective belief in common origins and descent, however fictive, and thereafter by shared historical memories associated with a specific territory which they regard as their 'homeland'. On this basis arises a shared culture, often a common language or customs or religion, the product of the common historical experiences that give rise to shared memories.[38]

The implication of such statements is that a certain vision of the past, made up of certain transmitted memories, becomes the shared or common property of the members of a given society, and as such a constitutive element of their collective identity. The social memory processes that operate within such a society have, in such a view, an essentially integrative function: by foregrounding aspects of the past with which the disparate members of society can feel connection, and by moulding these aspects into a coherent vision of the society's past development as a collectivity, they supply a mental basis for the social collaborations in which the members of that society are expected to engage, and for the commitments they are expected to make to the larger social cause. Jan Assmann has spoken of the 'concretion of identity' that arises within a group or society from the encapsulation of certain memories in the objective forms of what he calls 'cultural memory':

> The concept of cultural memory comprises that body of reusable texts, images, and rituals specific to each society in each epoch, whose 'cultivation' seems to stabilize and convey that society's self-image. Upon such collective knowledge, for the most part (but not exclusively) of the past, each group bases its awareness of unity and particularity.[39]

If such a way of talking about social memory has become widespread, it is no doubt partly because it does indeed capture an important aspect of what goes on when the collective past is remembered in society. If pressed too far, however, it presents us with a dangerously idealized picture of social memory's functions. Any account of how these processes operate in practice must recognize that conflict and contestation, and the use of power by some groups against others, are endemic features of most collective experiences. This is important in two ways. It means, firstly, that impressions generated by conflicts and contestations in the past are part of what is carried in social memory, and that this legacy of awkward and divisive recollection may complicate and disrupt any effort that is made to establish a stable and integrative conception of the collective past. Wars, revolutions, experiences of oppression and exploitation are not effortlessly assimilated into a vision of the past that everyone can agree on and relate to equally and uniformly. When Ernest Renan argued that 'the possession in common of a rich legacy of memories' was a vital constituent in nationhood, he took care to observe that the individuals who composed such a nation had also to 'have forgotten many things' (for example, in the French case, the massacre of Saint-Bartholomew or the atrocities in the Midi in the thirteenth century).[40] Such 'forgetting' is usually, to some extent, actively managed: those with an interest in promoting and shaping a society's sense of the past produce accounts in which certain experiences are centralized and others marginalized if not excluded; divisive episodes are reinterpreted as phases in a larger movement towards unity.

This shaping of the way the past is represented is likely, secondly, to be influenced by the operations of power, and the tensions and conflicts that those operations generate, within contemporary society. Particular visions of the past can be used either to legitimize present political and social arrangements or to supply a standpoint from which these may be criticized or resisted. Those who seek either to consolidate and extend or to capture or to resist power therefore have a vested interest in shaping the ways in which the past is represented; those who seek to influence the directions that a society or political community takes in the present and future will seek to mould and to propagate an understanding of the past that legitimizes their present agendas. The understandings of the past that appear to be dominant in a given society at a given moment will be the product not of some unitary collective process in which a society reflects on its past experiences, but of complex political interactions, in which different interests vie for ascendancy, influence and survival – and in which some interests will be more successful at asserting themselves than others. Thus, for example, recent studies of commemorative practice have often called in question the harmonizing and integrating effects that such practices are ostensibly geared to promoting: the outcomes of the commemorative project's efforts to co-ordinate the remembering of

individuals and of groups, John Gillis remarks, 'may appear
consensual when they are in fact the product of processes of intense
contest, struggle, and, in some cases, annihilation'.[41] In early
twentieth-century Spain, Carolyn Boyd asserts, 'the politics of
commemoration served to disrupt rather than to forge bonds
of social and political solidarity', while Kirk Savage's perception of
the marginalization of black Americans and of slave emancipation
in American Civil War monuments leads him to see 'a story of
systematic cultural repression, carried out in the guise of reconciliation and harmony'.[42] Beneath the idealized view that commemorations offer of a society whose past is stably ordered and stably
connected to its present, a more complex play of exclusions and
impositions can usually be detected.

What is true here of commemorations is true, more generally,
of the ways in which a sense of the collective past is cultivated. The
projection of organized understandings of such a past, and their
articulation in the public arena, is always, at least potentially, a
tension-ridden or conflictual business. Modern nationalism, especially, hinges on the presentation of the nation as a community
whose members are bound together by powerful ties of common
interest, common background and common destiny. The claims
of this community are advanced both externally, in relation to
other nations, and internally, in relation to the nation's own
members or to groups within it. Conflicts can arise in either of
these directions, and the politics of the past are one of the obvious
territories on which they can develop.

Thus, for example, conflicts may occur where different national
communities, or those who claim to speak on their behalf, lay claim
to the same symbolic commodities, or incorporate in their self-
images uses of those commodities that seem derogatory to other
nations. One nation's defining victories – the defeat of the Armada,
Trafalgar – may be defeats which another would prefer to forget;
two nations may compete for 'ownership' of the same heroic
ancestors (Greece and Macedonia for Alexander the Great, France
and Germany for Charlemagne). The ways of viewing the collective
past that are current within one national community may imply a
need for attitudes of shame or apology on the part of another –
apology for war crimes or for past imperialist aggressions, for
example – which those who identify with the latter may be unwilling
to accord. Contests between nations may be simply over the use

that is made of certain historical references, but they may also involve concrete issues of occupation or possession – of symbolic objects (such as the Benin bronzes or the Elgin marbles) which one nation is felt to have plundered from another, or of territory that is disputed between two national (or would-be national) communities (Jews and Palestinians within Israel, France and Germany in Alsace-Lorraine). Here the tensions that arise from symbolic appropriation (evident, for example, in the imposition of different sets of placenames on a territory in which different communities have an investment) are often aggravated by issues of physical displacement. The presence of cultural objects claimed by one national community in the art collections of another adds new layers to their significance: they function as symbols not just of the past glories of the native civilization that produced them, but of the painful histories of imperialist exploitation that account for their present location. Evocations of places in disputed territories from which populations have been evicted have, in many cases, a similar double function, offering reminders both of the longer past of the community that had those places as its original setting and of the experiences of exile or displacement which may be central to the way collective identity is currently constructed.[43]

In other cases, the tensions that are produced as visions of the collective past are articulated and often at least indirectly reflected in the representations that emerge, are internal to the national community whose contours such visions purport to define. Here a variety of scenarios are possible, and a range of conceptual frameworks have been employed by scholars seeking to describe them. One common type of conceptualization assumes the central role of political and social elites, usually operating through the state apparatus and with the support of other powerful cultural agencies (such as those of a dominant religion or of an elite-controlled newspaper press) in seeking to co-ordinate the way in which the past is remembered in any given society. Such elites are seen as promoting an 'official' or 'dominant' reading of the past, whose function is basically to maintain their own conception of the national community and to legitimize their ascendancy within it. Groups or individuals within society may either acquiesce in the official or dominant reading, allowing it to mould their conception of their own experience and tacitly suppressing any aspects of that experience that cannot readily be assimilated to this vision, or may in some way resist it, or be passively alienated by it. Resistance to the 'dominant' reading may remain fragmentary and sporadic, or may – perhaps with the assistance of some counter-hegemonic social agency, such as a revolutionary political party or a dissident religious or intellectual movement – develop into something that is itself organized and socially rooted, and that has the potential to challenge and destabilize, and even possibly in the end to over-throw, the previously hegemonic reading. Within this basic model, different scholars have used different terminology to develop slightly different emphases. In the early 1980s, for example, the Popular Memory Group urged oral historians to help to stimulate the emergence of forms of 'popular memory' robust enough to challenge the hegemony of the 'dominant memory' that was promoted by the 'historical apparatus' at the service of the state and ruling elites, by prompting ordinary members of society to re-remember their own experience in ways which focused on those elements in it which were at odds with the dominant version.[44] Other scholars have preferred the term 'countermemory' to 'popular memory'. For George Lipsitz, 'counter-memory is a way of remembering and forgetting that starts with the local, the immediate, and the personal', and which 'looks to the past for the hidden histories excluded from the dominant narratives'. Ultimately, he argues, such remembering has the capacity to force a revision of existing histories through the opening up of previously unrecognized perspectives.[45] Somewhat similarly, Yael Zerubavel posits an opposition between the 'master commemorative narrative' of the Jewish and Israeli past, which serves the interest of the ruling Israeli elite, and the 'countermemory' which 'challenges this hegemony by offering a divergent commemorative narrative representing the views of marginalized individuals or groups within the society'. Here again, 'countermemory' serves as a fairly flexible term, covering on the one hand cases where specific details of the 'master commemorative narrative' are denied or subverted through the circulation of stories in which the episodes are construed differently, and on the other the possible eventual emergence of 'an alternative overview of the past that stands in opposition to the hegemonic one', and which may even in the end have the potential to replace it as the dominant account. Through the development of countermemory of the latter kind, Zerubavel argues, the com-memoration of the past becomes 'a contested territory in which groups engaging in a political conflict promote competing views of the past in order to gain control over the political centre or to legitimize a separatist orientation'.[46] A spectrum of scenarios is thus evoked, ranging from ones in which an oppressively dominant official version of the past is met with only minimal and fragmentary shows of dissent to ones in which contradiction to the dominant version becomes an effective and organized vehicle of political opposition.

Other models, designed with somewhat different scenarios in mind, highlight the idea of transaction, rather than of open conflict, between the standpoints on the past that are promoted within a dominant or official mindset on the one hand, and those which reflect more local or sectional interests on the other. In a wide-ranging study of civic commemorative activities in twentieth-century America, for example, John Bodnar posits 'public memory' as a terrain of interaction and negotiation between 'official' and 'vernacular' cultures. Official culture, for Bodnar, is largely unitary, and employs a generalized patriotic language to promote an idealized conception of the nation which legitimizes elite agendas. Vernacular cultures are multiple, and are rooted in the concrete grass-roots experience of different groups within society, for example, ethnic, religious or local communities. Although public memory ultimately reflects the uneven distributions of power within society, it is also the field within which different groups and communities seek to establish the legitimacy of their interests and the terms of their past and continuing participation in the larger national society.[47] The tensions that arise in such a scenario arise not from the presence of conflicting total visions of national history, but from the difficulties of symbolically integrating conceptions of identity that are founded in different patterns of social experience with a larger national conception.

Memory conflicts within national communities do not, however, always fit easily into the conceptual frameworks that 'elite versus popular' or 'dominant versus counter memory' or 'official versus vernacular' models of social memory propose. Episodes of national division, such as civil wars, revolutions or genocidal atrocities, can have varied impacts on the public framing of remembrance and recollection. In some cases, such an episode may produce a seemingly definitive victory of one side over another, allowing the victors to impose their own reading of the episode as the official and hegemonic version, and reducing the memories of the vanquished to a private or fugitive status, deprived of legitimacy and of public recognition. (Such was the case, for example, in Finland after the Civil War of 1918.)[48] In other cases, an ostensibly irenic spirit may generate forms of public remembrance that are geared specifically to reconciling former antagonists, but which may, in practice, only achieve this by subjugating the interests and marginalizing the memories of some of those who had a stake in the original conflict. Thus, as David Blight has argued, the forms of commemorative culture that allowed Northern and Confederate veterans to embrace each other in the decades after the American Civil War had as their corollary the more or less systematic forgetting of the war's status as a struggle for and against the institution of slavery. By focusing not on the conflict's causes, but on a romanticized conception of it as a tragic but ennobling drama whose participants were bound together in 'an endearing mutuality of sacrifice' – a struggle 'in which devotion made everyone right, and no one truly wrong' – the pattern of post-war remembrance was part of a set of mental reactions that served, in effect, to perpetuate racial injustice by denying experiences and memories of slavery and emancipation their crucial place in the nation's history.[49] In a further set of cases, however, the legacy of conflict is less easily summarizable in terms of dominance and suppression; rather, the public arena witnesses the unresolved persistence of rival conceptualizations of the nation's character and destiny, each of which retains the backing of imposing social and institutional forces, and each of which stakes its claims through an appeal to different traditions in a past that is essentially contested. In the France of the early Third Republic, for example, secular Republicans and royalist or nationalist Catholics faced each other across an ideological divide which was defined most obviously by their conflicting attitudes to the French Revolution and its legacy, but which was also articulated in conflicts over the interpretation of other moments in French history – for example, in the struggle for commemorative ownership of the symbolic figure of Joan of Arc, upheld by the left as a heroine of popular patriotism and victim of clerical and monarchical perfidy, and by the right as a divinely inspired champion of Christian monarchy.[50] In early twentieth-century Spain, as Carolyn Boyd has shown, the drive to commemorate the twelve hundredth anniversary of the second battle of Covadonga (718) similarly brought into focus the rivalry between traditionalist Catholic and modernizing liberal (as well as regionalist) conceptions of Spain's historical identity. Although the Church and the right were the public victors on this occasion, other conceptions of Covadonga's significance remained in play and, though eventually driven underground by the right's triumph in the Civil War of the 1930s, have re-emerged publicly since the end of the Francoist regime.[51] In both the French and the Spanish cases, particular ways of viewing the past might be politically dominant under particular regimes, but different understandings remained deeply entrenched not just in popular opinion but within the structures of social and of institutional power.

The ability to shape people's understanding of what the nation is and of where its interest lies is a crucial lever of power in modern societies, and the ability to secure credit for particular readings of the national past and to discredit alternative readings is an important aspect of how this power is exercised. But while it may be naïve and misleading to see the representations and under-standings of the past that are current within a given society as an unproblematic expression of some kind of agreed collective self-knowledge, it may also in many cases be too simple to dismiss them as nothing but the cultural instruments of elite domination. Rather than regarding conflict and consensus as the terms that define two starkly opposing theories of social memory, it may be best to focus on the ways in which elements of the two are interwoven in the ways that the past is constructed and engaged with.[52] In the case of nations, Alon Confino is right in hoping to divert some of the attention that has been paid to conflicts of social memory into investigating the 'common denominators of variousness' that allow a nation to hold together as something resembling a community of memory despite such conflicts.[53] It is also helpful to be reminded that public 'silences' over the memory of certain events are not always and inevitably the implicit markers of oppressions and exclusions, but may sometimes be a necessary (and even to some extent an agreed) condition for the healing of social wounds.[54] A host of terms designating states intermediate between those of irreducible antagonism and easy harmony – tension, friction, rivalry, contestation, ambiguity, negotiation, compromise, transaction, re-conciliation, amnesty – may be useful in describing social memory's dynamic processes in particular cases. It remains important, however, to remember that the collective past is always a constructed past (and continually under reconstruction), that its construction is part of the process by which societies do not smoothly inherit but actively thrash out and negotiate forms of collective identity, and that this thrashing out and negotiating is always at least latently and potentially problematic and disharmonious – an affair of claims and counter-claims, of power and resistance, and not just of mutual recognition and collective celebration.

The individual and the collective past

Any account of all this will be a thin one, however, if it fails to incorporate an account of what a sense of the collective past means for individuals. For in the end, the potency of any conception of the collective past that is promoted in the public arena depends not just on the cultural resources and political muscle that are mustered behind it, but on the ability and willingness of individuals to draw meanings from it that have resonance for their own existence: as Confino puts it, such a conception 'must steer emotions, motivate people to act, be received; in short, it must become a sociocultural mode of action'.[55] The tensions, conflicts and negotiations that arise when a sense of the past is formulated are thus not only ones between different conceptions of the past as a collective property, but ones also between such conceptions and the memories and understandings that individuals have of their own unfolding existence as social beings caught up in the processes of history. We need here to consider, on the one hand, the contribution that the remembering and narrating of individual life experiences can make to the ways in which collective pasts are understood and represented; and, on the other, the ways in which individuals may relate to, make use of, or reject the generalizations and interpretative categories that are offered in the public arena in seeking to comprehend and to articulate their own experiences of living.

Not every meaningful engagement with a collective past need be a wholesale investment in a comprehensively encompassing narrative of the past in question; nor does every such engagement require the same level of personal commitment. Societies vary in the extent to which their ordinary members are expected actively to embrace a particular vision of the past, to make it part of their mental furniture, and to participate publicly in affirming it. Even where compliance in a particular vision is actively insisted on – as happens, for example, when a particular narrative is vigorously and exclusively promoted through the educational system – the practicalities of compliance will vary from individual to individual, along a spectrum from sulky public acquiescence (perhaps accompanied by private rejection or tacit resistance) to enthusiastic adoption. In dealing with the 'consumption' (or reception) of official historical narratives in Soviet and post-Soviet Russia, James Wertsch distinguishes helpfully between two levels of acceptance of the textual resources through which such narratives are articulated: 'mastery' and 'appropriation'. To have 'mastered' a particular narrative is to have developed the kind of working familiarity with it that allows one to recall its essential features reliably, and to make use of it in speech and discussion. Mastery involves a cognitive understanding of the meanings that are assigned to the past in a discourse that has been learnt, rather than an emotional commitment. Appropriation, by contrast, 'means bringing something into oneself or making it one's own': a text or narrative that is appropriated becomes available as 'an identity resource – a means for anchoring or constructing one's sense of who one is'.[56] Mastery allows an individual to pay the required lip-service to a particular conception of the past, and allows him or her to participate in debates and negotiations that are premised on outward acceptance of this conception. But there is nothing in the mastery of a narrative that prevents one from simultaneously mastering other – and perhaps conflicting – historical conceptions: mastery of an official narrative can therefore serve, sometimes, as a cover for discreet or private resistance to that narrative's implications. A narrative that has been appropriated, on the other hand, becomes operative as a framework for self-understanding that tends to exclude other influences. In practice, however, this exclusive kind of appropriation is often hard to sustain, partly because individuals have to operate in a range of social contexts, in some of which other conceptions of the past may be powerfully present, and partly because the 'official line' on the past is not always stable, and may therefore sometimes engender doubt by contradicting its earlier positions. In practice, therefore, the boundaries between appropriation, mastery and resistance are generally uncertain: individuals may oscillate between them as they move from one context to another.[57]

Rejection, mastery and appropriation are relationships that individuals may consciously enter into with narratives of the collective past that are explicitly articulated in a relatively highly developed form – that are taught in schools, enshrined in formal historical accounts, encapsulated in public commemorative programmes. For many people, however, and in many societies, the engagement with the past is not so obviously a deliberate engagement with a fully articulated narrative account. Scholars such as Raphael Samuel and David Lowenthal have highlighted the enormous range of social and cultural practices (running from genealogy to amateur archaeology, from country house visiting to the reading of historical novels, from spiritism to the collecting of antique or reproduction furniture) by which members of modern western societies lay claim to evoke, investigate, seek or happen to come into contact with pasts of one kind or another, giving a kind of historical texture to their mundane awareness and everyday enthusiasms, which may well not easily be translated into the categories either of academic historical understanding or of official commemorative discourse.[58] An awareness of the past has many potential points of focus, and individuals may be selective – or merely influenced by proximity – in which they find personally meaningful. (A historical re-enactor may be ardently committed to recapturing the lifestyles and experiential textures of the ancient Romans or the American Civil War, but not remotely interested in connecting these to earlier or later periods.[59]) The past of the larger community may be approached through an interest in something more restricted – a family, a locality, a province, a specific historical period, a particular set of historical remains. Scholars have explored, for example, the ways in which the notion of *Heimat* served, in nineteenth- and early twentieth-century Germany, as 'a mediating concept between the immediate local life and the abstract nation', articulating a form of patriotism that rooted the sense of nation in an attachment to place and local community.[60] A telling survey of popular attitudes to history in contemporary America by Roy Rosenzweig and David Thelen suggests similarly that ordinary people's readiness to find meaning in a larger collective past tends to arise not from the way history is taught in school, but as an outgrowth of their interest in the more intimate pasts of family or local or ethnic community. Rather than 'mechanically storing and retrieving fully formed representations of the past', Thelen argues, respondents to his and

Rosenzweig's survey 'constructed and used pasts as products and by-products of living their own lives'. This is not to say that the sense of the past these respondents articulated was merely particularistic, but rather that the need to understand their own present and future was the starting-point for any larger historical reflections, and that the messages that they drew from history were ones that had obvious value in the understanding of individual lives – for example, the message that benefits (whether political or social or personal) are only to be achieved through hard work and struggle.[61] If, following Confino's advice, we seek to discover the memory of the past 'where it is implied rather than said, blurred rather than clear',[62] in ordinary people's reactions and attitudes rather than merely in the realms of formal historiography and official commemoration, such transactions between the personal and the more general are part of what we have to investigate.

We should not start, however, by positing too formal a conceptual separation between the remembered life experiences of ordinary people and the categories of thought that govern the formation of larger narratives of collective history. One of the drawbacks of an approach to social memory that focuses only on public articulations (political speeches, commemorative ceremonies, historiography, film, etc.) is precisely that it tends to overlook the important contribution that processes of personal recollection can make to the way that events and experiences are lodged in public consciousness. Historical episodes such as wars, revolutions or periods of economic depression affect many people simultaneously. Immediate individual experiences of these events may vary widely, as may the relationships those events are perceived to have to earlier or to later experiences, and differences in individual remembering will obviously result. But there are likely to be common elements to many people's experiences of these episodes and of their legacy, and in this sense the episodes are likely to give a common inflection to many different individual patterns of recollection. Although this may, under certain circumstances (for example, ones of political oppression), remain submerged and unarticulated, it may in other cases be reinforced and developed both by individuals' subsequent social interactions (which throw up occasions for mutual reminiscence, etc.) and by public debate. It may thus become an important element in the shaping of collective identities and currents of sensibility, and may contribute, for example, to the sense that individuals may have of belonging to a particular generation whose experiences have moulded it in a particular way. Oral historians such as Luisa Passerini and Alessandro Portelli have begun to explore such effects in relation to particular collective experiences.[63] Others have sought to conceptualize, from a somewhat different angle, the ways in which different narratives may coalesce into larger structures of awareness, which may either remain informal or be publicly articulated. 'In the construction of a myth of war', Samuel Hynes has written, 'memorials play a very small role, and personal narratives a very large one': through the juxtaposing of individual narratives, a mythical structure develops ('a combined story that is not told in any individual narrative, but takes its substance from the sum of many stories') which can then exert an influence on the way later recollections are framed.[64] Konrad Jarausch has detected somewhat similar processes at work in the shaping of social memory in Germany after the Second World War. Recollections of personal life experience, he argues, pass through 'a stage of collective remembrance that fixes them into a figurative pattern': by being narrated in particular ways, individual stories of survival, suffering or post-war recovery are blended together into broader 'figures of remembrance' that come to be widely accepted as expressive of particular collective experiences. Figurations of this kind are then drawn into the larger public process of selection and arrangement (in which vital roles are played by the media and by politicians) whose purpose would normally be the 'creation of a memory culture that defines how a country deals with its own past' – an objective that, in Jarausch's view, cannot be fully realized in Germany's case, because of the divisive and disruptive character of many of the memories that are evoked.[65]

Sometimes more specific and carefully managed connections may arise between the articulation of personal recollections and the formulation of public conceptions of recent historical experience. Robert Moeller has shown how the administrative and political need of the post-war West German authorities to gather information about Germans either held in Soviet captivity or expelled from the eastern parts of Germany by the Soviet advance involved them in the gathering and publication of substantial volumes of autobiographical and eye-witness testimony. The prominence given to personal recollections of loss, displacement and Soviet brutality helped, Moeller argues, to structure the public memory of the war in ways which shifted the focus from the earlier experiences of Nazi rule and German military aggression to images of Germans as sufferers and victims – thus implicitly absolving the nation from any need to explore issues of responsibility and complicity in relation to the Nazi era more generally. Never completely submerged even by the swing towards a more anguished reckoning with the Nazi past that dominated German politics in the 1960s and '70s, this imaginative configuration of wartime experience resurfaced as a significant element in public debates over German history in the '80s and '90s. A rather more interventionist kind of 'memory work' with individuals was carried out by the Bolshevik authorities in Russia in the 1920s. The aim of organizations such as Istpart (the Commission on the History of the October Revolution and of the Communist Party) was, as Frederick Corney describes it, to solicit and to orchestrate patterns of individual recollection whose cumulative effect would be to establish the status of the October Revolution of 1917 – the moment of the Bolsheviks' acquisition of power – as a defining and foundational moment in popular experience. The purpose, in short, was less that of collecting independently formulated memories of an event whose importance could be taken for granted, than that of stimulating a tradition of popular recollection that would establish that event's decisive significance, and thus validate the Bolsheviks' preferred reading of recent history: the project was 'not about "recovering" historical memory but rather about framing it in the very process of elicitation'. Corney draws attention not just to the templates and instructions that guided the production of memories and to the procedures for corroboration that were intended to ensure reliability, but also to the social dimension of the project, hinging on such events as evenings of reminiscence, at which groups of party members would interactively and collectively write themselves into the revolutionary narrative that was being constructed. Through the structured and co-ordinated activity of remembering that Istpart and other organizations promoted, October 1917 was worked into consciousness not just as the defining moment of a grand narrative, but as the vital focusing moment of a host of group and personal stories, each of which contributed to establishing and legitimizing the larger story, and drew its own dignity and legitimacy from the connection. Manipulative as it was, the work of Istpart plainly reflected the Bolsheviks' conviction of the importance of ordinary people's recollections as an ingredient in social memory.[66]

Cumulatively and through social interaction, processes of recollection focused on the individual experiences of ordinary people can have a powerful influence on the conceptions of the collective past that become operative in a given society. The relationship between the efforts of individuals to make coherent sense of their own remembered experiences (and of the related experiences of friends or family or local community) and the facilities for understanding that are offered by the larger and always evolving narratives of collective experience that hold sway within their society is always, however, potentially problematic. Some memories are given obvious recognition within dominant or prevailing narratives, and thus find easy means of expression; others find little support or are even tacitly discredited or contradicted, and as a result become harder to sustain. According to Alistair Thomson:

> The available public languages and forms that we use to articulate and remember experience do not necessarily obliterate experiences that make no acceptable public sense. Incoherent, unstructured and indeed unremembered, these unrecognised experiences may linger in memory and find articulation in another time and place, or in less conscious outlets.

For the time being, however, elements of memory that are hard to assimilate to the available public narratives can be not just untidy, but 'risky and painful' for the individual, inasmuch as they hinder that individual in composing an account of his or her existence that will be simultaneously faithful to remembered experience and socially acceptable.[67] Unless they can find in some other – less official and perhaps even clandestine – set of collectively validated narratives (for example in those of a counterculture, of a dissident community or of a private group of friends) the kind of sympathetic recognition that the dominant narratives withhold, memories of this kind are liable either to wither or to be so repressed into a realm of recalcitrantly private feelings that they become generators of social alienation.

Such effects are no doubt most apparent in 'totalitarian' scenarios. Here, an inflexibly monolithic – but highly selective – construction of past events is imposed with such a weight of coercive authority that the forgetting – or at least the non-articulation – of much of what ordinary people have experienced becomes an inescapable rule of social existence. 'Organized oblivion' of this kind, Claudia Koonz observes, 'imposes a single narrative that vindicates the leaders and vilifies their enemies, but it leaves average citizens cynical and alienated'.[68] Catherine Merridale has shown how, in the Soviet Union, the official patriotic commemorative narrative of the nation's struggles in the Second World War was framed in ways which not only deprived the wartime experiences of, for example, women or non-Russian nationalities of any obvious acknowledgement, but also crucially suppressed all recognition of the loss and suffering inflicted by Russia's other catastrophic twentieth-century experiences of war, famine and state-promoted terror. The grieving processes that might have allowed ordinary Russians to come to terms with loss and bereavement were further disrupted by attacks on traditional funereal practices, by the unavailability of records relating to deaths and disappearances, and by such features of the Stalinist terror as the requirement for repetitive denunciations of purge victims by their bereaved relatives. The effects of all of this on personal memory were quite complex, as Merridale shows. Elements of countermemory no doubt took shape among those whom the official commemorative cult excluded, and discordant personal memories (of arrests, disappearances, unacknowledged deaths, etc.) 'were kept alive as family secrets, private narratives rehearsed in kitchens, out at the dacha on long summer evenings, in whispers at the funerals of each survivor as they died'. On another level, however, Soviet citizens acquiesced in official strategies of forgetting, refraining from articulating memories out of a desire to leave painful past experiences behind them, and seeking comfort in commemorative activities that could at least link some of their sufferings to themes of collective sacrifice and victory. What was produced was not a simple repression of memory, but a disjunctural coexistence of different levels of remembering.[69]

Such a case may be interestingly compared with that of First World War remembrance in countries such as Britain. Recent studies of this have increasingly emphasized the extent to which public commemorative practice was shaped by local initiative and public attitudes.[70] Where 'totalitarian' regimes allow no social or institutional space within which personal impulses to remember can find the kind of organization and be accorded the degree of legitimacy that would allow them to exert an influence on official narratives or commemorative practices, in more liberal societies there are a host of intermediate bodies, ranging from veterans' associations to the agencies of local government. These can be involved in mobilizing and channelling the commemorative energies of local communities, and in mediating between the commemorative priorities of political, military and ecclesiastical elites on the one hand, and the desire of ordinary people to find meaningful symbolic focuses for mourning and consolation on the other. Conventionally keen though they might be to structure commemorative activities around themes of heroic victory, political and military authorities were unable to prevent crucial sites such as the Cenotaph or the Tomb of the Unknown Soldier from acquiring symbolic meanings and uses that were often differently inflected. Private memory – that of bereaved families especially – became an essential reference point in public remembrance. To say this is not, however, to say that the scope for individuals to feel alienated or excluded by the forms in which memories of the war were publicly cast was eradicated; in one sense, indeed, the involvement of a wider range of interests in negotiations over these forms must have multiplied the opportunities for friction. War veterans, themselves, for example, were apt to find their own memories of the war and their own claims to recognition marginalized in a culture of remembrance increasingly focused on the memories of bereaved civilians. They might also display varied and complex reactions to the mythical representations of their wartime exploits and experiences that public commemorative culture sometimes embodied. Thus, as Thomson has shown, a construct such as the 'Anzac legend', with its celebrations of the fighting spirit, manliness and mateship of the (supposedly) typical Australian digger, might provide many veterans with a helpfully positive affirmation of their own values and experiences and thus with a viable framework for composing the sense of a selfhood forged in the crucible of wartime experience. However, it might drive others, painfully sensitive to this mythical image's discrepancies with remembered personal experience, into an alienated withdrawal from the commemorative culture that the legend served to animate.[71] Even when the symbolic meanings laid upon recent historical experiences are not coercively imposed by dominant central authorities, social and psychological tensions and feelings of exclusion may be endemic features of the ways these meanings become established.

In practice, of course, neither the fields of intersection that pull personal memories and public understandings of the collective past together nor the zones of exclusion that sometimes separate them are static or immutable. One of the strengths of Thomson's analysis of Anzac memories lies precisely in its recognition that both the personal memories of the veterans he has interviewed and the public forms of the Anzac legend are constantly evolving, in ways which may periodically modify and give fresh significance to the relationship between them. Individuals who found it hard to identify with certain aspects of the legend (for example, its apparent insensitivity to issues of fear and trauma), or who struggled to reconcile it with other sources of meaning in their lives (for example, a commitment to radical politics) could find, in old age and retirement, that the practices of remembrance associated with the legend offered social and discursive spaces within which it was possible to come to terms in new and reconciling ways with their past experience. The opportunities for such re-orientations arose partly because time (with its attendant effects of ageing and distancing, bereavement and moving on) had wrought changes in the individuals themselves, but also because time (through other attendant effects such as social or political change, generational transition, revisionist scrutiny and reaffirmation) had similarly remoulded the legend itself, preserving its central themes but recasting them in ways which paid new attention to (for example) the elements of dismal anguish and suffering that were an integrally constitutive part of many soldiers' remembered experience. 'As personal circumstances and needs shift, and as the public narratives and meanings of Anzac change over time', Thomson reports, 'the possibilities for remembering, and for fashioning new identities, also change'.[72] Private remembering and public representation are brought into new conjunctions and develop new mutual accommodations.

The ways in which this happens are inevitably complex, but may have far-reaching effects both on private self-perception and on the narratives in which a sense of the past is publicly embodied. In another study focusing on Australian subject matter, the historian Bain Attwood has traced the evolving forms and significance of personal stories embodying the memories generated – whether in the children themselves or among those from whom they were separated – by the separations or enforced removals of many Aboriginal children (or ones of supposedly 'mixed descent') from their homes and communities, in execution of government policies during the early twentieth century. Attwood's study distinguishes three phases or moments in the development of these stories' significance. In the first phase, references to personal experiences of separation or removal were confined to individual narratives, whose separateness and lack of conceptual co-ordination – to say nothing of the political and cultural factors inhibiting their public expression – effectively excluded these experiences from any recognition within the prevailing narratives either of the Aboriginal past or of Australian national history. In the second, such individual stories were not only articulated more widely and more self-consciously; the sense attached to them was also refocused through their connection to a larger and increasingly homogeneous general narrative of collective dispossession – the 'stolen generations narrative' – which began to assume a central place in Aboriginal historical consciousness, and to exert an increasingly powerful influence on the definition of Aboriginal cultural and political identities. In the third phase, this symbolically-charged and collectively-resonant narrative was brought finally into the broader Australian public domain and into the mainstream discourse of Australian history, where it has come to function as a troubling symbolic reminder of the racial oppressions that have been intrinsic to the emergence of Australian nationhood, and whose legacies require to be confronted. Viewed from one angle, then, what Attwood is studying is (as he puts it) a process of 'narrative accrual' or 'narrative coalescence' – the piling-up and bringing-together of stories, each of which is anchored in separate individual experiences, but which acquire, through the identification of their common elements, a kind of cumulative force which allows them in the end not simply to break down the barriers which have previously excluded certain kinds of oppression and suffering from public recognition, but also in some measure to transform the larger historical narratives through which collective identities are interpreted. It is no doubt possible also to conceptualize this process in terms of memory – not as a simple resurgence of memories that have been previously repressed (for Attwood insists that the emergence of the 'stolen generations narrative' subtly transforms the ways in which the memories in question are formulated) but as a process through which the activity of remembering is gradually suffused with broader (and empowering) kinds of social or political awareness. Attwood's analysis is principally geared, however, to revealing the complex interplay of cultural and political agencies and of different public discourses that contributed to the production of the 'stolen generations narrative' as the crucial co-ordinating structure for the framing and narrating of Aboriginal memories of removal and separation. An understanding of what has given the narrative shape and prominence cannot, he contends, be based solely on an appreciation of the memories that it brings into focus, but must take account also of the vital role of historians in labelling and defining historical phenomena, of the discourses and interactions that are promoted by organizations which seek to reunite victims of removal with their original families and communities, of the larger effects of popular interest in genealogy and family history, of the ways in which themes of justice and reconciliation were woven into discourses of national self-understanding in the rhetoric of public bodies such as the Human Rights and Equal Opportunity Commission and the Council for Aboriginal Reconciliation, and of a range of other factors. It is only through such complex conjunctions of influences in the public arena, Attwood's argument implies, that spaces are created – whether institutional or discursive – through which multiple individual memories may be fashioned into operative influences on the way the collective past is constructed, and may themselves be reconfigured in the process.[73]

Memory in crisis?

Complex and shifting relationships between public and private meaning, between personal experience and ideological assertion, between formal expression and informal assumption, as well as between different centres of power and different social interests, are always involved in shaping the ways in which the past is talked about and put to use in human societies. While some accounts of it may be socially dominant, the remembered past is, in practice, always multiple and contestable, mutable and elusive. It always, therefore, falls short of the expectations of those who want social memory to supply a stable and consensual foundation on which society can rely in shaping its own future development. In recent decades, however, fears have arisen, not simply that things which ought to be being remembered are getting forgotten, but that memory itself – the whole set of processes by which a sense of the past is sustained in human societies, and by which individuals sustain themselves as beings whose experiences of social living are temporally rooted and organized – is in a state of crisis. One intriguing aspect of recent discussions on this subject is that the current cultural preoccupation with memory, manifest both in recent spates of public commemorative activity (over anniversaries of the Second World War or the Holocaust, for example) and in scholarly developments such as the turn to memory in historical studies, is often seen as one of the symptoms of the crisis that is detected. Such a fascination with memory is not, some critics argue, a reflection of a healthy mnemonic condition, but a kind of neurotic bingeing – something excessive and obsessive, at once concealing and revealing an insistent insecurity.

Three kinds of development, overlapping and interlocking, are commonly seen as contributing to such a crisis in social memory. The first lies in the general long-term implications for social memory of the breakdown in traditional forms of social community. The erosion of traditional forms of communal living means, according to this argument, the breakdown of functioning communities of memory. The retention of information about the past ceases to be a selective process anchored in the practical experience and functional needs of specific communities, and becomes an unregulated mania fuelled by endemic social uncertainty. Pierre Nora has memorably described such a situation:

> The less memory is experienced from within [i.e. as the active memory of a specific community], the greater its need for external props and tangible reminders of that which no longer exists except *qua* memory – hence the obsession with the archive that marks an age and in which we attempt to preserve not only all of the past, but all of the present as well. The fear that everything is on the verge of disappearing, coupled with anxiety about the precise significance of the present and uncertainty about the future, invests even the humblest testimony, the most modest vestige, with the dignity of being potentially memorable. [. . .] What we call memory is in fact a gigantic and breathtaking effort to store the material vestiges of what we cannot possibly remember, thereby amassing an unfathomable

collection of things that we might someday need to recall. [. . .] As traditional memory has vanished, we have felt called upon to accumulate fragments, reports, documents, images and speeches – any tangible sign of what was – as if this expanding dossier might some day be subpoenaed as evidence before who knows what tribunal of history.

Modern societies suffer, according to Nora, from a 'hypertrophy of memory' (i.e. of memory in the sense of archived information) that testifies not to the strength, but to the crumbling away of memory as something genuinely rooted in social experience.[74] Contemporary history's interest in what Nora calls 'lieux de mémoire' – the symbolic places, objects or concepts that serve as focal points for social memory – is, in his analysis, simply another expression of modern society's uneasy sense of loss. By the time that history becomes interested in identifying them and analysing them, 'lieux de mémoire' are no longer vibrant centres of spontaneous mnemonic activity: they are vestigial markers of traditions that have become inoperative, or that can persist only by being artificially stimulated. According to Nora, '*lieux de mémoire* exist only because there are no longer any *milieux de mémoire*, settings in which memory is a real part of everyday experience'.[75]

But if the disruption and non-replacement of traditional forms of community produced in recent centuries by processes of urbanization, industrialization, migration and technological innovation supplies one ingredient in the perceived memory crisis, the assumption is generally that the effects of these developments on social memory were at least partially concealed for most of the nineteenth and twentieth centuries by the ideological ascendancy of the nation as an imagined community. The nation provided, as we have seen, a powerful focus for social remembering, capable of compensating on one level for the disruption of other types of social consciousness, and historians in particular, as well as governments, nationalist politicians and others, laboured hard to supply the symbolic and narrative ingredients that could give this focus substance. Crucial to the nationalist vision was the assumption not simply that nations had a past that could and should be remembered, but that they were the moral entities into which society was organized for the present and future. Nations were moral projects, rooted in the past, but extending into the future. Their pasts were presumed to be replete with the potential of further liberation, further fulfilment, further contributions to progress and civilization. The breakdown of these nationalist certainties, and of the broader faith in historical progress to which they were linked, chiefly through the twentieth-century's experiences of genocide and total war, is the second element that is woven into many accounts of the memory crisis. Some, such as Andreas Huyssen, have gone so far as to speak of 'a reorganization of the structure of temporality', in which the assumption of a unitary progressive movement from remembered past to optimistically envisioned future has been jettisoned. [76] Other critics have focused more specifically on the political aspects of such a process. According to Charles Maier, the half century since the Second World War has witnessed 'the end, or at least the interruption, of the capacity to found collective institutions that rest on aspirations for the future'. Conceptions of nationhood have dwindled into a narrow focus on ethnic claims to recognition, rather than on the need to give embodiment to civic values. For Maier, the contemporary preoccupation with memory does not combat such a movement, but reflects and reinforces it, by seeking the essential foci for national remembering not in symbolic textual reminders of the nation as a moral project (such as constitutions and laws), but in places, territories, landscapes – symbols of location and of origin, rather than of purpose and direction. In such a preoccupation, Maier detects 'a sign, not of historical confidence but of a retreat from transformative politics'.[77]

The concomitant of this breakdown in the progressivist conceptions that had nations as their central point of focus is, for many critics at least, a fragmentation and privatization of social memory processes. The effects of this are aggravated, it is often argued, by the third (and in many accounts the most important) element in the crisis scenario – the massive impact of the new media of mass culture and communication: film, television, the internet. By subjecting individuals with powerful immediacy to a delirious stream of images and information, evocative of a multitude of past and present situations, modern technologies, it is argued, relentlessly blur the distinctions between different phases of past experience, between past and present, between reality and simulation, between knowledge and entertainment, and between what is experienced personally and what is experienced vicariously, on which the individual's participation in a stable formation of social memory depends. We are beset, in Geoffrey Hartman's formulation, by an 'information sickness' – a 'sensory and information overload' that reduces us to a benumbed and bewildered passivity. 'We used to struggle *with* experience, and no doubt still do so', Hartman writes, 'but now we also struggle *for* experience, for a more than abstract sense of the past, or virtual sense of the present'.[78] Andreas Huyssen argues in similar vein:

> the very organization of this high-tech world threatens to make categories like past and future, experience and expectation, memory and anticipation themselves obsolete. The jumble of the non-synchronous, the recognition of temporal difference in the real world thus clashes dramatically with the draining of time in the world of information and data banks. But the borders between real world and its construction in information systems are of course fluid and porous. The more we live with new technologies of communication and information cyber-space, the more our sense of temporality will be affected.

Unlike some critics, Huyssen views the recent wave of interest in memory (the 'memory boom') not as a quasi-neurotic obsession, but as a fundamentally healthy reaction to mass culture's dissolving tendencies – 'an expression of the basic human need to live in extended structures of temporality', and thus to resist being drawn into 'a cocoon of timeless claustrophobia and nightmarish phantasms and simulations'.[79]

Anxieties over information overload are often coupled with anxieties over the commercialization and commodification of the past that mass culture makes possible. The logic of market capitalism, it is suggested, turns references to the past into items whose circulation and exchange is no longer restricted by any need to relate them to actual contexts of experience. Detached from such contexts, such references become available for inclusion in ever more synthetic, technology-assisted, market-driven combinations, in which the idea that a past is being meaningfully referred to becomes a mere residual illusion. In such a vein, Tony Horwitz memorably describes the laser show at Stone Mountain (Georgia) that he attended while investigating contemporary manifestations of Civil War memory in the American South. Here, Stone Mountain's connotations as a focus for specifically Confederate commemorative piety (centred on its massive granitic bas-relief of Lee, Jackson and Davis) get dissolved in a mishmash of allusions:

hackneyed images referring to Civil War experiences both northern and southern get crossed with assorted icons from a vaguely pro-gressive (or merely commercial) patriotic repertoire – the Statue of Liberty, 'God Bless the USA', Martin Luther King, Elvis and Coca-Cola. Horwitz muses on the experience:

> I sat there a while, letting 'Dixie' and the 'Battle Hymn' and Lee and Lincoln and Elvis all jangle around in my head. The show was a puddle of political correctness. The message seemed to be that there was no message – no real content to any of the divisive figures or songs or historic episodes the laser show depicted in its fast-paced cartoon. Why debate who should or shouldn't be remembered and revered when you can just stuff the whole lot inside a blender and spew it across the world's biggest rock?[80]

While there is little doubt that modern societies and information systems have evolved in ways which are disruptive of earlier patterns in the formation of social memory, not all of those who comment on such changes do so in the language of terminal crisis. For some, these developments carry the potential not for a disintegration of social memory, but rather for its transformation. Thus, for David Thelen, the dwindling of ordinary Americans' interest in a collective history conceived of as 'the story of the nation and of national institutions, events, policies, and cultures' is indicative not of a kind of moral purposelessness, but of a widespread conviction that the institutional frameworks of the nation may no longer provide the most appropriate arenas 'in which people can control their lives or fulfil a civic heritage'. The path is opened, according to Thelen, for the development of a more genuinely participatory historical culture, 'in which using the past could be treated as a shared human experience and opportunity for understanding, rather than a ground for division and suspicion'.[81]

Similarly, where some see the individual's exposure to mass culture as a source only of mnemonic disorientation, Alison Landsberg, for example, sees a more positive value in the scope for 'prosthetic memory' that such a culture can generate. Landsberg recognizes the ways in which the commodification of the past dismantles the traditional association between particular 'pasts' and particular communities:

> Commodification enables memories and images of the past to circulate on a grand scale; it makes these memories available to all

who are able to pay. Prosthetic memory, therefore, unlike its medieval and nineteenth-century precursors, is not simply a means for consolidating a particular group's identity and passing on its memories; it also enables the transmission of memories to people who have no 'natural' or biological claims to them.[82]

In Landsberg's view, however, the emergence of this newly 'portable, fluid, and nonessentialist form of memory' is a potentially healthy development, precisely because it challenges the assumption that particular memories, and therefore the past experiences to which the memories refer, can be regarded as the exclusive mental property of particular groups. When individuals make use of media such as film and television to forge mental connections to pasts of which they have no direct personal experience, they are not necessarily – as the prophets of memory crisis tend to assume – mindlessly registering whatever sensory stimuli the media throw their way, or vacuously picking and mixing from a pool of historical references that have become detached from any real context of structured knowledge. Rather, Landsberg argues, 'prosthetic' memories are established when individuals who are exposed to particular images of the past through the experiences of mass culture find ways of relating these images empathetically to their own life experience. Such memories have, therefore, the potential not only to constitute a genuine extension of the individual's subjectivity, but also to fashion new conceptions of social responsibility, rooted not in the limited collective experience of communities based on blood or family or heredity, but in patterns of 'mediated collective identification' in which people from different social backgrounds can simultaneously participate. Without denying the need to be wary of the dangers of a commodification of the past that is undeniably driven by capitalist impulses, Landsberg is concerned to stress the ways in which the technologies that implement this commodification can also be used to generate new types of mnemonic awareness that can help to transform the political arena.[83]

Discussions of memory crisis remain profoundly speculative: whether offering like Huyssen a dystopian nightmare of a future without memory, or like Landsberg a 'utopian dream'[84] of ethical development through mass culture, critics know that what they are describing is not something as yet fulfilled. Optimism and pessimism in such a case depend as much on the faith that is placed in the human mind's adaptive capacities as it does on empirical observation. Memory has never been changeless: its history is one of shifting definitions and evolving uses, as human beings, individually and collectively, have adapted themselves to new social and technological conditions. Such adaptations have often been socially and psychologically stressful: as new uses and conceptions of memory have taken shape, older ones in which individuals and societies had invested heavily and which had been built into their culture have been sometimes brutally discarded. The anxieties this generates have never been confined to those who find themselves culturally marginalized by new developments, as is clear for example from Plato's lamentations over the way that memory was threatened by writing.[85] The unprecedented rapidity of developments in the technologies of communication in recent decades, and the social fluidity (in terms of geographical and social mobility, career patterns, etc.) that has often accompanied these developments, makes it not surprising that these anxieties are nowadays sometimes acute, and are powerfully articulated even – perhaps especially – by people such as academics who are themselves active users of new technology. Nor is it surprising, however, that others see, in the same developments, the scope for further adaptive transformations – and perhaps regenerations – of memory as a social resource. That our sense of what memory is and our sense of that always elusive thing, the past, to which memory is assumed to give us a kind of access are evolving seems certain. That they might one day evolve to a point where neither memory nor the past in anything like our current conceptions of them seemed socially meaningful is possible. For the moment, what is apparent is rather a tension of perspectives, an uncertainty over memory's current meanings and social significance. This makes it all the more important to develop new ways of exploring, both conceptually and empirically, the multiple and ever changing ways in which understandings of the past are produced, debated and modified, over longer and shorter periods of time, through the ceaseless interactions of individual and collective structures, within our own society and others, past and present.

Notes

1 See, for example, P. Hamilton, 'Sale of the century? Memory and historical consciousness in Australia', in Hodgkin and Radstone (eds), *Contested Pasts*, esp. p. 139.

2 For interesting discussion of the latter issue, see E. Buettner, 'Cemeteries, public memory and Raj nostalgia in postcolonial Britain and India', *History and Memory* 18:1 (2006), pp. 5–42.

3 E. Hobsbawm, 'The sense of the past', in Hobsbawm, *On History*, pp. 13–31.

4 J. Olick, 'Genre memories and memory genres: a dialogical analysis of May 8, 1945 commemorations in the Federal Republic of Germany', *American Sociological Review* 64 (1999), p. 382. Olick applies this idea especially to commemorative performance; for an application to written texts, see the remarks on 'narrative dialogicality' in Wertsch, *Voices of Collective Remembering*, pp. 90–1.

5 J. Davis, 'The social relations of the production of history', in E. Tonkin, M. McDonald, M. Chapman (eds), *History and Ethnicity* (London, 1989), p. 104–17.

6 See above, pp. 88–9.

7 For an example, see the discussion of the 'triumph-over-alien forces schematic narrative template' and other templates in Soviet and post-Soviet Russian writing in Wertsch, *Voices of Collective Remembering*, pp. 93–115.

8 E. Zerubavel, *Time Maps: Collective Memory and the Social Shape of the Past* (Chicago, 2003), pp. 34–6, 82–8 and generally.

9 See, for example, M. Kammen, *Mystic Chords of Memory: the Transformation of Tradition in American Culture* (New York, 1991); Y. Zerubavel, *Recovered Roots: Collective Memory and the Making of Israeli National Tradition* (Chicago, 1995); A. Confino, *The Nation as a Local Metaphor: Württemberg, Imperial Germany and National Memory, 1871–1918* (Chapel Hill, 1997); D. Cressy, *Bonfires and Bells: National Memory and the Protestant Calendar in Elizabethan and Stuart England* (Berkeley, 1989).

10 See, for example, P. Joutard, *La légende des camisards: une sensibilité au passé* (Paris, 1977); R. Flores, *Remembering the Alamo: Memory, Modernity, and the Master-Symbol* (Austin, 2002); D. Blight, *Race and Reunion: the Civil War in American Memory* (Cambridge, Mass., 2001); C. Ó Gráda, *Black '47 and Beyond: the Great Irish Famine in History, Economy and Memory* (Princeton, 1999).

11 The literature on these is too massive to summarize here, but see (besides items listed in note 70 below), for example, J. Winter and E. Sivan (eds), *War and Remembrance in the Twentieth Century* (Cambridge, 1999); T. Ashplant, G. Dawson, M. Roper (eds), *Commemorating War: the Politics of Memory* (London, 2000); P. Fussell, *The Great War and Modern Memory* (Oxford, 1975); J. Winter, *Sites of Memory, Sites of Mourning: the Great War in European Cultural History* (Cambridge, 1995); G. Mosse, *Fallen Soldiers: Reshaping the Memory of World Wars* (New York, 1990); F. Capelletto (ed.), *Memory and World War II: an Ethnographic Approach* (Oxford, 2005); P. Friedlander, *Memory, History, and the*

Extermination of the Jews of Europe (Bloomington, 1993); G. Hartman (ed.), *Holocaust Remembrance: the Shapes of Memory* (Oxford, 1994); J. Young, *The Texture of Memory: Holocaust Memorials and Meaning* (New Haven, 1993); T. Segev, *The Seventh Million: the Israelis and the Holocaust* (New York, 1991); P. Novick, *The Holocaust in American Life* (Boston, 1999).

12 H. Nyyssönen, *The Presence of the Past in Politics: '1956' After 1956 in Hungary* (Jyväskylä, 1999); M. Sturken, *Tangled Memories: the Vietnam War, the AIDS Epidemic and the Politics of Remembering* (Berkeley, 1997); S. Nuttall and C. Coetzee (eds), *Negotiating the Past: the Making of Memory in South Africa* (Cape Town, 1998).

13 The description 'reputation studies' was coined, so far as I know, by Olick and Robbins, 'Social memory studies', p. 130. On the examples listed here, see, for example, B. Schwarz, *George Washington: the Making of an American Symbol* (Ithaca, NY, 1990); M. Elliott, *Robert Emmet: the Making of a Legend* (London, 2003); M. Warner, *Joan of Arc: the Image of Female Heroism* (New York, 1981); C. Hamilton, *Terrific Majesty: the Powers of Shaka Zulu and the Limits of Historical Invention* (Cambridge, Mass., 1998); P. Fara, *Newton: the Making of a Genius* (London, 2002); T. Connelly, *The Marble Man: Robert E. Lee and his Image in American Society* (Baton Rouge, 1977); S. Riches, *Saint George: Hero, Martyr and Myth* (Stroud, 2000); N. Higham, *King Arthur: Myth-Making and History* (London, 2002).

14 Cressy, *Bonfires and Bells*, pp. 114–23.

15 For an interesting discussion of the event's construction in memory, see C. Reardon, *Pickett's Charge in History and Memory* (Chapel Hill, 1997).

16 On the latter example, see G. Cubitt, 'Making historical connections: the political uses of seventeenth-century English history in Bourbon Restoration France', *Historical Journal* 50:1 (2007), pp. 73–95.

17 There is a considerable literature on the Enola Gay affair: see especially, E. Linenthal and T. Engelhardt (eds), *History Wars: the Enola Gay and Other Battles for the American Past* (New York, 1996); the articles in a 'round table about history after the Enola Gay controversy' in *Journal of American History* 82:3 (1995); M. Hogan, 'The Enola Gay controversy: history, memory, and the politics of persuasion', in M. Hogan (ed.), *Hiroshima in History and Memory* (Cambridge, 1996).

18 S. Kroen, *Politics and Theater: the Crisis of Legitimacy in Restoration France, 1815–1830* (Berkeley, 2000), ch. 1: 'The counterrevolutionary state and the politics of *oubli* (forgetting)'.

19 H. Rousso, *The Vichy Syndrome: History and Memory in France Since 1944* (Cambridge, Mass., 1991), pp. 10–11, and Part I generally.

20 Ibid., p. 220.

21 L. Valensi, *Fables de la mémoire: la glorieuse bataille des trois rois* (Paris, 1992), esp. pp. 266–70.

22 B. Schwartz, 'The reconstruction of Abraham Lincoln', in Middleton and Edwards (eds), *Collective Remembering*, pp. 81–107 (quotation, p. 102).

23 W. Sater, *The Heroic Image in Chile: Arturo Prat, Secular Saint* (Berkeley, 1973).

24 For general discussion of this point, see M. Schudson, 'The present in the past versus the past in the present', *Communication* 11 (1989), pp. 105–13; A. Appadurai, 'The past as a scarce resource', *Man* 16 (1981), pp. 201–19; Irwin-Zarecka, *Frames of Remembrance*, pp. 14–18. For a case study explicitly arguing and exploring the constraints on the reinvention of a particular historical image, see Hamilton, *Terrific Majesty*.

25 Schwartz, 'The reconstruction of Abraham Lincoln', pp. 95–6; and Schwartz, *George Washington*, pp. 196–8.

26 'Four score and seven years ago our fathers brought forth on this continent, a new nation, conceived in Liberty, and dedicated to the proposition that all men are created equal. Now we are engaged in a great civil war, testing whether that nation, or any nation so conceived and so dedicated, can long endure'. Text in G. Wills, *Lincoln at Gettysburg: the Words that Remade America* (New York, 1992), p. 263.

27 Zerubavel, *Recovered Roots*, pp. 221–8.

28 For sociological research exploring such issues of generational variation, see for example H. Schuman and J. Scott, 'Generations and collective memories', *American Sociological Review* 54 (1989), pp. 359–81; H. Schuman, R. Bell, K. Bischoping, 'The generational basis of historical knowledge', in Pennebaker, Paez, Rimé (eds), *Collective Memory of Political Events*, pp. 47–77. For other approaches, see Wertsch, *Voices of Collective Remembering*, ch. 7, and the classic account of the issue of generations in K. Mannheim, 'The problem of generations' (1928), in his *Essays in the Sociology of Culture* (London, 1952), pp. 276–322.

29 M. Frisch, 'American history and the structures of collective memory: a modest exercise in empirical iconography', *Journal of American History* 75 (1989), pp. 1133–43.

30 Zerubavel, *Recovered Roots*, pp. 7–10.

31 E. Zerubavel, 'Calendars and history: a comparative study of the social organization of national memory', in Olick (ed.), *States of Memory*, pp. 315–37 (quotation, p. 326).

32 Although commemorative calendars may be very important in structuring perceptions of the past in particular societies (see, for example, Cressy, *Bonfires and Bells*), we should not assume that they always supply a fundamental key even to the conceptions of the past that are being officially promoted: periods such as the Middle Ages

and the eighteenth-century, complete black holes in today's English commemorative calendar, may still figure prominently in, for example, English Heritage promotions.

33 B. Schwartz, 'The social context of commemoration: a study in collective memory', *Social Forces* 61:2 (1982), pp. 374–402 (quotations, pp. 394–6).

34 Olick, 'Genre memories', pp. 381–402.

35 C. Bushman, *America Discovers Columbus: How an Italian Explorer Became an American Hero* (Hanover, NH, 1992), pp. 165–90.

36 L. Spillman, *Nation and Commemoration: Creating National Identities in the United States and Australia* (Cambridge, 1997), esp. pp. 136–54. For the earlier significance of land and landscape in conceptions of the American past, however, see D. Lowenthal, 'The place of the past in the American landscape', in D. Lowenthal and M. Bowden (eds), *Geographies of the Mind: Essays in Historical Geography in Honor of John Kirtland Wright* (Oxford, 1976), pp. 89–117.

37 J. Vance, *Death So Noble: Meaning, Memory and the First World War* (Vancouver, 1997), p. 9.

38 A. D. Smith, *Myths and Memories of the Nation* (Oxford, 1999), p. 208.

39 J. Assmann, 'Collective memory and cultural identity', *New German Critique* 65 (1995), pp. 130, 132.

40 Renan, 'What is a nation?' (1882), (1996), pp. 45, 52.

41 J. Gillis, 'Memory and identity: the history of a relationship', in J. Gillis (ed.), *Commemorations: the Politics of National Identity* (Princeton, 1994), p. 5.

42 C. Boyd, 'The second Battle of Covadonga: the politics of commemoration in modern Spain', *History and Memory* 14:1/2 (2002), p. 40; Savage, 'The politics of memory', p. 143.

43 For interesting discussion of the sense of place in an Israeli/Palestinian context, see S. Slyomovics, *The Object of Memory: Arab and Jew Narrate the Palestinian Village* (Philadelphia, 1998).

44 Popular Memory Group, 'Popular memory: theory, politics, method', in R. Johnson et al (eds), *Making Histories: Studies in History-Writing and Politics* (Minneapolis, 1982), pp. 205–52.

45 G. Lipsitz, *Time Passages: Collective Memory and American Popular Culture* (Minneapolis, 1990).

46 Zerubavel, *Recovered Roots*, pp. 10–12. The concept of countermemory is applied by Zerubavel to dissident strands in a specifically Jewish debate on the Jewish and Israeli past, rather than to the other 'memories' which her 'master commemorative narrative' obviously excludes, namely those of Palestinians. On the latter, see, for example, T. Swedenburg, *Memories of Revolt: the 1936–1939 Rebellion and the Palestinian National Past* (Minneapolis, 1995).

47 J. Bodnar, *Remaking America: Public Memory, Commemoration and Patriotism in the Twentieth Century* (Princeton, 1991). For further relevant discussion, see, for example, O. Øverland, 'Homemaking myths: the creation of ethnic memory as a response to exclusive definitions of "American"', in W. Zacharasiewicz (ed.), *Remembering the Individual, Regional, National Past* (Tübingen, 1999), pp. 15–30.
48 See A. Heimo and U.-M. Peltonen, 'Memories and histories, public and private: after the Finnish Civil War', in Hodgkin and Radstone (eds), *Contested Pasts*, pp. 42–56.
49 Blight, *Race and Reunion*, esp. pp. 2–5; see also Savage, 'The politics of memory'.
50 See, for example, G. Krumeich, 'Joan of Arc between right and left', in R. Tombs (ed.), *Nationhood and Nationalism in France from Boulangism to the Great War, 1889–1918* (London, 1991), pp. 63–74.
51 Boyd, 'The second Battle of Covadonga', pp. 37–64 (quotation p.58).
52 See for example S. Scott, 'Dead Work: the construction and reconstruction of the Harlan Miners Memorial', *Qualitative Sociology* 19:3 (1996), pp. 365–93.
53 Confino, *The Nation as a Local Metaphor*, pp. 8–9.
54 On this point, and on the various forms of 'silence' more generally, see L. Passerini, 'Memories between silence and oblivion', in Hodgkin and Radstone (eds), *Contested Pasts*, pp. 238–54 (esp. pp. 246–7). For analysis of one such instance of constructive silence, see N. Loraux, *The Divided City: On Memory and Forgetting in Ancient Athens* (New York, 2002).
55 Ibid., p. 11.
56 Wertsch, *Voices of Collective Remembering*, pp. 119–223.
57 For further discussion, see ibid., pp. 123–48.
58 Samuel, *Theatres of Memory*; Lowenthal, *The Past is a Foreign Country*.
59 For insights into the mentality of American Civil War re-enactors, see T. Horwitz, *Confederates in the Attic: Dispatches from the Unfinished Civil War* (New York, 1998).
60 Confino, *The Nation as a Local Metaphor* (quotation p. 97); C. Applegate, *A Nation of Provincials: the German Idea of Heimat* (Berkeley, 1990). For discussion of how the sense of the past is filtered through the sense of locality in a different national context, see D. Glassberg, *Sense of History: the Place of the Past in American Life* (Amherst, 2001).
61 R. Rosenzweig and D. Thelen, *The Presence of the Past: Popular Uses of History in American Life* (New York, 1998), pp. 115, 193–4.
62 Confino, 'Collective memory and cultural history', p. 1395.
63 Passerini, *Autobiography of a Generation*; A. Portelli, *The Order Has Been Carried Out: History, Memory, and Meaning of a Nazi Massacre in Rome* (New York, 2003).

64 S. Hynes, 'Personal narratives and commemoration', in Winter and Sivan (eds), *War and Remembrance*, p. 207.

65 K. Jarausch and M. Geyer, *Shattered Past: Reconstructing German Histories* (Princeton, 2003), pp. 317–41 (quotations pp. 325, 331).

66 F. Corney, 'Rethinking a great event: the October Revolution as memory project', in Olick (ed.), *States of Memory*, pp. 25–39 (quotation, p. 29).

67 Thomson, *Anzac Memories*, p. 11.

68 C. Koonz, 'Between memory and oblivion: concentration camps in German memory', in Gillis (ed.), *Commemorations*, p. 258.

69 C. Merridale, 'War, death, and remembrance in Soviet Russia', in Winter and Sivan (eds), *War and Remembrance*, pp. 61–83 (quotation, p. 63).

70 On the themes outlined in this paragraph, see esp. A. King, *Memorials of the Great War in Britain: the Symbolism and Politics of Remembrance* (Oxford, 1998); A. Gregory, *The Silence of Memory: Armistice Day 1919–1946* (Oxford, 1994); D. Lloyd, *Battlefield Tourism: Pilgrimage and Commemoration of the Great War in Britain, Australia and Canada, 1919–39* (Oxford, 1998); and at a more general level, J. Winter, *Sites of Memory*.

71 A. Thomson, *Anzac Memories: Living with the Legend* (Melbourne, 1994), esp. p. 216.

72 Ibid., esp. ch. 9 (quotation p. 216).

73 B. Attwood, '"Learning about the truth": the stolen generations narrative', in B. Attwood and F. Magowan (eds), *Telling Stories: Indigenous History and Memory in Australia and New Zealand* (Crows Nest, NSW, 2001), pp. 183–212.

74 P. Nora, 'General introduction: Between memory and history', in P. Nora (dir.), *Realms of Memory: Rethinking the French Past*, vol. I: 'Conflicts and divisions' (ed. L. Kritzman) (New York, 1996 [French original 1984]), pp. 8–9.

75 Ibid., pp. 1, 6–7. Antze and Lambek (eds), 'Introduction', p. xiii, also put this nicely: memory becomes 'a monument visited' rather than 'a landscape inhabited', and 'we become the alienated tourists of our past'.

76 A. Huyssen, *Twilight Memories: Marking Time in a Culture of Amnesia* (New York and London, 1995), p. 8.

77 C. Maier, 'A surfeit of memory? Reflections on history, melancholy and denial', *History and Memory* 5:2 (1993), pp. 147–50.

78 G. Hartman, 'Public memory and modern experience', *Yale Journal of Criticism* 6:2 (1993), pp. 239–40.

79 Huyssen, *Twilight Memories*, pp. 7–9.

80 Horwitz, *Confederates in the Attic*, pp. 286–8.

81 Rosenzweig and Thelen, *The Presence of the Past*, pp. 190, 203.
82 A. Landsberg, *Prosthetic Memory: the Transformation of American Remembrance in the Age of Mass Culture* (New York, 2004), p. 18.
83 Ibid., pp. 21–2, 152–5.
84 Ibid., p. 155.
85 See Ong, *Orality and Literacy*, pp. 78–9, which interestingly compares Plato's critique of writing to present-day worries about computers.

INDEX

260   🌿 INDEX 🌿